Alternative

FAMILY MEDICAL

Medicine

D1337744

GEDDES &
GROSSET

Caution: Some substances used in aromatherapy and herbal medicine, when used inappropriately, can prove to be highly toxic. Do not undertake any course of treatment without the advice of a qualified practitioner.

This edition published 1997 by
Geddes & Grosset Ltd, David Dale House,
New Lanark, Scotland.

©1997 Geddes & Grosset Ltd.

24681097531

ISBN 1 85534 892 6

Printed and bound in France.
by Maury Eurolivres, Manchecourt

Contents

Acupuncture

Origins

Acupuncture is an ancient Chinese therapy that involves inserting needles into the skin at specific points of the body. The word 'acupuncture' originated from a Dutch physician, William Ten Rhyne, who had been living in Japan during the latter part of the 17th century and it was he who introduced it to Europe. The term means literally 'prick with a needle'. The earliest textbook on acupuncture, dating from approximately 400 BC, was called *Nei Ching Su Wen*, which means 'Yellow Emperor's Classic of Internal Medicine'. Also recorded at about the same time was the successful saving of a patient's life by acupuncture, the person having been expected to die whilst in a coma. Legend has it that acupuncture was developed when it was realized that soldiers who recovered from arrow wounds were sometimes also healed of other diseases from which they were suffering. Acupuncture was very popular with British doctors in the early 1800s for pain relief and to treat fever. There was also a specific article on the successful treatment of rheumatism that appeared in *The Lancet*. Until the end of the Ching dynasty in China in 1911, acupuncture was slowly developed and improved, but then medicine from the west increased in popularity. However, more recently there has been a revival of interest and it is again widely practised throughout China. Also, nowadays the use of laser beams and electrical currents are found to give an increased stimulative effect when using acupuncture needles.

yin and yang

The specific points of the body into which acupuncture needles are inserted are located along 'meridians'. These are the pathways or energy channels and are believed to be related to the internal organs of the body. This energy is known as *qi* and the needles are used to decrease or increase the flow of energy, or to unblock it if it is impeded. Traditional Chinese medicine sees the body as being comprised of two natural forces known as the *yin* and *yang*. These two forces are complementary to each other but also opposing, the yin being the female force and calm and passive and also representing the dark, cold, swelling and moisture. The yang force is the male and is stimulating and aggressive, representing the heat and light, contraction and dryness. It is believed that the cause of ailments and diseases is due to an imbalance of these forces in the body, e.g. if a person is suffering from a headache or hypertension then this is because of an excess of yang. If, however, there is an excess of yin, this might result in tiredness, feeling cold and fluid retention.

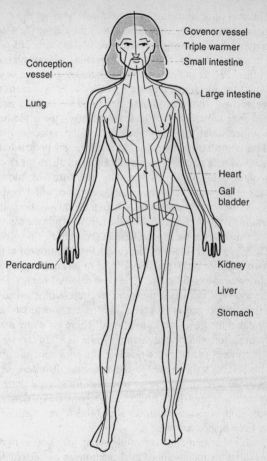

Govenor vessel

Triple warmer

Small intestine

Conception vessel

Large intestine

Lung

Heart

Gall bladder

Pericardium

Kidney

Liver

Stomach

The meridians

The aim of acupuncture is to establish whether there is an imbalance of yin and yang and to rectify it by using the needles at certain points on the body. Traditionally there were 365 points but more have been found in the intervening period and nowadays there can be as many as 2,000. There are 14 meridians (12 of which are illustrated on page 9), called after the organs they represent, e.g. the lung, kidney, heart and stomach as well as two organs unknown in orthodox medicine—the triple heater or warmer, which relates to the activity of the endocrine glands and the control of temperature. In addition, the pericardium is concerned with seasonal activity and also regulates the circulation of the blood. Of the 14 meridians, there are two, known as the *du,* or governor, and the *ren*, or conception, which both run straight up the body's midline, although the du is much shorter, extending from the head down to the mouth, while the ren starts at the chin and extends to the base of the trunk.

There are several factors that can change the flow of qi (also known as shi or ch'i), and they can be of an emotional, physical or environmental nature. The flow may be changed to become too slow or fast, or it can be diverted or blocked so that the incorrect organ is involved and the acupuncturist has to ensure that the flow returns to normal. There are many painful afflictions for which acupuncture can be used. In the west, it has been used primarily for rheumatism, back pain and arthritis, but it has also been used to alleviate other disorders such as stress, allergy, colitis, digestive troubles, insomnia, asthma, etc. It has been claimed that withdrawal symptoms (experienced by people stopping smoking and ceasing other forms of addiction) have been helped as well.

Qualified acupuncturists complete a training course of three years duration and also need qualifications in the related disciplines of anatomy, pathology, physiology and diagnosis before they can belong to a professional association. It is very important that a fully qualified acupuncturist, who is a member of the relevant professional body, is consulted because at the present time, any unqualified person can use the title 'acupuncturist'.

The treatment

At a consultation, the traditional acupuncturist uses a set method of ancient rules to determine the acupuncture points. The texture and colouring of the skin, type of skin, posture and movement and the tongue will all be examined and noted, as will the patient's voice. These different factors are all needed for the Chinese diagnosis. A number of questions will be asked concerning the diet, amount of exercise taken, lifestyle, fears and phobias, sleeping patterns and reactions to stress. Each wrist has six pulses, and each of these stand for a main organ and its function. The pulses are felt (known as palpating), and by this means acupuncturists are able to diagnose any problems relating to the flow of qi and if there is any disease present in the internal organs. The first consultation may last an hour, especially if detailed questioning is necessary along with the palpation.

The needles used in acupuncture are disposable and made of a fine stainless steel and come already sealed in a sterile pack. They can be sterilized by the acupuncturist in a machine known as an autoclave but using boiling water is not adequate for this purpose. (Diseases such as HIV and hepatitis can be passed on by using unsterilized needles.) Once the needle is inserted into the skin it is twisted between the acupuncturist's thumb and forefinger to spread or draw the energy from a point. The depth to which the needle is inserted can vary from just below the skin to up to 12 mm (half an inch) and different sensations may be felt, such as a tingling around the area of insertion or a loss of sensation at that point. Up to 15 needles can be used but around five is generally sufficient. The length of time that they are left in varies from a few minutes to half an hour and this is dependent on a number of factors such as how the patient has reacted to previous treatment and the ailment from which he or she is suffering.

Patients can generally expect to feel an improvement after four to six sessions of therapy, the beneficial effects occurring gradually, particularly if the ailment has obvious and long-standing symptoms. Other diseases such as asthma will probably take longer before any definite improvement is felt. It is possible that some patients may not feel any improvement at all, or even feel worse after the first session and this is probably due to the energies in the body being over-stimulated. To correct this, the acupuncturist will gradually use fewer needles and for a shorter period of time. If no improvement is felt after about six to eight treatments, then it is doubtful whether acupuncture will be of any help. For general body maintenance and health, most traditional acupuncturists suggest that sessions be arranged at the time of seasonal changes.

How does it work?

There has been a great deal of research, particularly by the Chinese, who have produced many books detailing a high success rate for acupuncture in treating a variety of disorders. These results are, however, viewed cautiously in the west as methods of conducting clinical trials vary from east to west. Nevertheless trials have been carried out in the west and it has been discovered that a pain message can be stopped from reaching the brain using acupuncture. The signal would normally travel along a nerve but it is possible to 'close a gate' on the nerve, thereby preventing the message from reaching the brain, hence preventing the perception of pain. Acupuncture is believed to work by blocking the pain signal. However, doctors stress that pain can be a warning that something is wrong or of the occurrence of a particular disease, such as cancer, that requires an orthodox remedy or method of treatment.

It has also been discovered that there are substances produced by the body that are connected with pain relief. These substances are called endorphins and encephalins, and they are natural opiates. Studies from all over the world show that acupuncture stimulates the release of these opiates into the central nervous system, thereby giving pain relief. The amount of opiates released has a direct bearing on the degree of pain relief. Acupuncture is a widely used form of anaesthesia in China where, for suitable patients, it is said to be extremely effective (90 per cent). It is used successfully during childbirth, dentistry and for operations. Orthodox doctors in the west now accept that heat treatment, massage and needles used on a sensitive part of the skin afford relief from pain caused by disease elsewhere. These areas are known as trigger points, and they are not always situated close to the organ that is affected by disease. It has been found that approximately three-quarters of these trigger points are the same as the points used in Chinese acupuncture. Recent research has also shown that it is possible to find the acupuncture points by the use of electronic instruments as they register less electrical resistance than other areas of skin. As yet, no evidence has been found to substantiate the existence of meridians.

Auricular therapy

Auricular therapy is a method of healing using stimulation of different acupuncture points on the surface of the ear. Auricular therapists claim that there are over 200 points on the ear that are connected to a particular organ, tissue or part of the body. If a disorder is present, its corresponding point on the ear may be sensitive or tender to touch and pressure, or there may even be some kind of physical sign such as a mark, spot or lump. Stimulation of the ear is carried out by means of acupuncture needles, or minute electric currents or a laser beam may be used.

It is claimed that auricular therapy is helpful in the treatment of various chronic conditions such as rheumatism and arthritis and also problems of addiction. During a first consultation, the auricular therapist obtains a detailed picture of the patient's state of health, lifestyle and family background. A physical examination of the ears is carried out and any distinguishing features are recorded. The therapist passes a probe over the surface of the ear to find any sensitive points that indicate the areas requiring treatment.

The practice of manipulating needles in the ear to cure diseases in other parts of the body is a very ancient one. It has been used for many hundreds of years in some eastern and Mediterranean countries and in China. Although the method of action is not understood, auricular therapy is becoming increasingly popular in several countries of the world including Great Britain.

The Alexander Technique

Breaking the habit of bad posture

The Alexander Technique is a practical and simple method of learning to focus attention on how we use ourselves during daily activities. Frederick Mathias Alexander (1869–1955), an Australian therapist, demonstrated that the difficulties many people experience in learning, in control of performance, and in physical functioning are caused by unconscious habits. These habits interfere with your natural poise and your capacity to learn. When you stop interfering with the innate coordination of the body, you can take on more complex activities with greater self-confidence and presence of mind. It is about learning to bring into our conscious awareness the choices we make, as we make them. Gentle hands-on and verbal instruction reveal the underlying principles of human coordination, allow the student to experience and observe their own habitual patterns, and give the means for release and change.

Armouring

Most of us are unconsciously armouring ourselves in relation to our environment. This is hard work and often leaves us feeling anxious, alienated, depressed and unlovable. Armouring is a deeply unconscious behaviour that has probably gone on since early childhood, maybe even since infancy. Yet it is a habit we can unlearn in the present through careful self-observation. We can unlearn our use of excess tension in our thoughts, movements, and relationships.

Correct posture

The Alexander technique is based on correct posture so that the body is able to function naturally and with the minimum amount of muscular effort. F. M. Alexander was also an actor and found that he was losing his voice when performing but after rest his condition temporarily improved. Although he received medical help, the condition was not cured and it occurred to him that whilst acting he might be doing something that caused the problem. To see what this might be he performed his act in front of a mirror and saw what happened when he was about to speak. He experienced difficulty in breathing and lowered his head, thus making himself shorter. He realized that the strain of remembering his lines and having to project his voice, so that people furthest away in the audience would be able to hear, was causing him a great deal of stress and the way he reacted was a quite natural reflex action. In fact, even thinking about having to project his voice made the symptoms recur and from this he concluded that there must be a close connection between body and mind. He was determined to try and improve the situation and gradually, by watching and altering his stance and posture and his mental attitude to his performance on stage, matters improved. He was able to act and speak on stage and use his body in a more relaxed and natural fashion.

In 1904 Alexander travelled to London where he had decided to let others know about his method of retraining the body. He soon became very popular with other actors who appreciated the benefits of using his technique. Other public figures, such as the author Aldous Huxley, also benefited. Later he went to America, achieving considerable success and international recognition for his technique. At the age of 78 he suffered a stroke but by using his method he managed to regain the use of all his faculties—an achievement that amazed his doctors.

The treatment

The Alexander technique is said to be completely harmless, encouraging an agreeable state between mind and body and is also helpful for a number of disorders such as headaches and back pain. Today, Alexander training schools can be found all over the world. A simple test to determine if people can benefit is to observe their posture. People frequently do not even stand correctly and this can encourage aches and pains if the body is unbalanced. It is incorrect to stand with round shoulders or to slouch. This often looks uncomfortable and discomfort may be felt. Sometimes people will hold themselves too erect and un-bending, which again can have a bad effect. The correct posture and balance for the body needs the least muscular effort but the body will be aligned correctly. When walking one should not slouch, hold the head down or have the shoulders stooped. The head should be balanced correctly above the spine with the shoulders relaxed. It is suggested that the weight of the body should be felt being transferred from one foot to the other whilst walking.

Once a teacher has been consulted, all movements and how the body is used will be observed. Many muscles are used in everyday activities, and over the years bad habits can develop unconsciously, with stress also affecting the use of muscles. This can be demonstrated in people gripping a pen with too much force or holding the steering wheel of a car too tightly whilst driving. Muscular tension can be a serious problem affecting some people and the head, neck and back are forced out of line, which in turn leads to rounded shoulders with the head

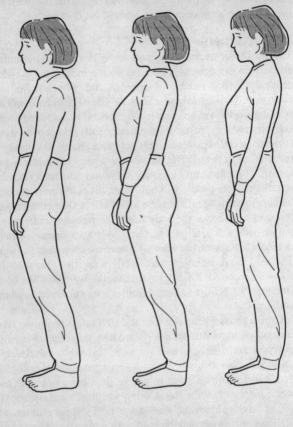

Slouching   Too unbending   Correct posture

held forward and the back curved. If this situation is not altered and the body is not re-aligned correctly, the spine will become curved with a hump possibly developing. This leads to back pain and puts a strain on internal organs such as the chest and lungs.

An Alexander teacher guides a person, as he or she moves, to use less tension. The instructor works by monitoring the student's posture and reminding him or her to implement tiny changes in movement to eradicate the habit of excess tension. Students learn to stop bracing themselves up, or to stop collapsing into themselves. As awareness grows, it becomes easier to recognize and relinquish the habit of armouring and dissolve the artificial barriers we put between ourselves and others.

An analogy of this process can be seen in the now familiar three-dimensional Magic Eye Art. With our ordinary way of looking we see only a mass of dots. When we shift to the 'Magic Eye' way of seeing, a three-dimensional object appears. Through the Alexander technique a similar type of experience is available. But the three-dimensional object we experience is ourselves.

No force is used by the teacher other than some gentle manipulation to start pupils off correctly. Some teachers use light pushing methods on the back and hips, etc, while others might first ensure that the pupil is relaxed and then pull gently on the neck, which stretches the body. Any bad postures will be corrected by the teacher and the pupil will be shown how best to alter this so that muscles will be used most effectively and with the least effort. Any manipulation that is used will be to ease the body into a more relaxed and natural position. It is helpful to be completely aware of using the technique not only on the body but also with the mind. With frequent use of the Alexander technique for posture and the release of tension, the muscles and the body should be used correctly with a consequent improvement in, for example, the manner of walking and sitting.

The length of time for each lesson can vary from about half an hour to three quarters of an hour and the number of lessons is usually between 10 and 30, by which time pupils should have gained sufficient knowledge to continue practising the technique by themselves. Once a person has learned how to improve posture, it will be found that he or she is taller and carrying the body in a more upright manner. The technique has been found to be of benefit to dancers, athletes and those having to speak in public. Other disorders claimed to have been treated successfully are depressive states, headaches caused by tension, anxiety, asthma, hypertension, respiratory problems, colitis, osteoarthritis and rheumatoid arthritis, sciatica and peptic ulcer.

The Alexander technique is recommended for all ages and types of people as their overall quality of life, both mental and physical, can be improved. People can learn how to resist stress and one eminent professor experienced a great improvement in a variety of ways: in quality of sleep; lessening of high blood pressure and improved mental awareness. He even found that his ability to play a musical instrument had improved.

The Alexander technique can be applied to two positions adopted every day, namely sitting in a chair and sitting at a desk. To be seated in the correct manner the head should be comfortably balanced, with no tension in the shoulders, and a small gap between the knees (if legs are crossed the spine and pelvis become out of line or twisted) and the soles of the feet should be flat on the floor. It is incorrect to sit with the head lowered and the shoulders slumped forward because the stomach becomes restricted and breathing may also be affected. On

Slumped posture

Comfortably balanced posture

Bad posture

Good balanced posture

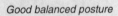

the other hand, it is also incorrect to hold the body in a stiff and erect position.

To sit correctly while working at a table, the body should be held upright but in a relaxed manner with any bending movement coming from the hips and with the seat flat on the chair. If writing, the pen should be held lightly and if using a computer one should ensure that the arms are relaxed and feel comfortable. The chair should be set at a comfortable height with regard to the level of the desk. It is incorrect to lean forward over a desk because this hampers breathing, or to hold the arms in a tense, tight manner .

There has been some scientific research carried out that concurs with the beliefs that Alexander formed, such as the relationship between mind and body (the thought of doing an action actually triggering a physical reaction or tension). Today, doctors do not have any opposition to the Alexander technique and may recommend it on occasions.

Although the Alexander technique does not treat specific symptoms, you can encourage a marked improvement in overall health, alertness, and performance by consciously eliminating harmful habits that cause physical and emotional stress, and by becoming more aware of how you engage in your activities.

Autogenic Training

Autogenic training is a form of therapy that seeks to teach the patient to relax, thereby relieving stress. This is achieved by the patient learning a series of six basic exercises that can be undertaken either lying flat on the back, sitting in an armchair or sitting towards the edge of a chair with the head bent forwards and the chin on the chest. The six exercises concentrate on (a) breathing and respiration (b) heartbeat (c) the forehead to induce a feeling of coolness (d) the lower abdomen and stomach to induce a feeling of warmth (e) the arms and legs to induce a feeling of warmth (f) the neck, shoulders, arms and legs to induce a feeling of heaviness.

It is now well established that a number of illnesses and disorders are related to, or made worse by, stress. By learning the techniques and exercises of autogenic training, the person is able to achieve a state of relaxation and tranquillity, sleeps better and generally has more energy and a greater feeling of wellbeing. Autogenic training is taught at group sessions involving a small number of people (about six is usual).

Patients with a variety of disorders may benefit from autogenic training, which can also help people who feel under stress without particular physical symptoms. Illnesses that may be helped include irritable bowel syndrome, digestive disorders, muscular aches and cramps, ulcers, headaches and high blood pressure. Also, anxieties, fears and phobias, insomnia and some other psychological illnesses. This form of therapy can benefit people of all age groups, although it is considered that children under the age of six may not be able to understand the training. Therapists in autogenic training usually hold medical or nursing qualifications and expect to obtain a full picture of the patient's state of health before treatment begins. Therapy is both available privately and through the National Health Service in some areas of Great Britain.

Ayurvedic Medicine

A holistic approach to health care that, alongside orthodox medicine, is a major form of therapy in India and is gaining an increasing number of followers in Western Countries. A great deal of emphasis is placed on preventative measures to maintain good health. Hence the practitioner in Ayurvedic Medicine obtains a detailed picture of all aspects of the patient's life and has frequent consultations with the person. If any aspect of the patient's life undergoes a change the practitioner may advise some form of treatment to prevent any problems from occurring. Methods of treatment include a great variety of medicines that are derived from plant and mineral sources, meditation, yoga and other exercises, religious ceremonies, water and steam baths, massage and specially planned diets.

In the Ayurvedic philosophy, everything in life is held to be controlled by three forces which are called *pitta*, *vata* and *kapha*. Pitta is said to be like the sun, a great source of energy and in control of all metabolic processes and bodily functions. Vata resembles the wind, which is a continual source of movement and controls the workings of the brain and nervous system. Kapha is like the moon and its tidal influences, and controls the fluids of the body and the growth and regeneration of cells. Also, in Ayurvedic medicine all disorders are grouped into four broad categories (although a holistic approach is still maintained). These are: (1) Mental, covering disorders or symptoms with an emotional basis especially the stronger feelings such as jealousy, fears and phobias, hatred, rage and depression; (2) physical, covering most illnesses and internal disorders; (3)

accidental, covering illnesses and disorders that are caused by some form of external trauma; (4) natural disorders or symptoms that are particularly associated with certain ages or stages in life.

In Ayurvedic medicine it is believed that good health results from the three forces of *pitta*, *kapha* and *vata* being balanced and in harmony with one another. If one force becomes relatively stronger or weaker than the others, then disorder arises causing symptoms of illness. A person 'inherits' his or her own particular balance of forces at the moment of conception. Imbalance in any of the three forces may arise as a result of stressful life events or due to a lack of care in maintaining the balance.

There are an increasing number of practitioners of Ayurvedic medicine in Great Britain. Many believe that its greatest strength lies in its emphasis on the maintenance of good health and prevention of problems or illnesses before they arise. The fact that the physician and the patient need to have a close working relationship no doubt provides reassurance for many of the followers of Ayurvedic medicine.

Chiropractic

Origins

The word chiropractic originates from two Greek words *kheir*, which means 'hand', and *praktikos*, which means 'practical'. A school of chiropractic was established in about 1895 by a healer called Daniel Palmer (1845–1913). He was able to cure a man's deafness that had occurred when he bent down and felt a bone click. Upon examination Palmer discovered that some bones of the man's spine had become displaced. After successful manipulation the man regained his hearing. Palmer formed the opinion that if there was any displacement in the skeleton this could affect the function of nerves, either increasing or decreasing their action and thereby resulting in a malfunction i.e. a disease.

Chiropractic is used to relieve pain by manipulation and to correct any problems that are present in joints and muscles but especially the spine. Like osteopathy, no use is made of surgery or drugs. If there are any spinal disorders they can cause widespread problems elsewhere in the body such as the hip, leg or arm and can also initiate lumbago, sciatica, a slipped disc or other back problems. It is even possible that spinal problems can result in seemingly unrelated problems such as catarrh, migraine, asthma, constipation, stress, etc. However, the majority of a chiropractor's patients suffer mainly from neck and back pain. People suffering from whiplash injuries sustained in car accidents commonly seek the help of a chiropractor. The whiplash effect is caused when the head is violently wrenched either forwards or backwards at the time of impact.

Another common problem that chiropractors treat is headaches, and it is often the case that tension is the underlying cause as it makes the neck muscles contract. Athletes can also obtain relief from injuries such as tennis elbow, pulled muscles, injured ligaments and sprains, etc. As well as the normal methods of manipulating joints, the chiropractor may decide it is necessary to use applications of ice or heat to relieve the injury.

Children can also benefit from treatment by a chiropractor, as there may be some slight accident that occurs in their early years that can reappear in adult life in the form of back pain. It can easily happen, for example, when a child learns to walk

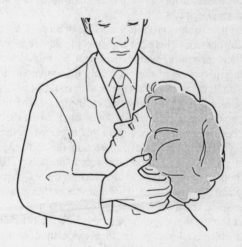

Chiropractic treatment of the neck

and bumps into furniture, or when a baby falls out of a cot. This could result in some damage to the spine that will show only in adult life when a person experiences back pain. At birth, a baby's neck may be injured or the spine may be strained if the use of forceps is necessary, and this can result in headaches and neck problems as he or she grows to maturity. This early type of injury could also account for what is known as 'growing pains', when the real problem is actually damage that has been done to the bones or muscles. If a parent has any worries it is best to consult a doctor and it is possible that the child will be recommended to see a qualified chiropractor. To avoid any problems in adult life, chiropractors recommend that children have occasional examinations to detect any damage or displacement in bones and muscles.

As well as babies and children, adults of all ages can benefit from chiropractic. There are some people who regularly take painkillers for painful joints or back pain, but this does not deal with the root cause of the pain, only the symptoms that are produced. It is claimed that chiropractic could be of considerable help in giving treatment to these people. Many pregnant women experience backache at some stage during their pregnancy because of the extra weight that is placed on the spine, and they also may find it difficult keeping their balance. At the time of giving birth, changes take place in the pelvis and joints at the bottom of the spine and this can be a cause of back pain. Lifting and carrying babies, if not done correctly, can also damage the spine and thereby make the back painful.

It is essential that any chiropractor is fully qualified and registered with the relevant professional association. At the initial visit, a patient will be asked for details of his or her case history, including the present problem, and during the examination painful and tender areas will be noted and joints will be checked to see whether they are functioning correctly or not. X-rays are frequently used by chiropractors since they can show signs of bone disease, fractures or arthritis as well as the spine's condition. After the initial visit, any treatment will normally begin as soon as the patient has been informed of the chiropractor's diagnosis. If it has been decided that chiropractic therapy will not be of any benefit, the patient will be advised accordingly.

For treatment, underwear and/or a robe will be worn, and the patient will either lie, sit or stand on a specially designed couch. Chiropractors use their hands in a skilful way to effect the different manipulative techniques. If it is decided that manipulation is necessary to treat a painful lumbar joint, the patient will need to lie on his or her side. The upper and lower spine will then be rotated manually but in opposite ways. This manipulation will have the effect of partially locking the joint that is being treated, and the upper leg is usually flexed to aid the procedure. The vertebra that is immediately below or above the joint will then be felt by the chiropractor, and the combination of how the patient is lying, coupled with gentle pressure applied by the chiropractor's hand, will move the joint to its furthest extent of normal movement. There will then be a very quick push applied on the vertebra, which results in its movement being extended further than normal, ensuring that full use of the joint is regained. This is due to the muscles that surround the joint being suddenly stretched, which has the effect of relaxing the muscles of the spine that work upon the joint. This alteration should cause the joint to be able to be used more naturally and should not be a painful procedure.

There can be a variety of effects felt after treatment—some patients may feel sore or stiff, or may ache some time after the treatment, while others will experience the lifting of pain at once. In some cases there may be a need for multiple treatments, perhaps four or more, before improvement is felt. On the whole, problems that have been troubling a patient for a considerable time (chronic) will need more therapy than anything that occurs quickly and is very painful (acute).

Although there is only quite a small number of chiropractors in the UK—yet this numbers is increasing—there is a degree of contact and liaison between them and doctors. It is generally accepted that chiropractic is an effective remedy for bone and muscular problems, and the majority of doctors would be happy to accept a chiropractor's diagnosis and treatment, although the treatment of any general diseases, such as diabetes or asthma, would not be viewed in the same manner.

Chinese Medicine

About 2500 years ago, deep in the mountains of Northern China, Taoist priests practised Qi Gong—meditative movement revealing and cultivating the vital life force. They believed this force, *qi* (pronounced 'chi' in China, 'ki' in Japan), was inseparable from life itself. They discovered that qi animated not only body and earth, but was the energetic force of the entire universe. Traditional Chinese medicine is a philosophy of preserving health, and is based first and foremost on an understanding of the ultimate power of qi. In contrast to much of Western medicine, traditional Chinese medicine is a preventative practice, strengthening the immune system to ward off disease.

In traditional Chinese medicine, qi is manifested both as *yin* (cold, dark and 'interior'), and *yang* (warm, light and 'exterior'). In fact, qi is present in all the opposites we experience, such as night and day, hot and cold, growth and decay. And although yin and yang may be perceived as opposites, they are actually inseparable. The recognition of one is essential to the recognition of the other. The balance between them is like the motion of night and day; at the instant darkness reaches its zenith at midnight, the cycle has begun to flow steadily towards dawn. At noon, the zenith of light, the day begins slowly to turn towards the darkness of night. All the internal organs of the body are subject to this nocturnal-diurnal swing of the universe.

This world view further holds that qi, manifesting as yin/yang, makes up the universe in the form of five elements: wood, fire, earth, metal and water. These five elements also represent our bodily constitution as human beings, making us one with the universe. Qi flows into our bodies, up from the earth in its yin form and down from the heavens in its yang form. The energy channels in our bodies through which it moves are called 'meridians'.

These meridians do not directly correspond to any anatomical component recognized by Western medicine. The best way to understand the flow of qi through the meridians is to compare it to the flow of blood in our veins and arteries. If our blood does not reach our toes, they become dead. If our blood does not flow freely, we have high or low blood pressure. If our blood clots, we have an embolism or a stroke. Similarly, unbalanced or stagnant qi can cause many diseases and ailments. In fact, traditional Chinese medicine is based on the principle that every illness, ailment and discomfort in the body can be explained in terms of an imbalance of qi.

Each meridian is related to one of the five elements. For example, the heart meridian is related to the element fire, the kidney and bladder to water. Along the meridians are pressure points, or 'gateways', special places where qi can become blocked. With the help of a trained practitioner, its flow can be freed and balance restored.

Colour Therapy

Colour therapy uses coloured light to treat disease and disorder
and to help restore good health. It is well known that human
beings respond to coloured light and are affected in different
ways by rays of various wavelengths. This even occurs in people who are blind, so the human body is able to respond in
subtle ways to electromagnetic radiation. Colour therapists believe that each individual receives and absorbs electromagnetic
radiation from the sun and emits it in a unique 'aura'—a pattern of colours peculiar to that person. It is believed that the
aura can be recorded on film by a photographic technique known
as Kirlian photography. If disease is present, this manifests itself as a disturbance of the vibrations that form the aura, giving
a distorted pattern. During a consultation, a colour therapist
pays particular attention to the patient's spine as each individual
vertebra is believed to reflect the condition of a particular part
of the body. Hence the aura from each vertebra is believed to
indicate the health of its corresponding body part. Each vertebra is believed to be related to one of the eight colours of the
visible spectrum. The eight colours are repeated in their usual
sequence from the top to the base of the spine.

The treatment consists of bathing the body in coloured
light with appropriate colours being decided upon by the therapist. Usually one main colour is used along with a complementary one, and the light is emitted in irregular bursts. Treatment
sessions last for a little less than twenty minutes and are continued for at least seven weeks. The aim is to restore the natural
balance in the pattern of the aura. A therapist also advises on

the use of colours in the home and of clothes and soft furnishings, etc.

In orthodox medicine it is accepted that colours exert subtle influences on people, especially affecting their state of mind and psychological wellbeing. Colour therapy may well aid healing, but there is no scientific evidence to explain the way in which this might work.

Dance and Music Therapy

Dance movement therapy

Dance movement therapy is aimed at helping people to resolve deep-seated problems by communicating with, and relating to others through the medium of physical movements and dance. The ability to express deep inner feelings in 'body language' and physical movements is innate in human beings. Young children express themselves freely in this way and without inhibition, and dancing would appear to be common to all past and present races and tribes of people. However, in modern industrial societies, many people find themselves unable to communicate their problems and fears either verbally or physically and may repress them to such an extent that they become ill. Dance movement therapy aims to help people to explore, recognize and come to terms with feelings and problems that they usually repress, and to communicate them to others. This therapy can help emotional, psychological and stress-related disorders, anxiety and depression, addiction, problems related to physical or sexual abuse, and learning disabilities. Children are often very responsive to this therapy and may have behavioural or intellectual problems, autism or other mental and physical disabilities.

People of any age can take part in dance movement therapy as the aim is to explore gently physical movements that are within each person's capabilities. The therapist may suggest movements, but hopes to encourage patients to learn to take the initiative. Eventually some groups learn to talk over feelings and problems that have emerged through taking part and are better able to resolve them.

Dance therapy sessions are organized in some hospitals and 'drop-in' and day-care centres. This form of therapy is regarded as particularly beneficial for people suffering from a number of disorders, particularly those with psychological and emotional problems or who are intellectually disadvantaged.

Music therapy

Making music has always been important in all cultures and societies, as a means of self-expression and communication. Many people have experienced the powerful effects of music, which may stimulate feelings of excitement, tranquillity, sadness or joy. Music therapy consists of creating music, using a range of different instruments and the human voice, as a means of helping people to communicate their innermost thoughts, fears and feelings.

Music therapy can help people with a variety of different disorders. It is especially valuable in helping people with intellectual impairment or learning difficulties. However, those who are physically disabled in some way may also benefit, especially people who need to improve their breathing or extend their range of movements. The sessions are conducted by a trained therapist who has a qualification in music, and the treatment may be available at some hospitals. Many therapists work in residential homes and schools and the demand for the service greatly exceeds the number of people working in this field. The approach taken depends upon the nature of the patient's problems. If the person is a child who is intellectually impaired and who perhaps cannot talk, the therapist builds up a relationship using instruments, vocal sounds and the shared experience of music-making. With a patient who is physically disabled or who has psychological or emotional problems, a different approach with more discussion is likely to be adopted.

Since most people react in some way to music and enjoy the experience of music-making, this form of therapy is usually highly beneficial and successful. Anyone can benefit and the person need not have any previous musical ability, knowledge or experience. Music therapy is especially helpful for children with intellectual and/or physical disabilities.

Hydrotherapy

The healing quality of water

Hydrotherapy is the use of water to heal and ease a variety of ailments, and the water may be used in a number of different ways. The healing properties of water have been recognized since ancient times, notably by the Greek, Roman and Turkish civilizations but also by people in Europe and China. Most people know the benefits of a hot bath in relaxing the body, relieving muscular aches and stiffness, and helping to bring about restful sleep. Hot water or steam causes blood vessels to dilate, opens skin pores and stimulates perspiration, and relaxes limbs and muscles. A cold bath or shower acts in the opposite way and is refreshing and invigorating. The cold causes blood vessels in the skin to constrict and blood is diverted to internal tissues and organs to maintain the core temperature of the body. Applications of cold water or ice reduce swelling and bruising and cause skin pores to close.

Physiotherapy

In orthodox medicine, hydrotherapy is used as a technique of physiotherapy for people recovering from serious injuries with problems of muscle wastage. Also, it is used for people with joint problems and those with severe physical disabilities. Many hospitals also offer the choice of a water birth to expectant mothers, and this has become an increasingly popular method of childbirth. Hydrotherapy may be offered as a form of treatment for other medical conditions in *naturopathy,* using the techniques listed above. It is wise to obtain medical advice before proceeding with hydrotherapy, and this is especially important for elderly persons, children and those with serious conditions or illnesses.

Treatment techniques in hydrotherapy

Hot baths

Hot baths are used to ease muscle and joint pains and inflammation. Also, warm or hot baths, with the addition of various substances such as seaweed extract to the water, may be used to help the healing of some skin conditions or minor wounds. After childbirth, frequent bathing in warm water to which a mild antiseptic has been added is recommended to heal skin tears.

Most people know the relaxing benefits of a hot bath. A bath with the temperature between 36.5°C and 40°C (98°F and 104°F) is very useful as a means of muscle relaxation. To begin with, five minutes immersion in a bath of this temperature is enough. This can be stepped up to ten minutes a day, as long as no feelings of weakness or dizziness arise. It is important to realize that a brief hot bath has quite a different effect from a long one.

There is nothing to be gained by prolonging a hot bath in the hope of increasing the benefit. Immersion in hot water acts not only on the surface nerves but also on the autonomic nervous system (which is normally outside our control), as well as the hormone-producing glands, particularly the adrenals, which become less active. A hot bath is sedative, but a hot bath that is prolonged into a long soak has quite the opposite effect.

Cold baths

Cold baths are used to improve blood flow to internal tissues and organs and to reduce swellings. The person may sit for a moment in shallow cold water with additional water being splashed onto exposed skin. An inflamed, painful part may be immersed in cold water to reduce swelling. The person is not allowed to become chilled, and this form of treatment is best suited for those able to dry themselves rapidly with a warm towel. It is not advisable for people with serious conditions or for the elderly or very young.

Neutral bath

There are many nerve endings on the skin surface and these deal with the reception of stimuli. More of these are cold receptors than heat receptors. If water of a different temperature to that of the skin is applied, it will either conduct heat to it or absorb heat from it. These stimuli have an influence on the sympathetic nervous system and can affect the hormonal system. The greater the difference between the temperature of the skin and the water applied, the greater will be the potential for physiological reaction. Conversely, water that is the same temperature as the body has a marked relaxing and sedative effect on the nervous system. This is of value in states of stress, and has led to the development of the so-called 'neutral bath'.

Before the development of tranquillizers, the most dependable and effective method of calming an agitated patient was the use of a neutral bath. The patient was placed in a tub of water, the temperature of which was maintained at between 33.5°C and 35.6°C (92°F to 96°F), often for over three hours, and sometimes for as long as twenty-four hours. Obviously, this is not a practical proposition for the average tense person.

As a self-help measure, the neutral bath does, however, offer a means of sedating the nervous system if used for relatively short periods. It is important to maintain the water temperature at the above level, and for this a bath thermometer should be used. The bathroom itself should be kept warm to prevent any chill in the air.

Half an hour of immersion in a bath like this will have a sedative, or even soporific, effect. It places no strain on the heart, circulation or nervous system, and achieves muscular relaxation as well as a relaxation and expansion of the blood vessels: all of these effects promote relaxation. This bath can be used in conjunction with other methods of relaxation, such as breathing techniques and meditation, to make it an even more efficient way of wiping out stress. It can be used daily if necessary.

Steam baths

Steam baths, along with saunas and Turkish baths, are used to encourage sweating and the opening of skin pores and have a cleansing and refreshing effect. The body may be able to eliminate harmful substances in this way and treatment finishes with a cool bath.

Sitz baths

Sitz baths are usually given as a treatment for painful conditions with broken skin, such as piles or anal fissure, and also for ailments affecting the urinary and genital organs. The person sits in a specially designed bath that has two compartments, one with warm water, the other with cold. First, the person sits in the warm water, which covers the lower abdomen and hips, with the feet in the cold water compartment. After three minutes, the patient changes round and sits in the cold water with the feet in the warm compartment.

Hot and cold sprays

Hot and cold sprays of water may be given for a number of

different disorders but are not recommended for those with serious illnesses, elderly people or young children.

Wrapping

Wrapping is used for feverish conditions, backache and bronchitis. A cold wet sheet that has been squeezed out is wrapped around the person, followed by a dry sheet and warm blanket. These are left in place until the inner sheet has dried and the coverings are then removed. The body is sponged with tepid water (at blood heat) before being dried with a towel. Sometimes the wrap is applied to a smaller area of the body, such as the lower abdomen, to ease a particular problem, usually constipation.

Cold packs

Cold packs were described by the famous 19th-century Bavarian pastor, Sebastian Kniepp, in his famous treatise *My Water Cure*, in which he explained the advantages of hydrotherapy. A cold pack is really a warm pack—the name comes from the cold nature of the initial application.

For a cold pack you need:

A large piece of cotton material; a large piece of flannel or woollen (blanket) material; a rubber sheet to protect the bed; a hot water bottle; safety pins.

First, soak the cotton material in very cold water, wring it out well and place it on the flannel material that is spread out on the rubber sheet on the bed. Lay the person who is having the treatment on top of the damp material, fold it round his trunk and cover him up at once with the flannel material. Safety-pin it all firmly in place.

Now pull up the top bed covers and provide a hot water bottle. The initial cold application produces a reaction that draws fresh blood to the surface of the body; this warmth, being well insulated, is retained by the damp material. The cold pack turns into a warm pack, which gradually, over a period of six to eight hours, bakes itself dry. Usually lots of sweat will be produced, so it is necessary to wash the materials well before using again.

The pack can be slept in—in fact it should encourage deeper, more refreshing sleep. Larger, whole body packs can be used, which cover not only the trunk but extend from the armpits to the feet, encasing the recipient in a cocoon of warmth.

If a feeling of damp coldness is felt, the wet material may be inadequately wrung out, or the insulation materials too loose or too few.

Flotation

A form of sensory deprivation, flotation involves lying face up in an enclosed, dark tank of warm, heavily salted water. There is no sound, except perhaps some natural music to bring the client into a dream-like state. It is exceptionally refreshing and induces a deep, relaxing sleep.

Kinesiology

The function of kinesiology

Kinesiology is a method of maintaining health by ensuring that all muscles are functioning correctly. It is believed that each muscle is connected with a specific part of the body such as the digestive system, circulation of the blood and specific organs, and if a muscle is not functioning correctly this will cause a problem in its related part of the body. The word is derived from *kinesis*, which is Greek for 'motion'. Kinesiology originated in 1964 and was developed by an American chiropractor named George Goodheart who realized that while he was treating a patient for severe pain in the leg, by massaging a particular muscle in the upper leg, the pain experienced by the patient eased and the muscle was strengthened. Although he used the same method on different muscles, the results were not the same. Previous research done by an osteopath named Dr Chapman, in the 1900s, indicated that there were certain 'pressure points' in the body that were connected with particular muscles and, if these were massaged, lymph would be able to flow more freely through the body. Using these pressure points, Chapman found which point was connected to each particular muscle and realized why, when he had massaged a patient's upper leg muscle, the pain had lessened. The pressure point for that leg muscle was the only one that was situated above the actual muscle— all the other points were not close to the part of the body with which they were connected.

The use of pressure points

In the 1930s it was claimed that there were similar pressure points located on the skull and, by exerting a light pressure on these, the flow of blood to their related organs could be assisted. Goodheart tested this claim, which originated from an osteopath called Terence Bennett, and discovered that after only fingertip pressure for a matter of seconds, it improved the strength of a particular muscle. After some time he was able to locate sixteen points on the head, the back of the knee and by the breastbone that were all allied to groups of important muscles. Goodheart was surprised that so little force applied on the pressure point could have such an effect on the muscle, so to further his studies he then applied himself to acupuncture. This is a form of healing that also makes use of certain points located over the body but that run along specific paths known as meridians. After further study, Goodheart came to the conclusion that the meridians could be used for both muscles and organs. The invisible paths used in kinesiology are exactly the same as the ones for acupuncture.

Energy and lymph

A kinesiologist will examine a patient and try to discover whether there is any lack of energy, physical disorders or inadequate nutrition that is causing problems. Once any troublesome areas have been located, the practitioner will use only a light massage on the relevant pressure points (which, as mentioned, are generally not close to their associated muscle). For example, the edge of the rib cage is where the pressure points for the muscles of the upper leg are situated. In kinesiology it is maintained that the use of pressure points is effective because the flow of blood to muscles is stimulated and therefore a good supply of lymph is generated too. Lymph is a watery fluid that takes toxins from the tissues and if muscles receive a good supply of both lymph and blood they should function efficiently. As in acupuncture, it is maintained that there is an unseen flow of energy that runs through the body and if this is disrupted for any reason, such as a person being ill or suffering from stress, then the body will weaken due to insufficient energy being produced. The way in which a kinesiologist assesses the general health of a patient is by testing the strength of the muscles as this will provide information on the flow of energy. It is claimed that by finding any inbalance and correcting it, kinesiology can be used as a preventive therapy. If there is a lack of minerals and vitamins in the body or trouble with the digestive system, it is claimed that these are able to be diagnosed by the use of kinesiology. If a person is feeling 'below par' and constantly feels tired, it is believed that these conditions are aggravated by a sluggish flow of the internal body fluids such as the circulation of blood. Kinesiologists can treat the disorder by stimulating the flow of lymph and blood by massaging the pressure points.

Although it is claimed that kinesiology can be of help to all people, it is widely known for the treatment of people suffering from food allergies or those who are sensitive to some foods. It is believed that the chemicals and nutrients contained in food cause various reactions in the body, and if a particular food has the effect of making muscles weak, then it would be concluded that a person has an allergy to it. Allergic reactions can cause other problems such as headaches, tension, colds, tiredness and a general susceptibility to acquiring any passing infections.

There are two simple tests that can easily be tried at home to determine if there is any sensitivity or allergy to certain foods. This is done by testing the strength of a strong muscle in the chest, and to carry this out the person being tested will need the

help of a partner. There is no need to exert real force at any
time, just use the minimum amount needed to be firm but gentle. To test the chest muscle, sit erect, holding the left arm straight
out at right angles to the body. The elbow should be facing
outwards and the fingers and thumb drooping towards the table. The partner will then place his or her right hand on the
person's nearest shoulder (the right) and the two fingers only
on the area around the left wrist. A gentle downward pressure
will then be exerted by the partner on the person's wrist who
will try to maintain the level of the arm, whilst breathing in a
normal fashion. This downward pressure should be exerted for
approximately five seconds. If the person was able to resist the
downwards pressure and the muscle felt quite firm, then the
allergy test can be tried. However, if this was not the case and
the person was unable to keep the arm level, the muscle would
not be suitable for use in the subsequent test. It would therefore
be advisable to use another muscle such as one in the arm. To
do this, place an arm straight down at the side of the body with
the palm of the hands facing outwards. The partner will then
use the same amount of pressure to try and move the arm outwards, again for a similar amount of time. If the person is unable to keep the arm in the same position, then it would be
advisable to get in touch with a trained kinesiologist.

To undertake the allergy test, hold the left arm in the same
way as for testing the muscle (*see* page 50, figure A). If, for
example, the food that is suspected of causing an allergy is
chocolate, a small piece of this should be put just in the mouth,
there is no need for it to be eaten. This time as well as applying
the pressure on the wrist as before, the partner should put his or
her first two digits of the left hand below the person's right ear.
Once again, the person tries to resist the downwards force and
if successful, it is claimed that there is no sensitivity or allergy

A—determining sensitivity or allergy to foods

connected with that food. However, if this does not happen and
the arm is pushed downwards or even feels slightly weak, then
kinesiology would suggest that this food, if eaten at all, should
never be consumed in any great amount.

It is claimed that the use of kinesiology can be of benefit to
people who suffer from irrational fears or phobias. An example
of this is the recommendation that the bone below the eye, just
level with the pupil, is softly tapped. Neck and back pain can
be treated without any manipulation of joints and some of the
methods can be learnt by patients for use at home. An example
of this for the alleviation of back pain is for a patient to massage the muscle situated on the inside of the thigh. This is said
to be of benefit for any muscles that are weak as they are the
reason for a painful back.

A number of other practitioners, such as homoeopaths, herbalists and osteopaths make use of kinesiology, so if there is a problem connected with the ligaments, muscles or bones it may be advisable to contact a chiropractor or osteopath who is also qualified in kinesiology. If the problem is of a more emotional or mental nature, then it might be best to select a counsellor or psychotherapist who also practises kinesiology. It is important always to use a fully qualified practitioner and the relevant association should be contacted for information. At the first consultation, detailed questions will be asked concerning the medical history, followed by the therapist checking the muscles' ability to function effectively. For instance, a slight pressure will be exerted on a leg or arm while the patient holds it in a certain way. The patient's ability to maintain that position against the pressure is noted and if the patient is unable to do so, then the therapist will find the reason why by further examination. Once the areas in need of 'rebalancing' have been identified, he therapist will use the relevant pressure points to correct matters. It is believed that if some of the points are painful or sore to the touch, this is because there has been an accumulation of toxins in the tissues, and these toxins stop the impulses between muscles and the brain. If this is the case, the muscle is unable to relax properly and can cause problems in areas such as the neck and shoulders.

There are ways of identifying any possible problems. For example, if there is any weakness in the shoulder muscle it may be that there is some problem connected with the lungs. To test for this, the patient sits upright with one arm raised to slightly below shoulder level and the other arm lower and out to the front. The therapist grasps the patient's upper arm and presses gently downwards on the raised arm at the elbow (*see* page 52, figure B). If the mucle is functioning correctly then

B—determining whether there is weakness in the shoulder
muscle

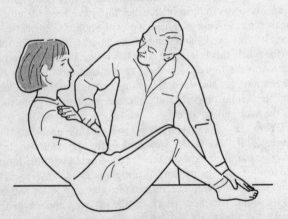

C—determining whether there are weak
muscles in the stomach

this downwards force should not be allowed to move the arm lower. If the patient is suffering from pain in the back, the probable cause lies with weak muscles in the stomach. To test for this, the patient sits on the floor with the knees raised, the arms crossed on the chest and then they lean backwards (*see* page 52 figure C). The therapist checks the stomach muscles' efficiency by pushing gently backwards on the patient's crossed arms. If all is well the patient should be able to maintain the position and not lean back any further.

After treatment by massage of the pressure points, there may well be some tenderness experienced for one or two days as the toxins in the tissues dissipate gradually. However, there should be an overall feeling of an improvement in health and in particular with the problem that was being treated.

Although there has been an increase in the use of kinesiology by doctors to help discover the cause of an ailment, there has been little scientific research carried out. Therefore, the majority of doctors using conventional medicine do not believe that the flow of electrical energy present in the body can be changed by the use of massage or similar methods.

Massage

Introduction

Origins

We massage ourselves nearly every day. The natural reaction to reach out and touch a painful part of the body—such as a sprain—forms the basis of massage. As long ago as 3000 BC massage was used as a therapy in the Far East, making it one of the oldest treatments used by humans. In 5 BC in ancient Greece, Hippocrates recommended that to maintain health, a massage using oils should be taken daily after a perfumed bath. Greek physicians were well used to treating people who suffered from pain and stiffness in the joints. The relaxation and healing powers of massage have been well documented over the past 5,000 years.

The therapeutic value of applying oils and rubbing parts of the body to lessen pain and prevent illness was recognized among the ancient Mediterranean civilizations. In ancient times scented oils were almost always used when giving massages, creating an early form of aromatherapy massage.

Popularity

Massage increased in popularity when, in the 19th century, Per Henrik Ling, a Swedish fencing master and academic, created the basis for what is now known as Swedish massage. Swedish massage deals with the soft tissues of the body.

Swedish massage is a combination of relaxing effects and exercises that work on the joints and muscles, but it is still based on the form that was practised in ancient times. More recently, a work was published in the 1970s called *The Massage Book,* by George Downing, and this introduced a new concept in the overall technique of massage, that the whole person's state should be assessed by the therapist and not solely the physical side. The emotional and mental states should be part of the overall picture. Also combined in his form of massage were the methods used in reflexology (*see* page 94) and shiatsu (*see* page 170), and this was known as therapeutic massage. The aim of this is to use relaxation, stimulation and invigoration to promote good health.

Uses

Massage is commonly used to induce general relaxation, so that any tension or strain experienced in the rush of daily life can be eased and eliminated. It is found to be very effective, working on the mind as well as the body. It can be used to treat people with hypertension (high blood pressure), sinusitis, headaches, insomnia and hyperactivity, including people who suffer from heart ailments or circulatory disorders. At the physical level, massage is intended to help the body make use of food and to eliminate the waste materials, as well as stimulating the nervous and muscular system and the circulation of blood. Neck and back pain are conditions from which many people suffer, particularly if they have not been sitting correctly, such as in a slightly stooped position with their shoulders rounded. People whose day-to-day work involves a great deal of physical activity, such as dancers and athletes, can also derive a great deal of benefit from the use of massage. Stiffness can be a problem that they have after training or working, and this is relieved by encouraging the toxins that gather in the muscles to disperse. Massage promotes a feeling of calmness and serenity, and this is particularly beneficial to people who frequently suffer from bouts of depression or anxiety. Once the worry and depression have been dispelled, people are able to deal with their problems much more effectively and, being able to do so, will boost their self-confidence.

Medical use

An aid to recovery

In hospitals, massage has been used to ease pain and discomfort as well as being of benefit to people who are bedridden, since the flow of blood to the muscles is stimulated. It has also been used for those who have suffered a heart attack and has helped their recovery. A more recent development has been the use of massage for cancer patients who are suffering from the after-effects of treatment, such as chemotherapy, as well as the discomfort the disease itself causes. Indeed, there are few conditions when it is not recommended. However, it should not be used when people are suffering from inflammation of the veins (phlebitis), varicose veins, thrombosis (clots in the blood) or if they have a raised temperature such as occurs during a fever. It is then advisable to contact a doctor before using massage. Doctors may be able to recommend a qualified therapist, a health centre may be able to help or contact can be made with the relevant professional body.

Psychological benefits

Along with the diagnosis element of massage there are great psychological benefits—the enjoyment of touch and of being stroked and caressed by another person. During a massage the patient is coaxed from emotional and occupational stresses and brought into the intense arena of the here and now. The importance of this kind of one-on-one nonverbal communication can never be underestimated in our increasingly impersonal and detached society.

Massage has a wide range of uses for a variety of disorders. Its strengths lie in the easing of strain and tension and inducing relaxation and serenity, plus the physical contact of the therapist. Although doctors make use of this therapy in conjunction with orthodox medicine, it is not to be regarded as a cure for diseases in itself and serious problems could occur if this were the case.

Benefits

Massage affects the whole body through rhythmically applied pressure. Gentle pulling and stroking movements increase the circulation of the blood and cause the blood vessels to dilate. The stimulation of nerves and blood will also affect the internal organs. Lymph is a milky white liquid that carries waste substances and toxins away from the tissues via the lymphatic system. Inactivity can cause an unhealthy build-up of this substance, and as the circulation of the lymph is largely dependent on muscle contractions, so massage will help speed the lymph's progress through the system. Active people can also benefit from massage as strenuous activity burns up the muscle, producing an increase of waste products in the muscle tissue. Massage will help to balance the system in both cases and can increase oxygen capacity by 10–15 per cent.

Massage can go a long way to repairing our damaged postures. Inactive lifestyles and sedentary occupations have created a society of people with cramped, stooped and neglected postures. Not only does massage help to coax the spine and corresponding physiology back into position, it also makes us more aware of our bodies. Relieved of muscle tension, the body feels lighter and can therefore be borne more naturally and with more poise. Used in conjunction with postural therapies such as Pilates or the Alexander technique (*see* page 15), massage can help achieve a relaxed yet controlled posture.

Women in labour have found that the pain experienced during childbirth can be eased if massage is performed on the buttocks and back. The massage eases the build-up of tension in the muscles, encouraging relaxation and easing of labour pains. It is said to be more effective on women who had previously experienced the benefits and reassurance of massage.

Many of the benefits of massage come through the healer/patient contact. Our hands are one of the most sensitive parts of our body, and we experience much of our sense of touch through our hands. An experienced masseur is able to use his or her hands to communicate feelings of harmony and relaxation. A practised masseur will also be able to diagnose the patient through touch. He or she can 'listen' to tension and stress through the texture of the skin, knotted muscles and stiff joints. Old and current sprains, congestion and swelling should all be obvious to a good masseur. The actions of massage—the stroking, kneading and pulling—detoxify the body, improving circulation and lymphatic drainage. After tension and weaknesses in the body have been pinpointed and relieved, the patient is left feeling, relaxed and energized.

The massage session

Preparation

A session may be undertaken in the patient's home, or he or she can attend the masseur or masseuse at a clinic. At each session the client will undress, leaving only pants or briefs on, and will lie on a firm, comfortable surface, such as a table that is designed especially for massage. The massage that follows normally lasts from 20 minutes to one hour.

If performed by professionals, massage is not a technique for the unduly modest. It achieves best results if the person receiving the massage is either naked or else dressed in the scantiest of underwear. For anyone who is competent and wishes to provide some simple massage for a partner, there are some basic rules to follow. The room should be warm and peaceful. The surface on which the person lies should be quite comfortable but firm. Use a mid-thigh level table or the floor. A futon (a quilted Japanese mattress) can be used, and to relieve the upper part of the body from any possible discomfort, a pillow should be placed underneath the torso. Any pressure that may be exerted on the feet can be dispelled by the use of a rolled-up towel or similar placed beneath the ankles. Both people should be relaxed, and to this end soft music can be played. All the movements of the hand should be of a continuous nature. It is suggested that the recipient always has one hand of the masseur or masseuse placed on him or her. If you wish you can buy a perfumed massage oil from a chemist or health shop, or mix your own using a blend of aromatherapy oils. Vegetable oil (about one teaspoonful) is suitable but should not be poured straight on to the person. It should be spread over the hands by rubbing, which will also warm it sufficiently for use. Should the masseur or masseuse get out of breath, he or she should stop for a rest, all the while retaining a hand on the person.

Basic techniques

Massage can be divided into four basic forms, and these are known as *percussion* (also known as drumming); *friction* (also called pressure); *effleurage* (also called stroking) and *petrissage* (also called kneading). These methods can be practised alone or in combination for maximum benefit to the patient.

Percussion (drumming or tapotement)

Percussion is also called tapotement, which is derived from *tapoter*, a French word that means 'to drum', as of the fingers on a surface. As would be expected from its name, percussion is generally done with the edge of the hand with a quick, chopping movement, although the strokes are not hard. This type of movement would be used on places like the buttocks, thighs, waist or shoulders where there is a wide expanse of flesh.

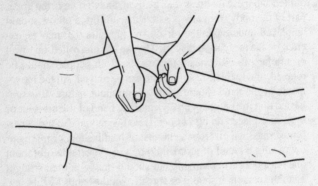

Percussion

Friction (pressure)

Friction strokes are used to penetrate into deep muscle tissue. Friction is often used on dancers and athletes who experience problems with damaged ligaments or tendons. This is because the flow of blood is stimulated and the movement of joints is improved. Friction can be performed with the base of the hand, some fingers or the upper part of the thumb. It is not advisable to use this method on parts of the body that have been injured in some way, for example where there is bruising.

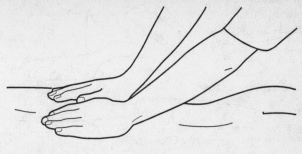

Friction

Effleurage (stroking)

Effleurage is performed in a slow, rhythmical, controlled manner using both hands together with a small space between the thumbs (A). If the therapist wishes to use only light pressure he or she will use the palms of the hands or the tips of the fingers with light gliding strokes, working away from the heart. Light gliding strokes have a relaxing effect on the nervous system. For increased pressure the knuckles or thumbs will be used in an upwards stroking motion towards the heart. Stronger pressure has more of an effect on the blood circulation and the nervous system.

Effleurage can be used on the upper leg as far up as the hip on the outside of the leg. Once the person is lying face downwards (with support under the chest), continue to use effleurage movements on the back of the lower leg. Continue as before but work on the upper leg (B), avoiding the knee. The muscles in the buttocks can be worked upon with both hands to squeeze but making sure that the hands are moving in opposite ways (C).

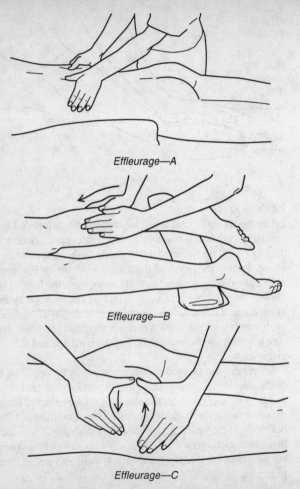

Effleurage—A

Effleurage—B

Effleurage—C

Petrissage (kneading)

Petrissage is ideal for unlocking aching or tense muscles, in particular the trapezium muscle between the neck and shoulders (A). Both hands work together in a rhythmic sequence, alternately picking up and gently squeezing the tense muscle. The kneading action gets deep enough to stimulate the lymph into removing the build-up of lactic acid. As the therapist works across each section, an area of flesh is grasped and squeezed, and this action stimulates the flow of blood and enables tensed muscles to relax. People such as athletes can have an accumu-

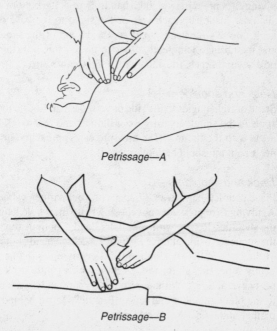

Petrissage—A

Petrissage—B

lation of lactic acid in certain muscles, and this is why cramp occurs. Parts of the body on which this method is practised are along the stomach and around the waist (B).

Neck and shoulder massage

What follows can be used to relieve headaches, loosen the shoulder muscles and provide a general feeling of relaxation.

Neck and shoulders—A

Stand behind your seated partner. Begin with effleurage, applying firm pressure with both hands. Start at the bottom of the shoulder blades up each side of the spine to the base of the neck. Move your hands apart across the top of the shoulders and then bring them gently down to the starting position. Repeat several times, finishing with a light return stroke.

Neck and shoulders—B

Stand at right angles to the side of your partner. Locate tension spots in the shoulders using your thumbs and then work these areas with the thumbs. The pressure can approach your partner's pain threshold but not exceed it.

Neck and shoulders—C

Place your left hand in an 'L' shape on your partner's shoulder. Applying firm pressure, move it slowly up the whole length of the shoulder. Repeat with your other hand. Continue repeating the sequence using alternate hands. Place one hand at the base of the back of the neck and move it gently up to the hairline, gently squeezing all the time. Return with a gentle stroke. Repeat several times. Without removing your hands, walk round to the other shoulder and repeat B and C. Move behind your partner and repeat A several times.

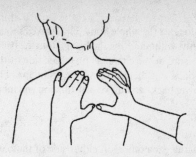

Neck and shoulders—A

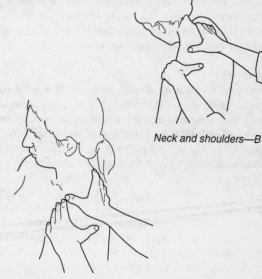

Neck and shoulders—B

Neck and shoulders—C

Back massage

Back massage helps to relax the whole body. The strokes should be carried out smoothly, without lifting the hands from the back. Applying thumb pressure to the channels on either side of the spine on the upper back will help respiratory problems. The same stroke on the lower back can relieve constipation and menstrual discomfort.

Back—A

Place your hands, facing each other, on either side of the base of the spine. Move them up the back, using your body weight to apply pressure. Take your hands round the shoulders and return lightly down the sides of the body. Repeat several times before stopping to knead the shoulders. Work on one shoulder and then the other. Repeat the movement.

Back—B

Place your hands at waist level, with your thumbs in the hollows on either side of the spine and your fingers open and relaxed. Push your thumbs firmly up the channels for about 2 ins (6 cm), relax them, and then move them back about 1 in (2 cm). Continue in this way up to the neck. Then gently slide both hands back to the base of the spine. Repeat. Follow with the sequence in A.

Back—C

Place your hand flat across one side of your partner's back at the base of the spine. Apply firm palm pressure and work up to the shoulders. Follow closely with your other hand. Repeat using alternate hands. Work through the same sequence on the other side of the back, then repeat on both side several times. Finish by working through A.

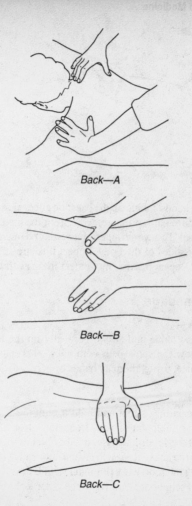

Back—A

Back—B

Back—C

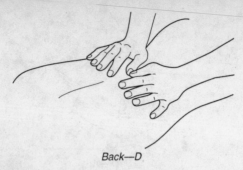

Back—D

Back—D

Place your hands, facing up the back, on either side of the spine. Applying firm palm pressure, work from the base of the spine to chest level. Turn your fingers outwards and move your hands apart to the sides of the body. Repeat this stroke at waist and hip levels. Repeat the first movement in A several times.

Limb massage

Limbs—A

Begin at the ankle and stroke vertically up the leg with one hand. Follow the same path with your other hand. Continue this sequence, using alternate hands.

Limbs—B

Raise your partner's foot and hold it with the knee at a right angle. Using the palm of your free hand, stroke firmly down the back of the leg from ankle to knee level. Use a light stroke to return to the ankle. Repeat the whole movement several times. If including the foot, work through D and E next before repeating the full sequence (A to B) on the other leg.

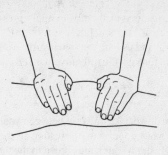

Limbs—A

Limbs—B

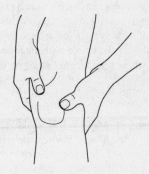

Limbs—C

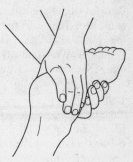

Limbs—D

Limbs—C

Help your partner to turn over, and begin by stroking with alternate hands up the whole leg, as in A. Then put your hands on either side of the knee and, using your thumbs to apply pressure, circle around the knee cap. If including the foot, bring your hands down to the ankle and use the sandwich stroke (D) on the front of the foot. Work through the full movement on the other leg.

Limbs—D

With your partner lying face down, take one foot between your hands, so that the palm of your upper hand is resting in the arch. Press firmly, and slowly draw your hands down to the tip of the foot. Use plenty of pressure for this 'sandwich' stoke.

Limbs—E

Hold the foot with your thumbs lying side by side behind the toes. Pull both thumbs back to the sides of the foot, then push them forward. Repeat this zig-zag movement as you work down to the heel. Then push firmly all the way back to the toes, keeping your thumbs side by side. Repeat the whole movement several times. Work through the whole sequence (D to E) on the other foot.

Limbs—F

Take hold of your partner's hand as in a firm handshake, and lift the arm up slightly, as far as the elbow. Gently place the palm of your fee hand across the top of the wrist and close your fingers round the raised arm. Apply firm pressure and slide your hand up to the elbow, or as far as the shoulder. Move your palm underneath the arm and use a light stroke to return to the wrist. Repeat several times.

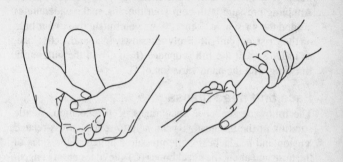

Limbs—E   *Limbs—F*

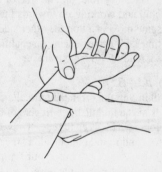

Limbs—G

Limbs—G

Place your thumbs across the inside of your partner's wrist. Applying pressure with both your thumbs, make wide circles around the wrist area. Repeat F. As you finish, relax your hold on the wrist and pull off firmly and slowly in a sandwich stroke, as in D. Repeat the full sequence (F to G) on the other arm, finishing with the hand variation of D.

Face and head massage

The following sequence encourages deep relaxation. Gentle stroking of the forehead (B) can help to relieve stress-related tension and headaches, while pressure applied to the sides of the nose and along the cheekbones (C) alleviates nasal congestion and sinus problems. Scalp massage (D) stimulates circulation.

Face and head—A

Use alternate hands to stroke up one side of the face, starting beneath the chin and working up towards the forehead. Work through the same movement on the other side of the face. Repeat several times. Finish by placing one palm across your partner's forehead, ready for the next stroke.

Face and head—B

Begin by stroking up the forehead with alternate palms. Then place the pads of the middle three fingers of both hands in the centre of the forehead between the eyes. Draw them gently apart across the brow and round the outside corner of the eyes. Lift off the middle two fingers and use your fourth fingers only to return under the eyes towards the nose.

Face and head—C

Position your thumbs on your partner's forehead. Using the

three middle fingers of both hands, press firmly against the sides of the nose. Continue along the top of the cheekbone, until you reach the temple. Keeping your thumbs in position, return to the nose, pressing along the middle of the cheekbone.

Face and head—D

Spread out the fingers and thumbs of both hands and place them on your partner's scalp. Keep them in position and begin to move the scalp muscle over the bone by applying gentle pressure and circling slowly and firmly on the spot. Stop occasionally to move to a different area, then begin again, working gradually over the whole scalp.

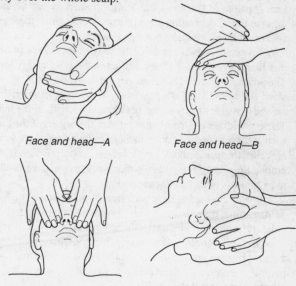

Face and head—A

Face and head—B

Face and head—C

Face and head—D

Acupressure

This is an ancient form of healing combining massage and acupuncture, practised over 3,000 years ago in Japan and China. It was developed into its current form using a system of special massage points and is today still practised widely in the Japanese home environment.

Certain 'pressure points' are located in various parts of the body and these are used by the practitioner by massaging firmly with the thumb or fingertip. These points are the same as those utilized in acupuncture. There are various ways of working and the pressure can be applied by the practitioner's fingers, thumbs, knees, palms of the hand, etc. Relief from pain can be quite rapid at times, depending upon its cause, while other more persistent problems can take longer to improve.

Acupressure is said to enhance the body's own method of healing, thereby preventing illness and improving the energy level. The pressure exerted is believed to regulate the energy that flows along the meridians,qi. As previously mentioned, the meridians are the invisible channels that run along the length of the body. These meridians are mainly named after the organs of the body such as the liver and stomach, but there are four exceptions, which are called the 'pericardium', 'triple heater', 'conception' and 'governor'. Specifically named meridian lines may also be used to treat ailments other than those relating to it.

Ailments claimed to have been treated successfully are back pain, asthma, digestive problems, insomnia, migraine and circulatory problems, amongst others. Changes in diet, regular exercise and certain self-checking methods may be recommended by your practitioner. It must be borne in mind that some painful symptoms are the onset of serious illness so you should always first consult your G.P.

Before any treatment commences, a patient will be asked

details of lifestyle and diet, the pulse rate will be taken along with any relevant past history relating to the current problem. The person will be requested to lie on a mattress on the floor or on a firm table, and comfortable but loose-fitting clothing is best so that the practitioner can work most effectively on the energy channels. No oils are used on the body and there is no equipment. Each session lasts from approximately 30 minutes to 1 hour. Once the pressure is applied, and this can be done in a variety of ways particular to each practitioner, varying sensations may be felt. Some points may feel sore or tender and there may be some discomfort such as a deep pain or coolness. However, it is believed that this form of massage works quickly so that any tenderness soon passes.

The number of treatments will vary from patient to patient, according to how the person responds and what problem or ailment is being treated. Weekly visits may be needed if a specific disorder is being treated while other people may go whenever they feel in need. It is advisable for women who are pregnant to check with their practitioner first since some of the acupressure methods are not recommended during pregnancy. Acupressure can be practised safely at home although it is usually better for one person to perform the massage on another. Common problems such as headache, constipation and toothache can be treated quite simply although there is the possibility of any problem worsening first before an improvement occurs if the pressure points are over stimulated. You should, however, see your doctor if any ailment persists. To treat headache, facial soreness, toothache and menstrual pain, locate the fleshy piece of skin between the thumb and forefinger and squeeze firmly, pressing towards the forefinger. The pressure should be applied for about five minutes and either hand can be used. This point is known as 'large intestine 4'.

To aid digestive problems in both adults and babies, for example to settle infantile colic, the point known as 'stomach 36' is utilized, which is located on the outer side of the leg about 75 mm (3 ins) down from the knee. This point should be quite simple to find as it can often feel slightly tender. It should be pressed quite firmly and strongly for about five to ten minutes with the thumb.

When practising acupressure massage on someone else and before treatment begins, ensure that the person is warm, relaxed, comfortable and wearing loose-fitting clothing and that he or she is lying on a firm mattress or rug on the floor. To discover the areas that need to be worked on, press firmly over the body and see which areas are tender. These tender areas on the body correspond to an organ that is not working correctly. To commence massage using fingertips or thumbs, a pressure

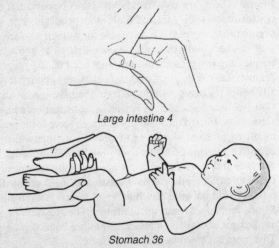

Large intestine 4

Stomach 36

of about 4.5 kg (10 lbs) should be exerted. The massage movements should be performed very quickly, about 50 to 100 times every minute, and some discomfort is likely (which will soon pass) but there should be no pain. Particular care should be taken to avoid causing pain on the face, stomach or over any joints. If a baby or young child is being massaged then considerably less pressure should be used. If there is any doubt as to the correct amount, exert a downwards pressure on bathroom scales to ascertain the weight being used. There is no need to hurry from one point to another since approximately 5 to 15 minutes is needed at each point for adults, but only about 30 seconds for babies or young children.

Using the 'self-help' acupressure, massage can be repeated as often as is felt to be necessary with several sessions per hour usually being sufficient for painful conditions that have arisen suddenly. It is possible that as many as 20 sessions may be necessary for persistent conditions causing pain, with greater intervals of time between treatments as matters improve. It is not advisable to try anything that is at all complicated (or to treat an illness such as arthritis) and a trained practitioner will obviously be able to provide the best level of treatment and help. To contact a reputable practitioner who has completed the relevant training it is advisable to contact the appropriate professional body.

Do-in

Do-in (pronounced doe-in) is another ancient type of massage that originated in China. It is a technique of self-massage and, as in other forms of alternative therapy, it is believed that there is a flow of energy throughout the body that travels along 'meridians' and that each of these is connected to a vital organ such as the lungs, liver and heart. Do-in has a connection with shiatsu (*see* page 170), and people of any age can participate, the only stipulation being that they are active and not out of condition. Clothing should not be tight or restrictive and adequate space is needed to perform the exercises.

If do-in is to be used as an invigorating form of massage, then the best time of day is as soon as possible after rising, but not after breakfast. After meals are the only times when do-in is to be avoided. It is generally recommended that people wishing to practise do-in should first go to classes so that when the exercises are done at home they are performed correctly. It is claimed that the use of do-in is preventive in nature since the vital organs are strengthened and therefore maintained in a healthy state.

Warming up

Before starting, it is best to do some warming-up exercises so that the body is not stiff. Begin by sitting on the ground with the knees up, grasp the knees and begin a rocking motion forwards and backwards. Then sit up, again on the floor, position the legs as if to sit cross-legged but put the soles of the feet touching each other. Hold the toes for a short time. These two exercises should help to make the body more supple (A).

A—warming up

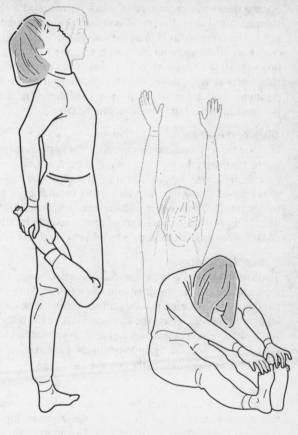

B—spleen meridian   *C—bladder meridian*

Spleen meridian

For the *spleen meridian* exercise, which is connected with the stomach, stand as near as possible in front of a wall. Place one hand palm-downwards high up the wall so that there is a good stretching action and with the other hand grasp the foot that is opposite to the raised arm. The neck and head should be stretched backwards, away from the wall. Maintain this stretched position, inhale and exhale deeply twice and then relax. Repeat the procedure using the other arm and leg (B).

Bladder meridian

For the *bladder meridian* exercise, and thereby the kidneys, sit on the floor with the legs straight out in front and ensure that the toes are tensed upright. The arms should then be stretched above the head and a breath taken. After breathing out, bend forwards from the shoulders with the arms in front and hold the toes. Maintain this for the length of time it takes to breathe in and out three times. Repeat the procedure again (C).

Pericardium meridian

To do the exercise for the *pericardium meridian*, which affects the circulation, sit on the floor with feet touching, but one behind the other, ensuring that the hands are crossed and touching opposite knees. Grasp the knees and incline the body forwards with the aim of pushing the knees downwards on to the floor. Do this exercise again but with the hands on opposite knees and the other foot on the outside.

Large intestine meridian

Using the exercise that strengthens the *large intestine meridian* and in turn the lungs, stand upright with the feet apart. Link the thumbs behind the back and then inhale. Exhale and at the same time place the arms outwards and upwards behind the back. To

D—Large intestine meridian

complete the exercise, lean forwards from the hips and then stand upright (D).

Gall bladder meridian

To strengthen the liver by stimulating the *gall bladder meridian*, sit upright on the floor with the legs the maximum distance apart. Then inhale, passing the arms along the length of the right leg so that the base of the foot can be held. There should be no movement of the buttocks off the floor. Maintain this stretched position while breathing deeply twice. Repeat the exercise using the other leg.

After all exercises have been accomplished, lie flat out on the floor with the legs apart and the arms stretched at the sides, palms uppermost. Then lift the head so that the feet can be seen and then put the head back on the floor again. The head and body should then be shaken so that the legs, arms and neck are loosened. To complete the relaxation, the eyes should be closed and the person should lie quietly for a few minutes.

Osteopathy

Introduction

An alternative medical treatment

Osteopathy is a technique that uses manipulation and massage to help distressed muscles and joints and make them work smoothly.

The profession began in 1892 when Dr Andrew Taylor Still (1828–1917), an American farmer, inventor and doctor, opened the USA's first school of osteopathic medicine. He sought alternatives to the medical treatments of his day which he believed were ineffective as well as often harmful.

Still's new philosophy of medicine, based upon the teachings of Hippocrates, advocated that 'Finding health should be the purpose of a doctor. Anyone can find disease.' Like Hippocrates, Still recognized that the human body is a unit in which structure, function, mind and spirit all work together. The therapy aims to pinpoint and treat any problems that are of a mechanical nature. The body's frame consists of the skeleton, muscles, joints and ligaments and all movements or activities such as running, swimming, eating, speaking and walking depend upon it.

A holistic treatment

Still came to believe that it would be safer to encourage the body to heal itself, rather than use the drugs that were then available and that were not always safe. He regarded the body from an engineer's point of view and the combination of this and his medical experience of anatomy, led him to believe that ailments and disorders could occur when the bones or joints no longer functioned in harmony. He believed that manipulation was the cure for the problem. Although his ideas provoked a great deal of opposition from the American medical profession at first, they slowly came to be accepted. The bulk of scientific research has been done in America with a number of medical schools of osteopathy being established. Dr Martin Littlejohn, who was a pupil of Dr Still, brought the practice of osteopathy to the UK around 1900, with the first school being founded in 1917 in London. He emphasized the compassionate care and treatment of the person as a whole, not as a collection of symptoms or unrelated parts. The philosophy and practices of A. T. Still, considered radical in the 1800s, are generally accepted principles of good medicine today.

Injuries and stress

Problems that prevent the body from working correctly or create pain can be due to an injury or stress. This can result in what is known as a tension headache since the stress experienced causes a contraction in muscles. These are situated at the back of the neck at the base of the skull and relief can be obtained by the use of massage. In osteopathy, it is believed that if the basic framework of the body is undamaged, then all physical activities can be accomplished efficiently and without causing any problems. The majority of an osteopath's patients suffer from disorders of the spine, which result in pain in the lower part of the back and the neck. A great deal of pressure is exerted on the spinal column, and especially on the cartilage between the individual vertebrae. This is a constant pressure due to the effects of gravity that occurs merely by standing. If a person stands incorrectly with stooped shoulders, this will exacerbate any problems or perhaps initiate one. The joints and framework of the body are manipulated and massaged where necessary so that the usual action is regained.

Athletes or dancers can receive injuries to muscles or joints such as the ankle, hip, wrist or elbow and they too can benefit from treatment by osteopathy. Pain in the lower back can be experienced by pregnant women who may stand in a different way due to their increasing weight and, if this is the case, osteopathy can often ease matters considerably. To find a fully qualified osteopath, it is advisable to contact the relevant professional body, or the G.P. may be able to help.

The treatment

The first visit
At the first visit to an osteopath, he or she will need to know the complete history of any problems experienced, how they first occurred and what eases or aggravates matters. A patient's case history and any form of therapy that is currently in use will all be of relevance to the practitioner. A thorough examination will then take place observing how the patient sits, stands or lies down and also the manner in which the body is bent to the side, back or front. As each movement takes place, the osteopath is able to take note of the extent and ability of the joint to function. The practitioner will also feel the muscles, soft tissues and ligaments to detect if there is any tension present. Whilst examining the body, the osteopath will note any problems that are present and, as an aid to diagnosis, use may also be made of checking reflexes, such as the knee-jerk reflex. If a patient has been involved in an accident, X-rays can be checked to determine the extent of any problem. It is possible that a disorder would not benefit from treatment by osteopathy and the patient would be advised accordingly. If this is not the case, treatment can commence with the chosen course of therapy.

A solution to tension

There is no set number of consultations necessary, as this will
depend upon the nature of the problem and also for how long it
has been apparent. It is possible that a severe disorder that has
arisen suddenly can be alleviated at once. The osteopath is likely
to recommend a number of things so that patients can help themselves between treatments. Techniques such as learning to relax, how to stand and sit correctly and additional exercises can
be suggested by the osteopath. Patients generally find that each
consultation is quite pleasant and they feel much more relaxed
and calm afterwards. The length of each session can vary, but it
is generally in the region of half an hour. As the osteopath gently manipulates the joint, it will lessen any tenseness present in
the muscles and also improve its ability to work correctly and
to its maximum extent. It is this manipulation that can cause a
clicking noise to be heard. As well as manipulation, other methods such as massage can be used to good effect. Muscles can
be freed from tension if the tissue is massaged and this will
also stimulate the flow of blood. In some cases, the patient may
experience a temporary deterioration once treatment has com-
menced, and this is more likely to occur if the ailment has ex-
isted for quite some time.

People who have to spend a lot of their life driving are susceptible to a number of problems related to the manner in which
they are seated. If their position is incorrect they can suffer
from tension headaches, pain in the back and the shoulders and
neck can feel stiff. There are a number of ways in which these
problems can be remedied such as holding the wheel in the
approved manner (at roughly 'ten to two' on the dial of a clock).
The arms should not be held out straight and stiff, but should
feel relaxed and with the arms bent at the elbow. In order that
the driver can maintain a position in which the back and neck

feel comfortable, the seat should be moved so that it is tilting backwards a little, although it should not be so far away that the pedals are not easily reached. The legs should not be held straight out, and if the pedals are the correct distance away the knees should be bent a little and feel quite comfortable. It is also important to sit erect and not slump in the seat. The driver's rear should be positioned right at the back of the seat and this should be checked each time before using the vehicle. It is also important that there is adequate vision from the mirror so its position should be altered if necessary. If the driver already has a back problem then it is a simple matter to provide support for the lower part of the back. If this is done it should prevent strain on the shoulders and backbone. Whilst driving, the person should make a conscious effort to ensure that the shoulders are not tensed, but held in a relaxed way. Another point to remember is that the chin should not be stuck out but kept in, otherwise the neck muscles will become tensed and painful. Drivers can perform some beneficial exercises while they are waiting in a queue of traffic. To stretch the neck muscles, put

Osteopathic treatment of the knee

the chin right down on to the chest and then relax. This stretching exercise should be done several times. The following exercise can also be done at the same time as driving and will have a positive effect on the flow of blood to the legs and also will improve how a person is seated. It is simply done by contraction and relaxation of the muscles in the stomach. Another exercise involves raising the shoulders upwards and then moving them backwards in a circular motion. The head should also be inclined forward a little. This should also be done several times to gain the maximum effect.

The figure on the previous page illustrates an example of diagnosis and treatment by manipulation, in which the osteopath examines a knee that has been injured. To determine the extent of the problem, the examination will be detailed and previous accidents or any other relevant details will be requested. If the practitioner concludes that osteopathy will be of benefit to the patient, the joint will be manipulated so that it is able to function correctly and the manipulation will also have the effect of relaxing the muscles that have become tensed due to the injury.

Another form of therapy, which is known as cranial osteopathy, can be used for patients suffering from pain in the face or head. This is effected by the osteopath using slight pressure on these areas including the upper part of the neck. If there is any tautness or tenseness present, the position is maintained while the problem improves. It is now common practice for doctors to recommend some patients to use osteopathy and some general practitioners use the therapy themselves after receiving training. Although its benefits are generally accepted for problems of a mechanical nature, doctors believe it is vital that they first decide upon what is wrong before any possible use can be made of osteopathy.

Polarity Therapy

Introduction

Origins

This is a therapy devised by Dr Randolph Stone (1890–1983) that amalgamates other healing therapies from both east and west. Dr Stone studied many of these therapies, including yoga (*see* page 194) and acupuncture (*see* page 7), and he was also trained to practise osteopathy (*see* page 82) and chiropractic (*see* page 28) among others. He began to search for a cure to the problem that he experienced with some of his patients when, although their disorder had been cured by the use of manipulation, they subsequently became unwell. Through his studies of eastern therapies he accepted the fundamental belief that a form of energy flows along certain channels in the body and that to keep good health the flow must be maintained. In India this energy is referred to as *prana* and in China it was called *chi* or *qi*. The western equivalent of this would probably be called a person's soul or spirit. It is believed that ailments occur when this flow of energy is blocked or is out of balance, and this could happen for different reasons such as tension or stress, disturbances in the mind or unhealthy eating patterns. This energy is purported to be the controlling factor in a person's whole life and therefore affects the mind and body at all levels. It is believed that once the flow of energy has been restored to normal, the ailment will disappear and not recur.

The underlying belief

Dr Stone's polarity therapy states that there are three types of relationships, known as *neutral*, *positive* and *negative*, to be maintained between various areas in the body and five centres of energy. These centres originate from a very old belief held in India, and each centre is held to have an effect on its related part of the body. The centres are known as *ether* (controlling the ears and throat), *earth* (controlling the rectum and bladder), *fire* (controlling the stomach and bowels), *water* (controlling the pelvis and glands), and *air* (controlling the circulation and breathing). The therapy's aim is to maintain a balance and harmony between all these various points, and Dr Stone slowly developed four procedures to do this. They are the use of *diet*, *stretching exercises*, *touch and manipulation*, and *mental attitude*, that is, contemplation allied with a positive view of life.

The treatment

Diet

To cleanse the body from a build-up of toxins caused by unhealthy eating and environmental pollution, the person will eat only fresh vegetables, fruit juices and fresh fruit. The length of time for this diet will vary according to the degree of cleansing required, but it is unlikely to be longer than a fortnight. Also available is a special drink that consists of lemon juice, olive oil, garlic and ginger. After the cleansing is complete, there is another diet to be followed that is said to promote and increase health, and finally one to ensure that the body maintains its level of good health.

Stretching exercises

Various positions may be adopted for the stretching exercises, such as on the floor with the legs crossed (A) or squatting or

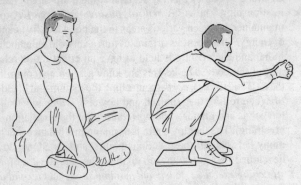

A—sitting with the legs
crossed

B—squatting

C—a change in the squatting
position

sitting with the hands held at the back of the head. It is believed that these exercises free the channels that carry the body's energy and strengthen the sinews, muscles, ligaments and spine. As a way of releasing any stress or tension, the person would be requested to shout out loud at the same time as exercising. For the first exercise, the person can sit on the floor cross-legged with the right hand taking hold of the left ankle and with the left hand holding the right ankle. The eyes should then be shut and the mind relaxed and quiet.

For the squatting exercise, once in this position, clasp the hands out in front for balance and then move backwards and forwards and also in a circular motion. For people unable to balance in this position, a small book or similar item put under the heels should help (B).

For a slight change on the basic squatting position, bend the head forward and place the hands at the back of the neck so that the head and arms are between the knees. Relax the arms a little so that they drop forward slightly and thus the backbone is stretched (C).

Another variation is to hold the hands behind the neck whilst squatting and push the elbows and shoulder blades backwards and inwards. Any tension or stress can be relieved by shouting at the same time as breathing deeply.

Another exercise in which stress can be eased by shouting is known as the *wood chopper*. This is a fairly simple one to perform, and it entails standing with the feet apart and the knees bent. The hands should be clasped above the head as if about to chop some wood and the arms brought down together in a swinging action ending with the arms as far between the legs as possible. As the hands are being swung downwards, the person should shout, so that any tension is relieved. This action can be repeated quite frequently as long as there is no discomfort (D).

Touch and manipulation

Touch and manipulation are used by the therapist to detect any stoppages in the flow of energy along the channels, which are believed to be the reason for disorders. It is said that by the use of pressure, of which there are three sorts, the therapist is able to restore the flow of energy. *Neutral pressure* is gentle and calming and only the tips of the fingers are used. *Positive pressure* is the use of manipulation over the whole of the body with the exception of the head. *Negative pressure* is the use of a firmer and deeper manipulation and touch.

Mental attitude

Mental attitude is the fourth procedure, and basically this encourages people to have a more positive view on all aspects of their lives. This is achieved by talking or counselling sessions, and it is believed that a negative view of things can make a person more susceptible to having an ailment. A positive attitude is regarded as being essential for harmony in the body and mind.

Polarity therapy is claimed to be of some benefit to all people who are ill, although it does not concentrate on a particular set of symptoms but is more concerned with the overall aspect of the patient's health and the achievement of internal harmony and balance. For the therapy to work successfully, each patient has to believe in it completely and be prepared to carry out the practitioner's instructions with regard to diet, exercises, and so on. It is, of course, always advisable to make sure that any therapist is fully qualified before beginning treatment. At the first consultation, the patient will be required to give a complete case history to the therapist, who will then assess the flow of energy through the body and also check on its physical make-up. Reflexes such as the knee-jerk reflex are tested, and any imbalances or blockages in the energy channels are detected by the reflex and pressure point testing. If there is a stoppage or imbalance of the flow, this will be manifested by some physical symptoms. One way in which it is believed a patient can help to speed the restoration of health is by remembering and concentrating on any thoughts, feelings or pictures in the 'mind's eye' that happen while a particular area is being treated. The patient should also have knowledge of the body's ability to heal itself. If a patient is receiving treatment on a painful knee joint, for example, he or she should focus attention on that part of the body whilst being receptive to any feelings that occur. It is believed that if the patient is aware of the overall condition, as a complete person and not just the physical aspect, this will encourage restoration of health. It is possible that a patient will need to keep details of all food consumed to enable the practitioner to detect any harmful effects, and a 'fruit and vegetable' diet may be advised (as described previously). It may be that the patient has some habit, view or manner of life that is not considered conducive to good health. If this is the case, the patient would be able to take advantage of a counselling service in order to help make a change. Other alternative therapies such as the use of herbal medicine may be used to effect a cure.

Polarity therapy has much in common with other eastern remedies that have the common themes of contemplation, exercise, touch or pressure, and diet and that can give much improvement. However, it is recommended that an accurate medical analysis of any condition is found in the first instance.

Reflexology

Introduction

Origins

Reflexology is a technique of diagnosis and treatment in which certain areas of the body, particularly the feet, are massaged to alleviate pain or other symptoms in the organs of the body. It is thought to have originated about five thousand years ago in China and was also used by the ancient Egyptians. It was introduced to Western society by Dr William Fitzgerald, who was an ear, nose and throat consultant in America. He applied ten zones (or energy channels) to the surface of the body, hence the term 'zone therapy', and these zones, or channels, were considered to be paths along which flowed a person's vital energy, or 'energy force'. The zones ended at the hands and feet. Thus, when pain was experienced in one part of the body, it could be relieved by applying pressure elsewhere in the body, within the same zone.

Subsequent practitioners of reflexology have concentrated primarily on the feet, although the working of reflexes throughout the body can be employed to beneficial effect.

Massage and energy flow

Reflexology does not use any sort of medication—merely a specific type of massage at the correct locations on the body. The body's energy flow is thought to follow certain routes, connecting every organ and gland with an ending or pressure point on the feet, hands or another part of the body. When the available routes are blocked, and a tenderness on the body points to such a closure, then it indicates some ailment or condition in the body that may be somewhere other than the tender area. The massaging of particular reflex points enables these channels to be cleared, restoring the energy flow and at the same time healing any damage.

The uses of reflexology are numerous, and it is especially effective for the relief of pain (back pain, headaches and toothache), treatment of digestive disorders, stress and tension, colds and influenza, asthma, arthritis, and more. It is also possible to predict a potential illness and either give preventive therapy or suggest that specialist advice be sought. The massaging action of reflexology creates a soothing effect that enhances blood flow, to the overall benefit of the whole body. Reflexology, however, clearly cannot be used to treat conditions that require surgery.

Reflex massage initiates a soothing effect to bring muscular and nervous relief. The pressure of a finger applied to a particular point (or nerve ending) may create a sensation elsewhere in the body, indicating the connection or flow between the two points. This is the basis of reflexology, and although pain may not be alleviated immediately, continued massage over periods of up to one hour will usually have a beneficial effect.

There are certain conditions for which reflexology is inappropriate, including diabetes, some heart disorders, osteoporosis, disorders of the thyroid gland, and phlebitis (inflammation of the veins). It may also not be suitable for pregnant women or anyone suffering from arthritis of the feet.

The best way to undergo reflexology is in the hands of a therapist, who will usually massage all reflex areas, concentrating on any tender areas that will correspond to a part of the body that is ailing. Reflexology can, however, be undertaken at home on minor conditions such as back pain, headache, etc, but care should be taken not to over-massage any one reflex point as it may result in an unpleasant feeling. Although there have not been any clinical trials to ascertain the efficacy of reflexology, it is generally thought that it does little harm and, indeed, much benefit may result.

Some practitioners believe that stimulation of the reflex points leads to the release of endorphins (in a manner similar to acupuncture). Endorphins are compounds that occur in the brain and have pain-relieving qualities similar to those of morphine. They are derived from a substance in the pituitary gland and are involved in endocrine control (glands producing hormones, for example, the pancreas, thyroid, ovary and testis).

The reflexes

Reflexes on the hands and feet
Reflexes on the feet—the soles of the feet contain a large number of zones, or reflexes, that connect with organs, glands or nerves in the body, as shown in the figures on pages 97–98. In addition, there are a small number of reflexes on the top and insides of the feet, as shown in the figures on page 99.

The *palms of the hands* similarly contain a large number of reflex areas, reflecting the arrangement seen on the soles of the feet, as shown in the figures on pages 100–101. The backs of the hands again mirror, to some extent, the tops of the feet, containing a smaller number of reflex areas (*see* the figures on page 102).

Use of the hands in reflexology
The hands are considered to have an electrical property, so that the right-hand palm is positive and the left-hand palm is nega-

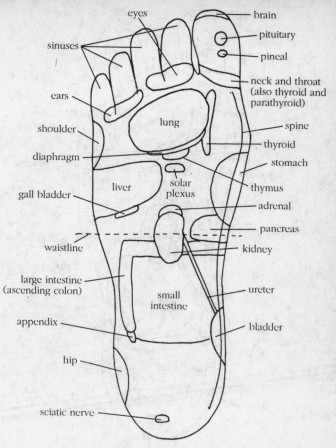

Major reflex points on the sole of the right foot

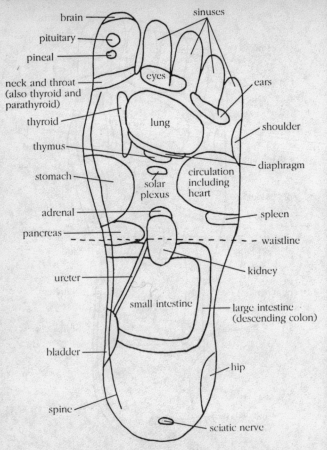

Major reflex points on the sole of the left foot

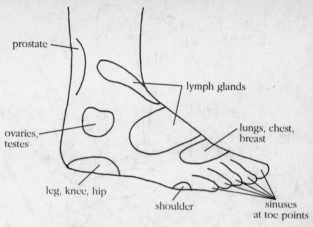

prostate

lymph glands

ovaries,
testes

lungs, chest,
breast

leg, knee, hip

shoulder

sinuses
at toe points

Reflex areas on the outside of the foot

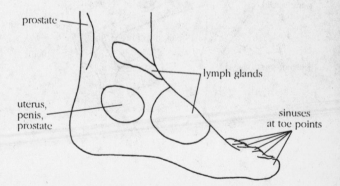

prostate

lymph glands

uterus,
penis,
prostate

sinuses
at toe points

Reflex areas on the inside of the foot

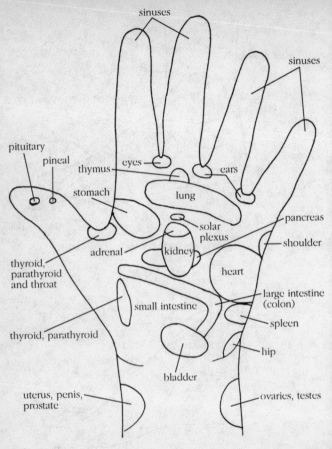

Major reflex points on the palm of the left hand

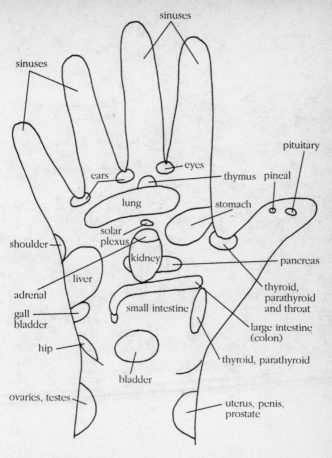

Major reflex points on the palm of the right hand

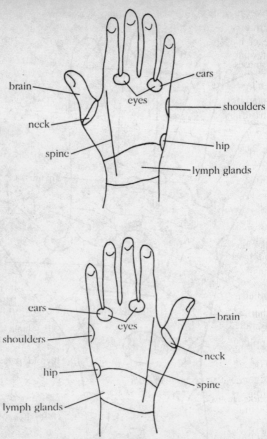

Reflexes on the backs of the hands

tive. In addition, the right hand has a reinforcing, stimulating effect while the left has a calming, sedative effect. The back of each hand is opposite to the palm, thus the right is negative and the left is positive. This is important when using reflexology because if the object is to revitalize the body and restore the energy flow that has been limited by a blockage then the right hand is likely to be more effective. The left hand, with its calming effect, is best used to stop pain.

Reflexes on the body

Reflexes on the body necessarily differ from those on the feet and hands in that there is less alignment with the ten zones (the figures on pages 104–105 show some of the reflexes on the body). Also, there are a number of reflex points on the body that correspond to several organs or glands. These reflex points are sometimes harder to find accurately and may be more difficult to massage.

The middle finger is thought to have the greatest effect, so this should be used to work the reflex point. Light pressure should be applied to each point, and if pain is felt it means there is a blockage or congestion somewhere. A painful point should be pressed until the discomfort subsides or for a few seconds at a time, a shorter rest being taken in between the applications of pressure.

The abdominal reflex

A general test can be applied by gently pressing into the navel, either with the middle finger or with one or both hands, with the individual lying in a supine position. The presence of a pulse or beat is taken to mean there is a problem in this area. To combat this, the same technique is used, holding for a few seconds (six or seven), releasing slightly, and keeping the fingers in the same area, gently massaging with a circular action. If it is nec-

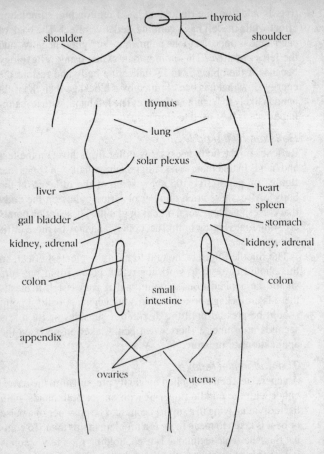

Major reflex areas on the body (female)

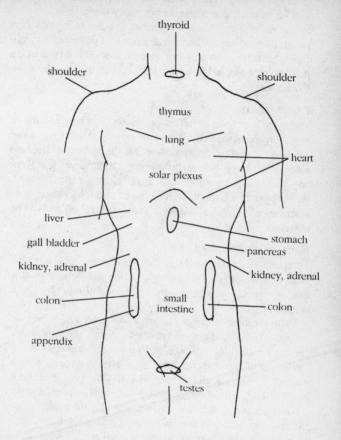

Major reflex areas on the body (male)

essary to press quite deep to feel the beat, then heavier massage will be required to provide the necessary stimulation.

The same principle can be applied to other reflex points in the abdominal region, and the absence of a pulse or beat indicates that there is no problem. In each case, should there be a painful response, holding for a few seconds invokes the sedative action.

Chest reflexes

There are a number of reflex points on the chest relating to major organs in the body. The same massage technique can be adopted for these reflex points as for the abdomen. Because many of the points lie over bone or muscle, however, it will not be possible to press in the finger as deeply as for the abdomen. However, pressure should be maintained over tender areas, with a subsequent circular massage, and a similar effect will be achieved.

Reflexes on the head

There are a surprisingly large number of reflex points on the head, although all may not be apparent immediately. With time and experience, such points are often located more by touch than by sight.

There are many important reflexes on the head including the stomach, kidneys, spleen and pancreas. Again, the middle finger can be used for massage, beginning in the middle of the forehead with a gentle circular motion. The massage should go through the skin to rub the bone beneath—the skin should not be rubbed. In so doing, a sensitive point may be felt (pituitary) and another one a little lower down, which is the pineal. (The pituitary gland secretes hormones that control many body functions and the pineal body is thought to regulate the natural variations in the body's activities over a 24-hour period.) This mas-

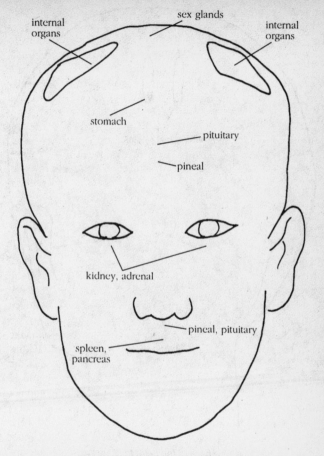

Some of the major reflex points on the head

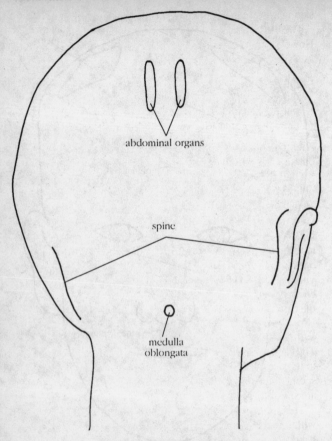

abdominal organs

spine

medulla
oblongata

*The back of the head to show the
medulla oblongata reflex*

saging action can be continued to check other parts of the body.

The back of the head also shows a large number of reflexes. However, there are a number of ways of stimulating the body as a whole through the head. These include:

- tapping the head gently with the fists, all over and very quickly for a period of about thirty seconds
- pulling handfuls of hair
- tapping the head gently with a wire brush

Each has a specific result, for example, stimulating the hair, but also enlivening organs and glands over the whole body.

One particularly important reflex point is the medulla oblongata. The medulla oblongata is the lowest part of the brain stem, which joins to the upper part of the spinal cord. It contains important centres for the control of respiration, swallowing, salivation and the circulation. This reflex point is located at the nape of the neck, towards the base of the skull. Massage of this point opens all channels within the body and generates a vitality, relieving nervous tension and producing almost instant energy. The point should be pressed and massaged to produce the desired effects.

Ear reflexes

The ear has long been used in acupuncture because, in addition to its ease of use, it contains scores of acupoints, which correspond to the reflex points in reflexology. Some of these points are shown in the figure on page 110.

The ear is perhaps the most difficult area of the body to work with because there are so many reflexes in such a small space. It becomes essentially a question of touch, pressing and exploring, and any sore point located can be massaged and worked out. By using a gentle squeeze-and-roll method on the tops of

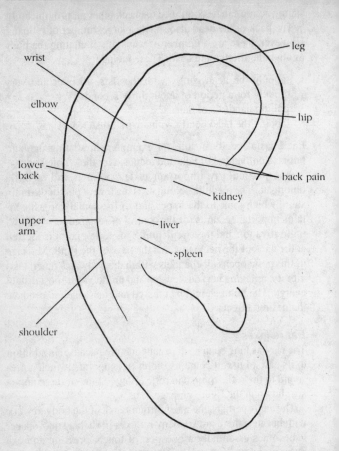

Some of the major reflex points on the ear

the ears and the ear lobes a number of areas can be stimulated. It has been reported that reflexology can help ear problems such as ringing in the ears, and the condition tinnitus may be alleviated to some extent.

Techniques and practice

Some indication of the massaging, manipulative procedures of reflexology have already been mentioned, but a number of general points of guidance can also be made.

The whole process of reflexology is one of calm, gentle movements in a relaxed state. The foot is probably used most in reflexology, in which case shoes and socks and stockings, etc, should be removed. A comfortable position should be adopted on the floor or bed, in a warm, quiet room with the back supported by pillows.

To begin, the whole foot is massaged, indeed both feet should ideally be worked on. However, if working on your own feet it is thought that the right foot should be massaged first (contrary to previous practice). It is considered that the right foot is linked with the past, hence these emotions must be released before the present and future aspects are dealt with in the left foot.

Techniques of massage vary, but a simple method with which to start involves placing the thumb in the middle of the sole of the foot. The thumb then presses with a circular and rocking motion for a few seconds before moving to another reflex. Reference can be made to the diagrams to determine which reflex is being massaged. In all cases, the massage should work beneath the skin, not on the skin. Another method involves starting the massage with the big toe and then moving on to each toe in turn. In using the thumbs to effect the massage, some refinements of motion can be introduced to give slightly different movements.

1 The thumb can be rocked between the tip and the ball, moving forwards over the relevant area. This, along with the circular massage already mentioned, relieves aches and pains.
2 Both thumbs can be used alternately to stroke the skin firmly. This creates a calming effect.
3 The area can be stroked with the thumbs, one moving over the other in a rotational sense. This action is intended to soothe and allow for personal development.

In addition to the procedures already mentioned, reflexology can be used to alleviate many symptoms and help numerous conditions. The following sections provide examples of these uses. Reflexology can be approached intuitively, so that the pressure of touch and the time factor can vary depending upon response and need.

The use of reflexology

The digestive system

The *stomach* is an organ that has thick muscular walls and in which food is reduced to an acidic semi-liquid by the action of gastric juices. There are many factors that can cause an upset stomach. To assess the general condition, the stomach body reflex (above the navel) can be pressed. Around it are several related reflexes such as the liver, gall bladder, intestines and colon. The reflex should be pressed for a few seconds and then released three times to activate the reflex.

On the *hands*, the web of soft tissue between the thumb and forefinger of the left hand should be worked with the thumb of the right hand for a few minutes. The hands can be reversed but the stronger effect will be gained this way, because the stomach lies mostly on the left side.

On the *feet*, the reflexes for the stomach are found primarily on the instep of the left foot, although they are also present on the right foot. These should be massaged, but there are further factors, in addition to the use of reflexology, that will aid digestion. These include eating a sensible diet with a minimum of artificial substances, and not overeating. The use of certain essential oils (aromatherapy) can also be of benefit. In this case peppermint oil can often be particularly effective.

The *colon* is the main part of the large intestine in which water and salts are removed from the food that enters from the small intestine. After extraction of the water, the waste remains are passed on to the rectum as faeces. If this system becomes unbalanced in any way, then the water may not be absorbed or the food remains pass through the colon so quickly that water cannot be absorbed. In such cases, the result is diarrhoea, which can be painful and inconvenient.

Both body and foot reflexes should be massaged for the stomach, intestines, colon and also the liver and kidneys. The thyroid reflex should also be worked to help regulation of the body functions. A useful body reflex is to press and rotate your finger about two inches above the navel for a couple of minutes. This can be repeated numerous times, each time moving the fingers a little clockwise around the navel until a complete circuit has been made.

It is important that the condition be stabilized as soon as possible as continued loss also leads to loss of vital salts and a general nutritional deficiency.

At the outset it is possible to work the colon reflexes on the hand to identify any tender areas. The right thumb should be pressed into the edge of the pad (around the base and side of the thumb) of the left palm and worked around to seek out any tender spots. Any tender reflex should be massaged and pressed for a few seconds. In each case, the tenderness should be worked out. Since there are many reflex points crowded onto the navel, it may not solely be the colon reflex that requires some attention. It is always useful to work the reflex on both sides of the body to ensure a balance is achieved.

A similar approach can be adopted for reflexes on the feet, starting at the centre, or waistline. By applying a rolling pressure, the foot is massaged along to the inner edge and then down the line of the spine and any tender points are worked through pressure and massage. It may be necessary to start with a very light pressure if the area is very tender, and then as the soreness lessens, the pressure can be increased.

Again, diet can be an important factor in maintaining the health of the body and the workings of the colon. Fibre is particularly important in ensuring a healthy digestive system and avoiding ailments such as diverticulitis.

Reflexology can be used for other conditions associated with the digestive system, notably ulcers. A peptic ulcer (in the stomach, duodenum or even the oesophagus) is caused by a break in the mucosal lining. This may be due to the action of acid, bile or enzymes because of unusually high concentrations or a deficiency in the systems that normally protect the mucosa. The result can be a burning sensation, belching and nausea.

To help alleviate the problem, which may often be stress-related, the reflexes in the feet should be massaged, as these are often the most relaxing. Obviously, the important reflexes are the stomach and duodenum, but it is also worthwhile to work on the liver and the endocrine glands (notably the pituitary). If the ulcer is a long-standing problem or if stomach complaints have been experienced for some time, then further medical help is probably needed.

The heart and circulatory system

The heart is obviously a vital organ. This muscular pump is situated between the lungs and slightly left of the midline. It projects forward and lies beneath the fifth rib. Blood returns from the body via the veins and enters the right atrium (the upper chamber), which contracts, forcing the blood into the right ventricle. From there it goes to the lungs where it gains oxygen and releases carbon dioxide before passing to the left atrium and left ventricle. Oxygenated blood then travels throughout the body via the arteries.

By using body reflexes, the heart can be maintained, and conditions can be dealt with by massaging the appropriate reflex points. A useful massage exercise is to work the muscles, rather than the reflex points, of the left arm in a side-to-side movement. This can be followed by the neck muscles and the chest muscles; in each case any tightness or tension should be massaged out. An additional preventive is a good diet, which should be low in fat and food high in cholesterol, but should contain adequate amounts of vitamins, notably the B group, C and E. Exercise is, of course, very important to maintain a good heart and circulation.

There is also a simple test that many reflexologists feel is useful in the diagnosis of possible heart problems. It may also be worth doing if strenuous activity is contemplated in the near future. Pressure is applied to the pad of the left thumb, at the top. The pressure should be quite hard. It is suggested that when this part of the pad hurts, it indicates a constriction in blood vessels, limiting supply. If the bottom of the pad hurts, this is indicative of congested arteries. If the area is too tender to touch (and there is no physical damage to the hand) then there is a possibility of a heart attack. This test thus provides advance warning and enables a medical doctor to be consulted. Should painful areas occur on both hands, this does *not* indicate a heart problem.

Many blood and circulatory disorders will benefit from the same sort of massage. In these cases the foot reflexes for the endocrine glands (hypothalamus, pituitary, pineal, thyroid and parathyroid, thymus, adrenals, pancreas, ovary or testis) should be worked well, as should those for the circulatory system and heart, lungs and lymphatic system.

Conditions that may benefit from such treatment include:

Angina
A suffocating, choking pain usually referring to angina pectoris, which is felt in the chest. It occurs when blood supply to the heart muscle is inadequate and is brought on by exercise and relieved by rest. The coronary arteries may be damaged by atheroma (scarring and buildup of fatty deposits). Of particular importance are the heart and circulatory reflexes (veins and arteries) and those of the lymphatic system.

Arteriosclerosis
A general term including atheroma and atherosclerosis (where arteries degenerate and fat deposits reduce blood flow), which results generally in high blood pressure and can lead to angina. Additional reflexes that should be worked include the liver.

Hypertension (high blood pressure)
This may be one of several types, the commonest being *essential* (due to kidney or endocrine disease or an unknown cause) and *malignant* (a serious condition that tends to occur in the younger age groups). In addition to the reflexes for the blood and circulation, those for the shoulders, neck and eyes should be worked, in combination with reflexes for the digestive system and liver.

Palpitations

An irregular heartbeat, often associated with heightened emotions. Also due to heart disease or may be felt during pregnancy. The lung and heart reflexes are particularly important, in addition to those of the circulation.

Some heart conditions are very serious and require immediate hospitalization, e.g. cardiac arrest (when the heart stops) and coronary thrombosis (a coronary artery blockage causing severe chest pain, vomiting, nausea and breathing difficulties. The affected heart muscle dies, a condition known as myocardial infarction). However, massage of appropriate reflexes may help, particularly in less serious cases. These should include the heart and circulation (veins and arteries), lungs, endocrine system and the brain. Each will have some beneficial effect in relieving stress and congestion.

Varicose veins

Veins that have become stretched, twisted and distended, and this often happens to the superficial veins in the legs. The possible causes are numerous and include pregnancy, defective valves, obesity and thrombophlebitis (the inflammation of the wall of a vein with secondary thrombosis). Phlebitis is inflammation of a vein and occurs primarily as a complication of varicose veins. Both these conditions can be treated by massaging the circulatory reflexes and also the leg and liver reflexes. In both cases, resting with the legs in an elevated position is beneficial.

The respiratory system

Asthma is one of the major problems of the respiratory system and its incidence seems to be escalating. The condition is caused by a narrowing of the airways in the lungs. It usually begins in early childhood and may be brought on by exposure to allergens (substances, usually proteins, that cause allergic reactions) exercise or stress.

There are certain body reflexes that can help in this instance. One reflex point is in the lower neck at the base of the V-shape created by the collar bones. Relief may be achieved by pressing the finger into this point with a downward motion for a few seconds. There are additional reflex points on the back, at either side of the spine in the general region of the shoulder blades. These can be worked by someone else with thumb or finger, who should press for a few seconds. Other reflexes that can be worked on the foot include the brain, endocrine glands such as the pineal, pituitary, thymus and thyroid, the lungs, and also the circulatory system. Particular attention should be paid to the lungs, which includes the bronchi and bronchioles, the branching passageways of the lungs where gaseous exchange (oxygen in, carbon dioxide out) takes place. At the point where the instep meets the hard balls of the feet, and along the base of the lung reflex area is the massage point for the diaphragm. Working the whole of this area will help alleviate symptoms of asthma. During an attack of asthma, both thumbs can be placed on the solar plexus reflexes immediately to initiate the soothing process.

The adrenal glands are found one to each kidney, situated on the upper surface of that organ. These are important endocrine glands because they produce hormones such as adrenaline and cortisone. Adrenaline is very important in controlling the rate of respiration and it is used medically in the treatment of bronchial asthma because it relaxes the airways. It is clear therefore, that the adrenal is an important reflex and it is located in the middle of each sole and palm.

Many other respiratory disorders can be helped by using massage of the same reflexes: brain, endocrine glands, lungs and diaphragm, neck and shoulders, augmented by the heart and circulatory system. Conditions responding to this regime include bronchitis, croup, lung disorders and emphysema (distension and thinning, particularly of lung tissue, leading to air-filled spaces that do not contribute to the respiratory process).

Infections of the respiratory tract leading to coughs and colds can also be helped primarily by working the reflexes mentioned above. For colds, the facial reflexes should be massaged, especially that for the nose. However, it is good practice to include the pituitary, and to work the index and middle fingers towards the tip to help alleviate the condition.

With such respiratory problems, there are complementary therapies that can help such as homoeopathy, aromatherapy and Bach flower remedies. There are also many simple actions that can be taken, for example a sore throat may be helped by gargling regularly with a dessertspoon of cider apple vinegar in a glass of water, with just a little being swallowed each time. Honey is also a good substance to take, as are onion and garlic.

The endocrine glands

Summary

Endocrine glands are glands that release hormones directly into the bloodstream, or lymphatic system. Some organs, such as the pancreas, also release secretions via ducts. The major endocrine glands are, in addition to the pancreas, the thyroid, parathyroid, pituitary, pineal, thymus, adrenal and gonads (ovaries and testes).

The endocrine glands are of vital importance in regulating body functions as summarized below:

pituitary	controls growth, gonads, kidneys; known as the master gland
pineal	controls the natural daily rhythms of the body
thyroid	regulates metabolism and growth
parathyroid	controls calcium and phosphorus metabolism
thymus	vital in the immune system, particularly pre-puberty
adrenal	control of heartbeat, respiration and metabolism
gonads	control of reproductive activity
pancreas	control of blood sugar levels

The fact that the endocrine glands are responsible for the very core of body functions means that any imbalance should be corrected immediately to restore the normality. There are some general points relating to massage of these reflex areas. It is good practice to massage the brain reflex first and then the pituitary. This is because the hypothalamus, situated in the forebrain, controls secretions from the pituitary gland. The pituitary gland then follows as this is the most important in the endocrine system. The reflexes should be gently massaged with thumb or finger for a few seconds and then gentle pressure exerted and held for a few seconds before releasing slowly.

The pituitary

An imbalance of pituitary gland secretions, often caused by a benign tumour, can lead to acromegaly (excessive growth of skeletal and soft tissue). Gigantism can result if it occurs during adolescence. There may also be consequent deficiencies in adrenal, gonad and thyroid activity. The brain and endocrine reflexes should be worked in order, supplemented by those for the circulation, liver and digestion. In addition to reflex points on the hands and feet, there is also one on the forehead. If any of these reflex areas is found to be tender, it should be massaged often to maintain the balance necessary for healthy growth.

The pineal

The pineal body, or gland, is situated on the upper part of the mid-brain, although its function is not fully understood. It would seem, however, to be involved in the daily rhythms of the body and may also play a part in controlling sexual activity. The pineal reflex points are found close to those of the pituitary on the big toes, thumbs and on the forehead and upper lip.

The thyroid

The thyroid is located at the base of the neck and it produces two important hormones, thyroxine and triiodothyronine. Under or overactivity of the thyroid leads to specific conditions.

If the thyroid is overactive and secretes too much thyroxine (hyperthyroidism), the condition called thyrotoxicosis develops. It is also known as Grave's disease and is typified by an enlarged gland, protruding eyes and symptoms of excess metabolism such as tremor, hyperactivity, rapid heart rate, breathlessness, etc. The important reflexes on which to concentrate are the brain and solar plexus, endocrine system and also the circulatory and digestive systems. The reflexes are found on the soles and palms and using the thumbs or fingers, the areas should be massaged, but in stages if the area is very tender.

Underactivity of the thyroid, or hypothyroidism, can cause myxoedema producing dry, coarse skin, mental impairment, muscle pain and other symptoms. In children a similar lack causes cretinism, resulting in dwarfism and mental retardation. The reflexes to be worked are essentially those mentioned for hyperthyroidism, and in addition (for both conditions) the liver reflexes on the right sole and palm should benefit from attention.

There are additional thyroid reflexes elsewhere on the body, notably on the neck roughly midway between jaw and collarbone and on either side. These points should be massaged gently with the thumb and fingers on opposite sides of the throat. Using a gentle gyratory motion, the massage can be taken down to the collarbone, the fingers and thumb of the other hand are then used (on opposite sides of the throat) and the procedure repeated.

Goitre is another condition associated with the thyroid and is a swelling of the neck caused by enlargement of the gland, typically due to overactivity of the gland to compensate for an iodine deficiency. The important reflexes to concentrate upon are the brain, solar plexus, endocrine system and circulatory system but working of all body reflexes will help.

The parathyroid

There are four small parathyroid glands located behind or within the thyroid. They control the use of calcium and phosphorus (as phosphate) in the body's metabolism. An imbalance of these vital elements can lead to tetany (muscular spasms), or at the other extreme, calcium may be transferred from the bones to the blood, creating a tendency to bone fractures and breaks.

The reflexes to these glands are found in the same location as those for the thyroid but it will probably be necessary to massage more strongly to achieve an effect. It is a good idea to work on these areas each time reflexology is undertaken as they are vital in maintaining the metabolic equilibrium of the body.

The thymus

The thymus is located in the neck (over the breastbone) and is a vital contributor to the immune system. It is larger in children and is important in the development of the immune response. After puberty it shrinks although seems to become more active later in life. Bone marrow cells mature within the thymus and one group, T-lymphocytes, are dependent upon the presence of the thymus. These are important cells as they produce antibodies.

The commonest disorder associated with the thymus is myasthenia gravis, which lowers the level of acetylcholine (a neurotransmitter) resulting in a weakening of skeletal muscles and those used for breathing, swallowing, etc. The thymus reflexes are found on the soles of the feet and palms of the hand, next to the lung reflexes. The thymus can also be stimulated by tapping with the finger over its position in the middle of the upper chest.

The adrenals

The two adrenals (also known as suprarenals) are situated one above each kidney and consist of an inner medulla and an outer cortex. The medulla produces adrenaline, which increases the rate and depth of respiration, raises the heartbeat and improves muscle performance, with a parallel increase in output of sugar from the liver into the blood.

The cortex of the adrenal glands releases hormones including aldosterone, which controls the balance of electrolytes in the body, and cortisone, which, among other functions, is vital in the response to stress, inflammation and fat deposition in the body.

On both the palms and soles, the adrenal reflexes are located above those for the kidneys and if this area is at all tender, it should be massaged for a few seconds. Because the kidney and adrenal reflexes are close together, the massage should be limited to avoid over-stimulation of the kidney reflexes. Disorders of the adrenal glands should be treated by working the endocrine reflexes starting with the pituitary and including the adrenal reflexes themselves, followed by the reflexes for the circulatory, liver and urinary systems.

Specific disorders include Cushing's syndrome, caused by an overproduction of cortisone, which results in obesity, reddening of the face and neck, growth of body and facial hair, high blood pressure, osteoporosis and possibly mental disturbances, and Addison's disease, which results from damage to the cortex and therefore a deficiency in hormone secretion. The latter was commonly caused by tuberculosis but is now due more to disturbances in the immune system. The symptoms are weakness, wasting, low blood pressure and dark pigmentation of the skin. Both these conditions can be treated by hormone replacement therapy but reflexology can assist, through massage of the endocrine, digestive and liver reflexes.

The gonads

The gonads, or sex glands, comprise the ovaries in women and testes in men. The ovaries produce eggs and also secrete hormones, mainly oestrogen and progesterone. Similarly, the testes produce sperm and the hormone testosterone. Oestrogen controls the female secondary sexual characteristics such as enlargement of the breasts, growth of pubic hair and deposition of body fat. Progesterone is vital in pregnancy as it prepares the uterus for implantation of the egg cell.

The reflexes for these and related organs are found near the ankles on the inside of the feet, just below the angular bone (*see* figure depicting the reflex areas on the inside and outside of the feet on page 99). The same reflex areas are also located on the arms, near the wrist. The ovaries and testes are on the outer edge, while on the opposite, inner edge, are the reflexes for the uterus, penis and prostate.

For any disorders that might involve the ovaries or testes, it is also useful to massage other systems such as the brain, other endocrine glands, the circulation and liver.

The pancreas

This is an important gland with both endocrine and exocrine functions. It is located behind the stomach, between the duodenum and spleen. The exocrine function involves secretion of pancreatic juice via ducts, into the intestine. The endocrine function is vital in balancing blood sugar levels through the secretion of two hormones, insulin and glucagon. Insulin controls the uptake of glucose by body cells and a lack of hormone results in the sugar derived from food being excreted in the urine, the condition known as diabetes mellitus. Glucagon works in the opposite sense to insulin, and increases the supply of blood sugar through the breakdown of glycogen in the liver, to produce glucose.

The primary reflexes for the pancreas are found on the soles and palms, near to the stomach. The thumb should be used, starting on the left foot, working across the reflex area and on to the right foot. If the area is tender, it should be worked until the tenderness goes. Because there are numerous reflexes in this area, there will be stimulation of other organs, to the general wellbeing of the body as a whole.

For other disorders of the pancreas, such as pancreatitis (inflammation of the pancreas) the reflexes associated with digestion should also be worked. Pancreatitis may result from gallstones or alcoholism and, if sufficiently severe, may cause diabetes.

The liver and spleen

The role of the liver

The liver is a very important organ and is critical in regulating metabolic processes. It is the largest gland in the body and is situated in the top right hand part of the abdominal cavity.

Among the functions, the liver converts excess glucose to glycogen, which is stored as a food reserve; excess amounts of amino acids are converted into urea for excretion; bile is produced for storage in the gall bladder and some poisons are broken down. The liver also recycles red blood cells to remove the iron when the cells reach the end of their life; it stores vitamins and produces blood clotting substances. Due to its high chemical and biochemical activity, the liver generates a lot of heat and is the major contributor of heat to the body.

The liver reflex points

The reflex area for the liver is a large area, reflecting the size of the organ, on the right palm and right sole, on the outer edge. As a general procedure, the area should be massaged with the left thumb, searching for tender points. More massage may be required for the liver than for other reflexes.

Hepatitis is inflammation of the liver due to viral infection or the presence of toxins. Alcohol abuse commonly causes hepatitis, and it may also be due to drug overdose or drug side effects. Viral infections such as HIV and glandular fever can also cause hepatitis. There are several types of hepatitis, designated A to E, and all may persist in the blood for a long time.

To combat such disorders, after removing the source of any toxins, the reflex for the liver and digestion should be worked and the reflexes for the eyes. Dietary restraint is also important and should involve natural foods with little or no alcohol, caffeine, nicotine and a low intake of fats.

Associated with the liver, anatomically, is the gall bladder. This is a small sac-like organ that stores and concentrates bile. When fats are digested, the gall bladder contracts, sending bile into the duodenum. Sometimes stones form here, and often gallstones can cause severe pain. The gall bladder reflex is found at the foot of the liver on the right palm and foot. On the body there is another reflex just below the ribs on the right-hand side, and below the liver reflex point. A steady pressure should be held around the point, beginning near the navel and working to the right side, maintaining pressure for a few seconds on any tender point.

The role of the spleen

The spleen is situated on the left side of the body behind and below the stomach. The spleen produces leucocytes (white blood cells), lymphocytes (a white blood cell involved in the immune system), blood platelets (involved in blood coagulation) and plasma cells. It also acts as a store for red blood cells, which are made available in emergencies (when oxygen demand is greater).

The spleen reflex point

The reflex area for the spleen is found on the left palm or sole, below the reflex for the heart. If a tender point is found in this reflex, it may indicate anaemia and it would then be wise to obtain a blood test.

The kidneys and bladder

The role of the kidneys and bladder

The kidneys are important organs in the body's excretory system. They are responsible for processing the blood continuously to remove nitrogenous wastes (mainly urea) and they also adjust salt concentrations. By testing the reflexes with the thumb, tender areas can be located and worked upon. However, prolonged massage should be avoided—it is better to use shorter periods of 15–20 seconds initially as the system becomes accustomed to the treatment.

It is not surprising, considering the pivotal role of the kidneys in removing body wastes, that any interference with their normal function can lead to serious illnesses. General kidney disorders, kidney stones, nephritis and pyelitis are all best aided by massaging the kidney reflex but also the reflexes for the central nervous system, the endocrine glands (especially the pituitary and adrenal glands), liver, stomach and circulation. Kidney stones are formed by the deposition of solid substances that are naturally found in the urine but that precipitate out for one reason or another. They are commonly salts of calcium, and the alteration in pH of the urine is often a contributory factor. Nephritis is inflammation of the kidney and pyelitis is when part of the kidney, the pelvis, becomes inflamed. If the whole kidney becomes affected, it is then called pyelonephritis.

The kidney and bladder reflex points

Disorders associated with the bladder tend to be infections such as cystitis or other physical manifestation of a problem whether through stress or a medical condition. The latter category includes enuresis (bed-wetting) and incontinence. In these cases, the bladder reflex should obviously be worked upon, and the reflexes for the brain, solar plexus and endocrine system.

The reflexes for the kidneys are found just off centre on the palms of both hands and soles of both feet. They are close to the pancreas and stomach. The bladder reflex is towards the base of the palm, near the wrist and on the feet it is found on the inside edge of both soles, towards the heel. There are also body reflexes for both organs.

The body reflexes for the kidney are at the side of the body, almost at the waistline, between the hip and rib cage. They also occur on the face, just beneath the eyes.

The alleviation of back pain and other skeletal disorders

The reflex points for the spine

Within the working population of most countries, back pain accounts for millions of days in lost production. This is not unexpected as the spine is the primary part of the skeleton, hence any problem with it will inevitably upset the body and its overall wellbeing.

On the soles of the feet, the reflex for the spine is located along the inner edge of both feet running from the base of the big toe almost to the heel. By working this line with the fingers, any tender points can be found and worked upon. The top end of the line, near the toe, is equivalent to the spine at the level of the shoulders.

Treatment of back disorders through reflexology

With back disorders, such as lumbago, additional reflexes should be worked including the brain and endocrine system. Because the body's musculature is a complementary and antagonistic system with the skeleton, creating all the movements of which the body is capable, the muscles are also important when dealing with back pain. It will help therefore to massage muscles, rubbing quite deeply with the fingers, and moving across the muscles.

Back pain can result from a problem elsewhere in the body with posture, tight muscles or even flat feet. It is important to be aware of the possibilities and ensure that the treatment deals with the problem as a whole, and not just in part. Exercise is clearly beneficial and walking can help loosen and strengthen muscles associated with the back. A brisk walk is fine, but jogging is not necessarily the best remedy, as in some cases this can itself prove harmful.

Reflexologists often turn to the muscles in the legs to alleviate back pain, particularly in the area of the lower back. The muscles at the back of the thigh should be massaged with a pressing and pulling action, first with one hand and then the other. The whole of the thigh should be treated, from the top of the leg, to the knee. Massage of both legs in this manner, concentrating on any 'tight' areas, will help improve the overall tone and assist in eliminating causes of back pain.

Study of the diagrams for the feet and hands reveals specific reflex areas for the shoulders, hip and neck. When working on skeletal disorders in general, it is wise to undertake a thorough massage of specific reflex areas such as neck and shoulders, plus those for the brain, solar plexus, the endocrine system, remainder of the skeletal system, endocrine glands, etc. For particular conditions such as bursitis (inflammation of a joint, as in housemaid's knee), general joint pain, stiff neck and similar complaints, a common regime of reflexological massage applies. This should include working the skeletal reflexes along with those for the nervous and endocrine system, digestive and circulatory systems. It is usually the case that the specific complaint will benefit from massage of its reflex area and most of those that comprise a whole body workout. It should always be remembered that there are occasions when surgery may prove essential, e.g. in the case of a hip replacement.

The knee joint can often be the source of pain and discomfort. It may help to apply gentle pressure on either side of the knee, just where the bone ends, using the thumb and middle finger. This should be held for a few seconds, pressing as much as possible (do not press hard if it is too painful) and then the same should be done below the knee.

Relief from arthritis with reflexology

Arthritis can be a crippling disease and many people suffer from it. It is an inflammation of joints or the spine, the symptoms of which are pain and swelling, restriction of movement, redness and warmth of the skin. Two forms of the condition are osteoarthritis and rheumatoid arthritis.

Treatment of osteoarthritis through reflexology

Osteoarthritis involves the cartilage in joints, which then affects the associated bone. What often happens is that the cartilage is lost, to be replaced by osteophytes at the edges of the bones. These are bony projections that occur with the loss of cartilage or with age. The projections affect the joint function, causing pain.

Treatment of rheumatoid arthritis through reflexology

Rheumatoid arthritis is the second commonest joint disease after osteoarthritis. It usually affects the feet, ankles, wrists and fingers in which there is a swelling of the joint and inflammation of the synovial membrane (the membraneous envelope around the joint). Then follows erosion and loss of cartilage and loss of bone. At its worst, the condition can be disabling.

Massage of the reflex areas for the affected areas should be worked but, as mentioned previously, it is important to massage the reflexes for the whole body to achieve a complete and balanced approach. The endocrine system is one important system in this respect.

In seeking ways to treat rheumatoid arthritis, the medical profession isolated the glucocorticosteroid hormone, cortisone, from the adrenal glands of cattle. It was found that the use of cortisone had dramatic effects on the symptoms of rheumatoid arthritis. However, the relief was only temporary, and an additional disadvantage was the occurrence of associated side effects, which could be severe, e.g. damage to muscle, bone, stomach ulcers, bleeding and imbalances in the hormonal and nervous systems. The medical use of this compound is therefore very restricted, but it is produced naturally by the adrenal cortex. Being a natural secretion, there are no detrimental side effects. There is a reflex point in the lower back, between the first and second lumbar vertebrae, which can be pressed. Finding this point will be hit and miss initially, but upon locating it (roughly 5 cm up from the coccyx or tailbone), apply gentle pressure, gradually increasing, and hold it for a few seconds. This should be repeated several times. This is helpful for other conditions, in addition to rheumatoid arthritis, such as asthma and bursitis.

As with back disorders, muscle condition is also felt to be important in the treatment of arthritis. The muscles in the area affected by arthritis should be massaged by pressing in with the fingers, either on or near to the area. The massage should be across the muscles, with a deep motion, although it may initially produce discomfort or soreness. Many practitioners regard this as an important supplementary technique in administering reflexology.

Stress and tension

The relaxing effects of reflexology
One of the additional beneficial effects of reflexology when dealing with a particular reflex area or point is that the treatment is very relaxing. If most of the body reflexes are massaged, a feeling of wellbeing is generated, and tension is released. Stress control and relief can be accomplished in a number of ways, some of which happen instinctively, such as deep breathing and, paradoxically, wringing the hands. The latter is

an obvious way of working the reflex points, albeit that it is mostly done unconsciously. A related method of calming the nerves is to intertwine the fingers, as in clasping the hands, which enables all the reflexes between the fingers to be pressed. This should be done several times. Deep breathing is a common method of relaxation that ultimately can envelop the whole body, providing that the focus of attention is the attainment of the correct pattern of breathing. Mental attitude is also an important aspect of reflexology. It clearly makes sense, while undergoing massage (with or without a practitioner or partner) to imagine, or listen to, pleasing sounds, rather than worrying about the pressures of modern life. If there is no access to relaxing sounds (bird song, running water, etc) it is perfectly possible to imagine it, and thereby to augment the physical relaxation with mental calm.

Reflex points for treating stress

The *endocrine glands* are considered important in combating stress because they are responsible for the hormonal balance of the body. All reflex areas for these glands, on both soles and palms, should be massaged and special attention given to the thyroid, which controls body temperature and can help restore calm. The adrenal reflex point, almost in the centre of the hand, is also important, and, because it is so near the solar plexus, receives equal attention. (The solar plexus is a network of nerves and ganglia in the sympathetic nervous system concerned with body functions not under conscious control. It is located behind the stomach).

Quite often stress and tension can result in a sore neck or back. A number of reflex points can be worked to relieve these sorts of complaint. The medulla oblongata is important in this respect as it controls some major body functions such as the circulation. The point on the back of the head (*see* the figure on page 108) should be held with the middle finger for a few seconds and then released, and repeated several times. The reflex points of the spine should also be worked starting at the neck reflex, which is found below the base of the big toe or thumb. By moving down the side of the foot, the whole spine can be covered. To relieve a sore back completely and effectively, other reflexes to be attended to should include the shoulders, hips, and the sciatic nerve. The sciatic nerve is made up of a number of nerve roots from the lower part of the spinal cord, and pain with this origin may be felt in the back of the thigh, buttock and the foot. The reflex point may at first be painful to the touch, but through careful massage it can be worked to assist in promoting relief.

Control of the heart rate is a natural, complementary procedure in promoting stress relief. If a situation, wherever it may be, results in you feeling stressed, massaging the reflex areas for the heart will help, whether on foot or hand.

Sound, restful sleep is refreshing and also contributes to a reduction in stress. Reflexology can also help in this respect through the feeling of relaxation that it induces. The clasping of the hands, mentioned earlier, can be used to combat sleeplessness. The fingers can be clasped on the chest and then worked over each other so that the length of each finger is massaged. The fingers should remain intertwined and simply be released a little to allow each finger over the first knuckle, when the fingers are squeezed together again. This, associated with deep breathing will encourage relaxation.

Reflexology and the reproductive system

Reflex points for the reproductive system
The major reflexes of the reproductive system are those for the

uterus, ovary and breast in the female, and the penis, testes and prostate in the male. The ovary reflexes are found on the outer side of the foot, just below the ankle (*see* figures on page 99). On the hand, these are found a little way beyond the wrist (*see* figures on page 102), on the outer edge. On both foot and hand, the breast reflex is found on the outer edge, a little below the base of the little toe or finger. The uterus reflex on the hand occupies a position opposite to the ovaries, i.e. just below the wrist, but on the inner edge of the arm. On the foot, this reflex mirrors that for the ovary, but it is on the inside of the foot, below the ankle.

The male reflexes

The male reflexes occupy the same positions as those of the female, thus the penis reflex is in the same position as that for the uterus and the testes is the same as the ovaries. The prostate gland reflexes are situated with the penis reflex and also at the back of the leg/foot, above the heel, (*see* the figures on page 99).

There are also reflex points on the head for the gonads (*see* sex glands on the diagram of the reflex points on the head on page 107). As well as working the various reflexes for the reproductive system, it is beneficial to pay attention to the endocrine gland reflexes as they have considerable control over the gonads (*see* endocrine glands, page 119). In particular, the pituitary, thyroid and adrenal glands and their hormonal secretions have a large influence on the reproductive system. All these points should be massaged to stimulate activity and ensure that hormone secretion is balanced and gonad activity is normal. The body reflexes can also be used to this end by pressing each point for a few seconds and repeating several times for all endocrine and sex glands.

If any of the endocrine glands are tender, it may be indicating a problem with the sex glands. By working the various reflex points, it is possible to ensure a healthy reproductive system. There are a number of reflexes to the penis and testes that can help in this respect. The sex reflex below the navel should be pressed with fingers or thumb and massaged for a few seconds. Additional reflex points on the legs, about 15 cm above the ankle on the inside of the leg, should also be massaged. Initially, massage here should be for half a minute or so, because any problems will make it tender. However, with further attention it will be possible to work out the soreness. A further point on the leg lies above the knee, in the soft area on the outer edge, above the kneecap. All these reflexes, if worked in turn, will contribute to a healthy system and lead to fewer problems, such as impotence.

Impotence itself can, however, be treated. In addition to undertaking the massage of reflex points and areas mentioned above, there are further techniques that may help. There is a particularly sensitive and stimulating area between the anus and scrotum, which should be pressed gently a number of times. It is also said that if gentle on-off pressure is applied to the scrotum, this will help.

Another problem faced by many men involves the prostate gland. This gland is situated below the bladder and opens into the urethra, which is the duct carrying urine out of the body and which also forms the ejaculatory duct. On ejaculation, the gland secretes an alkaline fluid into the sperm to help sperm motility. In older men particularly, the prostate gland may have become enlarged, causing problems with urination. Working the appropriate reflexes may help this situation as may massaging the base of the penis. However, it is advisable to check with a medical doctor to ensure that there is no other condition present.

The female reflexes

There are a number of female conditions that may be helped by reflexology. In most cases, the reflexes to be worked are very similar and the following complaints are therefore grouped in this way:

- *amenorrhoea* lack of menstruation, other than during pregnancy or pre-puberty
- *endometriosis* the occurrence of endometrial cells, normally found in the womb, elsewhere in the body, e.g. Fallopian tubes or peritoneum, causing pain and bleeding
- *fibroid* a benign tumour of the uterus that may cause pain, bleeding and urine retention
- *leucorrhoea* discharge of white/yellow mucus from the vagina, which may be normal before and after menstruation, but at other times large amounts signify an infection
- *dysmenorrhoea* painful menstruation
- *menorrhagia* excessive blood flow during menstruation

For these and related conditions, the general procedure should be to spend time on the specific female reflex, which in these cases is the uterus. In addition the endocrine gland reflexes should be massaged and to provide a balanced treatment, the reflexes for the other reproductive organs (ovary, etc) should be worked. Further areas to concentrate upon include the urinary and circulatory systems and the central nervous system (brain) with the solar plexus.

Premenstrual tension (or syndrome) is the condition typified by headache, nervousness, irritability, depression and tiredness (in addition to physical symptoms) several days before the start of menstruation. It is advisable, before menstruation starts, to have a thorough massage of the reflexes once or twice per week. Next, the reflexes for the uterus and ovaries should be worked. The uterus reflex is on the inside of the foot in the soft area beneath the ankle. The massage should work all around the ankle, beginning with a gentle pressure, and then working back towards the heel. The other foot should then be dealt with in the same way.

To help overcome depression the endocrine glands are very important to regulate hormones, maintain body rhythms and balance the biochemical functions—all of which have some effect on emotions. Other reflexes to work, in addition to the endocrine glands, include the solar plexus, brain and liver. The liver is very important in this respect and, although the area should not be overworked, it should not be forgotten.

The *menopause* is the time when a woman's ovaries no longer release an egg cell every month, and child-bearing is no longer possible. This usually occurs between the ages of 45 and 55. It may be preceded by a gradual decline in the frequency of menstruation or there may be an abrupt cessation. There is an imbalance in the sex hormones and this can cause a number of symptoms, including hot flushes, sweats, palpitations, depression and vaginal dryness. Over a longer period there may be a gradual loss of bone (osteoporosis) leading to a greater risk of bone fractures.

In this instance, the endocrine reflexes are once again very important. In conjunction with these, the reflexes for the spine and brain should be worked, the former to promote relaxation. As a general point, the reflexes to the spine can be massaged for any length of time whereas those for organs and glands should be worked periodically and for a few seconds each time.

To help combat hot flushes, the thyroid reflex should be worked since this is the endocrine gland responsible for the control of the metabolic rate. Regulation of breathing through deep breaths will also help.

The breasts are, of course, the mammary glands that produce milk at the appropriate time, but in today's society they have also become important from a cosmetic point of view. Disorders of the breasts can include lumps or cysts, pain or tenderness. Such conditions may be due to an hormonal imbalance but in any event will benefit from a complete treatment of all the reflexes on feet, hands or head. The breast reflex is found on the top of the foot or hand, at the base of the toes or fingers, and this should be worked regularly. Since the endocrine system is of great significance in the reproductive system, all glands reflexes should receive some attention. Reflexological massage can also be used as a general technique to maintain healthy breasts. Essentially the hand should form a cup around the breast with the fingers underneath and the nipple between thumb and forefinger. Using a circular movement the breast is massaged slightly upwards. This should help retain the shape of the breast, and maintain its tone.

Diseases of the immune system

Antibodies and the lymphatic system
The human body resists infection by means of antibodies and white blood cells. Antibodies are protein substances produced by the lymphoid tissue (spleen, thymus gland and the lymph nodes) that circulate in the blood. They react with their corresponding antigens (foreign bodies that cause antibodies to be formed) and make them harmless. There are a number of immunoglobulins (large protein molecules) that act as antibodies, and each has a particular function. For example, one is responsible for allergic reactions and another is produced to fight bacteria and viruses in the body.

The lymphatic system is also important in the body's immune response. Lymph nodes are swellings that occur at various points in the system. They are found in the neck, groin and armpit, and their main function is to remove foreign particles from the lymph, and to participate in the immune response. In this latter function they become enlarged and produce lymphocytes, a type of white blood cell, which locate and neutralize antigens, or produce antibodies, depending upon their type.

The lymph itself is a colourless, watery fluid. It is derived from blood and is similar to plasma. It contains 95 per cent water, with protein, sugar, salt and lymphocytes. It is circulated by muscular action, and pumped through the lymph nodes for filtering.

It is clear that the lymphatic system, and the immune system overall, are very important in maintaining good health. Any disorder or deficiency in this system will lead to illness, which in some cases may be life-threatening. Reflexology may prove useful in restoring the balance although the need for professional medical advice should always be borne in mind.

Reflex points for the immune system

A number of reflexes to the lymph glands can be worked, on the back of the hands, located over the wrists (*see* the figures on page 102) and on the top of the foot (*see* page 99). The spleen is also an important reflex because the spleen itself produces lymphocytes (amongst other things). Associated reflexes that should be worked are those for the endocrine glands, circulation and liver.

In the case of infectious diseases, many of which occur in childhood (such as measles, mumps and chickenpox), the infection will normally run its course and as a result confer immunity to further bouts. To minimize discomfort and aid the recovery, the reflexes for the brain, solar plexus, circulation, endocrine glands and liver should be massaged.

The same applies to most infectious conditions, even autoimmune diseases where the antibodies attack their own body cells. Here, the lymph gland reflexes are particularly important.

Reiki

Introduction

A complementary therapy

Reiki is a complementary therapy and one of the many facets of alternative medicine available today. It is a method of natural healing which is centred upon *universal life energy*, the meaning of the Japanese word *reiki*. The therapy was named after Dr Mikao Usui, a Japanese theologist, who rediscovered the art of healing using and by transferring this universal life energy. Following a prolonged period of meditation, Dr Usui acquired the ability of transferring reiki energy. He was also able to help others to act as channels for this energy.

To benefit fully from the technique, it is preferable to be initiated into the reiki energy. This is done by a reiki master. A number of reiki grand masters brought the practice to the West to allow many people to prepare themselves for self-discovery. Reiki is now used to heal, either the practitioner or others, in meditation and in conjunction with other therapies such as aromatherapy.

In many cases traditional reiki, as generated by Dr Usui, forms the basis of reiki-do, an amplification of the technique which essentially translates into using reiki as a way of life. This aspect of reiki will be discussed more fully in due course.

Reiki energy

Reiki energy is regarded as life energy at its most effective—with the maximum vibration. It is considered to have an almost divine quality and as such includes everything, in a world where problems and disorders are deemed to be due to the feeling of detachment from the world. There is no division of reiki energy into positive and negative forms but when a person undergoes a session of therapy, they allow the energy to be taken into themselves with beneficial effects. Essentially, those receiving reiki energy decide subconsciously just how much of the life energy is taken in.

Those who use reiki regularly often find they are more joyful, lively and their own inbuilt energy is enhanced—almost as if their batteries had been fully charged! Existing conflicts within the person are broken down and there is a greater vitality, leading to relaxation and a stimulation of the body. As this improvement develops, the natural processes of renewal and removal of toxins are enhanced and rendered more effective, ultimately opening up more of the body to the life energy.

Body organs such as the skin, and protective systems such as the immune system are improved providing the individual is prepared regularly to undertake reiki and in the first place to undergo an attunement or initiation into reiki energy. The initiation is merely a means whereby the universal life energy is bestowed through the reiki master. The master acts as a channel and a link with God to release the healing power.

An initiation is not absolutely essential but it allows the individual access to the universal life energy, which is used rather than their own life energy. Also, an initiation conveys a greater capacity for using reiki energy, with no associated tiredness and further, it provides a protective mechanism against any negative manifestations.

The treatment

Effects and limitations

There are several interrelated effects that result from taking in reiki energy:

- it enables the universal life energy to be received;
- it creates a feeling of deep relaxation;
- energy blockages are removed allowing a flow of life energy throughout the body;
- toxins of various sorts are removed; these and other waste products are removed from the system much more quickly.

When the toxins have been removed from the body, more energy can be received and the vital processes and functions become more highly tuned. When the body takes in more and more life energy, it is said that its frequency becomes higher, facilitating contact with the Universal Spirit and generating trust in the universal life energy.

Deep relaxation is central to reiki therapy and this is very much dependent upon the divine quality attributed to the energy. The extent to which reiki can work is defined by the receiver of the energy because only the necessary amount of energy is drawn in. A refusal to accept reiki, whether or not it is made consciously, will result in no energy flowing. This is, in a way, one limitation of reiki, albeit self-imposed. It should also be appreciated that attitude is very important and if someone attempts to use reiki in the wrong way, it will not work. Self-discovery must go hand in hand with everyday experience of real life and it is not possible to hide from the troubles of the real world through misplaced introspection

A qualified therapist in the appropriate discipline must be sought to deal with major problems and difficulties. Of course, adopting reiki in tandem with another therapy will be very beneficial as the reiki will maximise the treatment being received. This applies whether the therapist is a homoeopath, naturopath or medic.

The use of whole-body reiki

Because no one part of the body exists independently, and because a disease or disorder in one area will inevitably affect the whole body, the use of reiki is best applied in a whole-body way, to cleanse and revitalise the complete system.

Many practitioners undertake a particular routine before commencing a regime of whole-body treatment and the main elements are briefly described below.

Preparing for whole-body reiki

It is a good idea to prepare thoroughly for reiki treatment to capitalise fully upon the beneficial effects. The following is a possible routine:

Remove jewellery

Most people wear jewellery of some description, whether stones of a semiprecious or precious nature, metal rings or chains, leather thongs or one of a whole variety of objects. Some metals and stones are believed to attract energies which may interfere with the life energy of reiki. Other items such as watches create a closed circuit which reduces the flow of life energy. In a way, items of jewellery can be seen as objects which create interference in the 'signal' in much the same way that an engine or motor can generate annoying interference in the reception of a radio programme. Earrings can also be a problem because in the case of pierced ears the earrings conflict with the flow of energy—the ear is very important in other therapies such as acupuncture and must therefore be kept unencumbered.

Wash hands

The benefits of washing your hands are twofold. Firstly, there is the physical effect of cleaning which has the additional quality of making the hands pleasant to feel for the recipient of reiki. It is essential that hot, sticky hands are not used in reiki as this would hardly be conducive to the state of relaxation being sought.

The second benefit relates to the aura surrounding the body. This aura may be affected by contact with objects, people, etc over the course of the day and washing removes such influences which could, in sensitive people, have an adverse effect.

Say a prayer

It is helpful at this stage to recite a short prayer asking for healing and to concentrate upon and acknowledge your aims, self-perception and those of the person upon whom your hands will be placed.

Even out the aura

This is a means of gently making contact and starting the therapy, and may be carried out as follows:

- your partner/client/friend should lie down (*see* figure on page 146)
- sitting at their side put your left hand on your sacrum
- with your right hand held about 15–25 cm (6–9 inches)above the body and palm facing down, move your hand along the length of the body from the head to the toes
- return the hand to the starting point using a circular motion along the side of the body
- repeat this three or four times

This process can be repeated after the reiki therapy when your left hand can be placed on the sacrum of your partner/client/friend.

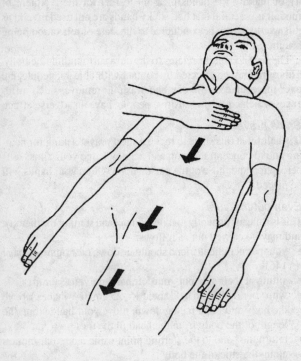

Even out the aura

Energise

When each reiki therapy session is complete the whole body may be energised via the root chakra (*see* page 165 for chakras). The hand is held vertically above the body and then quickly moved from the pelvis to the head.

These preparatory rituals should only be performed when they are perceived to have some significance. There is little point going through the procedures if you do not see the reason why, but clearly some aspects of the procedure can be understood easily and will be accepted readily by the recipient.

The practicalities of whole-body reiki

Before the treatment

There is great scope for variation in the number and sequence of positions used for whole-body treatment. It will depend greatly upon the practitioner and what is felt to be best for the recipient, but no one sequence can be deemed the best one for all. It is important to be certain that your client/partner is not suffering from any illness or condition that might require the attention of another health professional. Reiki has its particular uses but it is unwise to try to address problems that clearly fall beyond its scope. The client can easily ask advice from their doctor, or other professional, as to whether they should undergo reiki therapy.

When it is clear that therapy can go ahead the next commitment to be made is that of time. It is essential that both parties agree to pledge the time to make the most of the reiki therapy. It is likely that the practitioner will, in acting as a channel for the universal life energy, see their own status develop.

The extent of each session of reiki will vary depending upon circumstances and the individual receiving treatment. Certain positions may be better left out of the sequence or therapy may be focused on a particular area to help relieve blockages or deal with tension. If the recipient is currently on a regime of medication then a shorter session may be appropriate.

Similarly, if dealing with a small child or an elderly or infirm person, it is probably wise to limit the therapy to a session of 15 to 20 minutes. In all cases the reiki practitioner should be sensitive to and aware of the condition, needs and wellbeing of the recipient.

Positions in reiki therapy

The hands are clearly the 'instruments' of healing in reiki and although the position in which they are placed on the recipient is meaningful, it may not be possible, nor is it essential that the exact position is copied. Just placing the hands on the appropriate part of the body will suffice.

Reiki can be effected through clothing, as the energy will flow just as well, but many people prefer to have no material obstacles to the therapy. In this case, and particularly for partners, the reiki can be undertaken in the nude. If there are any physical blemishes such as a burn or other wound, the hands should be held a few inches above the skin at this area, around the corresponding acupuncture point, or reflex zone.

The head

On the *head*, the basic position is shown on page 149. The hands are placed either side of the nose, with the palms covering the eyes; the thumbs rest by the bridge of the nose and the fingertips cover the cheeks and reach the upper lip. This arrangement covers the sinuses, eyes, pituitary gland, teeth and is useful for dealing with colds, sinusitis, eye complaints, allergies, fatigue and general discontent.

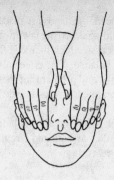

The basic position on the head

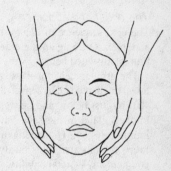

Alternative arrangement
on the head

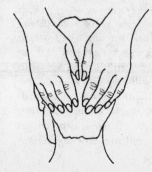

Hands on the back of the head

In the second arrangement for the head, the hands are placed over the ears, with the fingertips extending down the jawline to the neck , encompassing the ears of course which includes the semicircular canals, responsible for balance. The effect also extends to the pharyngeal area. Diseases and problems of these organs—colds, trouble with balance, hearing loss, etc—are dealt with in this arrangement.

If the hands are placed on the back of the head, this helps with conditions such as headaches, colds, asthma and circulatory problems. It generally promotes relaxation.

The chest and abdomen

The next sequence of hand arrangements is for the chest and abdomen. Once again there are many variations, but a selection is presented here.

The arrangement for the thymus, heart and lungs is as follows: one hand is laid across the thymus and the other is at 90° starting just below and between the breasts. The thymus is a bilobed gland in the neck which is an important part of the immune system. This arrangement therefore reinforces the immune system and helps the lymphatics, the heart, lungs and counters any general debility.

The next illustration in the sequence shows the hands placed either side of the navel and slightly to one side. The stomach and digestive organs are the focus of attention here and the conditions/symptoms addressed necessarily have a link with these body systems. As such this will help digestion and the metabolism in general terms, and specifically will combat nausea, heartburn, gastrointestinal diseases and indigestion. Because the presence of such conditions often results in tension and worry, the relief of symptoms will similarly help relieve anxiety and depression.

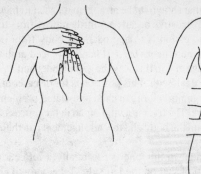

Arrangement for thymus, heart and lungs

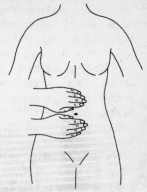

Arrangement for the stomach and digestive organs

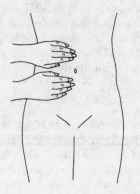

Focus on the gall bladder and liver

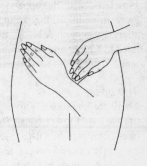

Focus on the appendix, intestines and urogenital organs

Next are two positions in which the hands are placed in a position similar to that shown in the arrangement used to focus on the stomach and digestive organs but further away from the body midline. One version is to approach the body from the right side of the partner/client. The left hand is placed around the base of the ribcage and in this way the gall bladder and liver are the organs to be dealt with. This position is for diseases and conditions of these important organs and associated problems of a metabolic nature. The liver is a vital organ in the process of removing toxins from the body and this arrangement can therefore be very important.

The position related to this one is essentially a reflection, where the hands are placed on the left side of the body to encompass the area of the bowels, spleen and some of the pancreas. Accordingly diseases of these organs, indigestion and healthy blood are all dealt with.

The position of the hands where the pelvic bones are covered and meet over the pubic area is for a number of ailments, many associated with the appendix, intestines and urinogenital organs. In addition, this arrangement is considered suitable for allergies, general debility, problems of a sexual nature and related to weight and is appropriate to reinforce the immune system.

The back

There are a number of arrangements which can be adopted on the back and lower back. The first figure on page 153 shows one such position with a number of effects but it is likely that by gently experimenting, a slightly different yet equally beneficial arrangement can be found. Here the hands are placed across the shoulder blades at mid to upper point, to influence the intestines, lung, heart and various muscles in the neck and

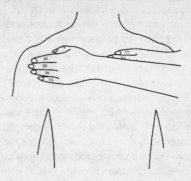

*Focus on the back to help lungs, heart,
muscular tension and headaches*

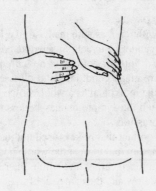

*Focus on the lower back to help
kidneys and adrenal glands*

shoulder region. This will help lung and heart diseases, muscular tension, headaches and related conditions.

If the hands are placed lower down the back, around the midriff (on the lower ribs) this position will accommodate the kidneys and adrenal glands. (The adrenal glands are situated one each on the upper surface of each kidney and are important because they manufacture hormones that control a variety of body functions, e.g. adrenaline is one hormone produced).

In addition to these specific positions, there are many other reiki positions to deal with a multitude of complaints and the reader is referred to a more extensive account for greater detail. It must always be remembered that serious conditions or diseases of a particular nature should be dealt with by the appropriate specialist.

The benefits of whole-body reiki

A reinforcing effect
It is believed with reiki, as with many similar forms of therapy, that the body cannot be treated in separate parts or as discrete organs that have little or nothing to do with other parts of the body. There are many conditions and diseases that affect the wellbeing of the individual as a whole or have a knock-on effect even though the symptoms may be less tangible, such as anxiety or depression.

It is thus important that reiki is used not just to counteract a particular symptom, but to treat the whole body to achieve the relaxation mentioned earlier and with it the removal of blockages in energy flow and the dispersal of toxins.

Long-term whole-body reiki should be adopted in all cases, and in a therapy session of 60 to 90 minutes all parts of the body will be addressed and receive reiki energy. Over a period of time, the general condition of the body is restored and the energy channels are opened to allow the body to deal properly and naturally with both stress and the buildup of toxins.

In cases of recovery from illness, reiki therapy provides the additional energy to bolster recovery and will reinforce the effects of any other method of natural healing. It can be used as a supplementary therapy almost as a general, ongoing, policy as it is a truly complementary system of treatment.

Reduction of side-effects

It is well-known that the use of drugs to combat say, an infection may at first seem very effective. However, it is becoming all too obvious that the excessive use of drugs is causing its own problems. In the case of many drugs, uncomfortable, distressing and even threatening side-effects can ensue. With antibiotics, there is now the problem of drug resistance in bacteria, leading to situations where hospital patients are vulnerable to infections from so-called superbugs or killer bugs. This has resulted specifically from the overuse of antibiotics and has reached the point where hospitals now have only one or two very powerful drugs to use in these circumstances.

Reiki therapy can be a very useful adjunct for anyone taking a course of drugs. It can help reduce some side effects and generally aid the body in recovery when the course has been completed. Postoperative recovery will benefit from reiki and it can also help after chemotherapy. In all these cases reiki therapy supplies that extra life energy, enabling the body to bounce back more quickly from the burdens of surgery and chemicals.

In some cases, use of reiki therapy after an operation will lessen pain and the natural healing processes will be accelerated. The key in all these examples is that the reiki therapy must be undertaken on a regular basis. The added benefit of this is that when a person is enjoying good health, the regular therapy increases the body's inbuilt defences which manifests itself as a confidence and outward harmony in dealing with everyday events. It also bestows a greater ability to deal with stressful situations. This very positive outlook can become possible because once the blockages and toxins have been removed from the system, the scope for personal advancement and growth becomes available. In general, the better metabolic functioning afforded by reiki therapy means that benefits and improvements may be experienced in many ways.

Reiki associations

It has already been mentioned that reiki therapy can be undertaken in conjunction with other methods of natural healing. In addition, it can be combined with activities such as meditation and crystal therapy. The following sections consider briefly a few of these combinations which for the present purpose have been called associations.

Reiki and the use of crystals

Crystal therapy is known to many people and involves the use of precious and semi- precious stones. The stones are thought to hold positive energy and they act as a conduit for healing from the practitioner to the recipient. It is also said that the stones generate a healing vibration that acts upon the body. In some cases the stone is placed on the body where treatment is focused, in others it may be positioned on the appropriate acupuncture point. Most therapists use quartz for physical healing, amethyst for spiritual healing and rose quartz to heal emotions. Fluorite may also be used to develop awareness and knowledge of a spiritual nature.

In reiki, three varieties of quartz are commonly used—amethyst, rose quartz and ordinary quartz (or rock crystal). The crystal structure of quartz is often taken to be related to the six chakras and the tip of the crystal to the seventh chakra. Practitioners recommend using rock crystal to avoid feeling overpowered by changes, mounting pressures and the stress of everyday life. Carrying the crystal or wearing it is meant to bring light into your workaday routines.

Rock crystal can also be used in conjunction with reiki meditation (of which see later), being held between, or in, the hands. In this way the energy emanating from the crystal is thought to go into the palms and then the rest of the body via the reflex zones. It is recommended by some in a variety of applications such as relaxation, wound-healing with other therapy and treating particular organs.

Rose quartz, with its soft pink coloration, is used for mending emotional problems. This may be dealing with problematic emotions, such as shutting out certain desires or it may be facing trauma and stress brought about by a separation.

The use of amethyst with reiki is varied. It can help promote the proper function of an organ that has been under treatment; placed on the Third Eye (centre of the forehead) it facilitates clearer vision in one's path through life; and it can reduce tension and fear.

Meditation with reiki

Meditation in its own right is a useful therapy. It needs concentration and time and a will to continue with the practice. Some of the benefits may happen straight away (such as a lowering of the blood pressure) while others require some proficiency. It has been reported that it helps with insomnia, and a high blood pressure can be lowered significantly, enough to allow the dependence on drugs to be reduced. Meditation is undertaken in a quiet room and it must be at least half an hour after consuming food or drink. Sitting comfortably, the mind is then concentrated upon excluding the hustle and bustle, problems, tension and overstimulating thoughts of modern life.

Reiki assists in this concentration, with the flow of energy aiding relaxation. There are some positions that can be adopted in reiki meditation to achieve particular goals. In the first position the legs are drawn up and the soles of the feet put together with the knees falling apart. This can be done while lying down or sitting against a wall or chair. The hands adopt a praying gesture. This is meant to complete the circuit of energy, allowing a flow around the body. The reiki energy removes any blockages and performed regularly, this becomes a powerful meditation exercise. It can be done for short periods initially, just a couple of minutes, and then built up in small increases.

To achieve complete harmony with your partner, there is a meditation exercise which can be done together. Sitting facing each other, the legs are spread, with the knees raised slightly. Moving closer, the legs of one are put over the legs of the partner and palms are put together. This allows a joint circuit of energy which strengthens the harmonious and loving relationship between two people. Done properly, this meditation may take up to half an hour.

Group meditation is also possible with reiki, in which the participants stand in a circle with hands joined.

Aromatherapy blended with reiki

Aromatherapy is covered in greater detail elsewhere in this volume (*see* page 211). It is essentially a healing method that employs essential oils extracted from plants, usually in a neutral oil base (carrier oil). The oils can be used in three ways: by direct application, bathing in water to which a few drops of the appropriate oil have been added, and inhalation.

When used in conjunction with reiki, some oils can be applied directly on particular areas of the body, or their aroma can be made to fill the room using an aroma lamp. Below a few oils are considered and their use compared to their therapeutic value in aromatherapy. It is very likely that someone with a knowledge of essential oils will be able to capitalize upon their experience and incorporate further oils in their reiki therapy.

- *Lavender*—in aromatherapy lavender is a tonic with relaxing effects. It is also antiseptic, an antispasmodic and stimulates the appetite. It is a widely-used and versatile oil that is used for minor burns and wounds. Its soothing effects render it helpful for headaches, tension and similar conditions.

  In reiki, lavender is associated primarily with patients/recipients who are sensitive and easily hurt, essentially introverts. It can be used in long sessions of reiki when the lavender helps to promote the calm and confidence necessary for a period of building and strengthening of the life force energy.

- *Sandalwood*—this oil is used in aromatherapy for its relaxing and antiseptic effects. It forms a very effective oil for application to the skin (especially facial), particularly for dry or sensitive skin.

  The use of sandalwood in reiki therapy is quite different. Its benefit seems to be in producing an ambience conducive to the reiki therapy itself because the oil is considered to elicit trust and confidence, between practitioner and recipient.

- *Clary sage*—this is a very useful oil with a number of qualities including tonic, antispasmodic, antidepressant, anti-inflammatory, bactericidal and more. It is also used to treat

colds, menstrual problems and its very low toxicity renders
it suitable for general use.

In a session of reiki therapy, clary sage has been used to
open blocked channels and to enhance sensitivity.

- *Patchouli*—apart from being accredited with some aphrodisiac qualities, patchouli is more commonly used in
aromatherapy to treat skin disorders and minor burns because of its anti-inflammatory and antiseptic qualities.

While patchouli is also used in reiki therapy for allergies
and impurities of the skin, the fundamental use and aim is to
enhance the sensual qualities and aspects of life.

Other reiki associations

Because reiki is very much a positive therapy and benign, it can
be undertaken in conjunction with other therapies with no harm.
However, there are some beneficial effects of reiki which may
affect in some way the activity of other courses of treatment.

- *Prescription drugs*—many reiki therapists believe that reiki
can readily affect the way in which such drugs work in the
body. It has already been mentioned that side effects of drugs
can be lessened through the use of reiki, and in some cases
it is reported that the process will be accelerated. In addition, reiki makes the body more receptive and therefore
therapy prior to a course of drugs may enhance the effect of
the drug. The relaxed state engendered by reiki may also
counter, to some extent, the efficacy of an anaesthetic. However, injections such as anaesthetics can more readily and
easily be released from the body with the help of reiki.

Although minor pains can often be remedied through the
use of reiki alone, stronger pain killers do not have their
effect lessened by reiki. The interaction between reiki and
drugs is neither well tested nor documented, but the overall

positive effect of the therapy means that it is not likely to cause any problems.

* *Homoeopathy*—in conjunction with this therapy, reiki provides a reinforcing effect by rendering the treatment more effective. Reiki can help avoid strain, improve the removal of toxins and increase the body's sensitivity. After treatment, whole-body reiki will help recovery. *See* page 331 for a full discussion of homoeopathy.

* *Bach remedies*—these are named after Edward Bach, an English doctor, who in the early years of this century gave up his Harley Street practice to concentrate upon finding plants with healing qualities. He identified 38 plants, the flowers of which he floated on clear spring water. This, he believed, transferred medicinal properties to the water which could be given to patients. This practice he developed to mimic the drops of dew on the plant which in the first instance were used. Intended for home self-help, the remedies are meant for treating the whole person. Stock solutions are diluted in water and a few drops taken.

Typical examples are:

      cherry plum for fear, tension, irrationality
      holly for envy, jealousy and hatred
      pine for guilt and constantly apologizing
      sweet chestnut for despair
      wild rose for apathy

In common with many other examples, reiki improves the effectiveness of Bach remedies.

Determining the need

Introduction
When undertaking reiki therapy it is often necessary to deter-

mine the need for therapy in the client or partner. As therapists work with reiki for longer, they become more sensitive and proficient and are better able to judge problem areas on what is called the subtle plane (the etheric body). Expertise comes only with experience, but it seems that there are certain reactions or feelings detected which may be indicative. Before trying to perceive a person's need, some practitioners 'sensitise' their hands. This involves holding the palms facing, about 40 to 50 cm apart and slowly bringing them together. The movement should be spread out over four or five minutes to allow an attunement and for changes to be perceived.

The following are some possible responses that may be experienced:

- *Attraction*—implies that reiki energy is needed at that point.
- *Repulsion*—suggests a long-established blockage is present which is restricting the flow of energy. This may require a considerable period of therapy to rectify.
- *Flow*—a positive feeling representing the flow of life energy which will be enhanced by further reiki energy, raising the entire system.
- *Heat*—if your hands feel warmer, it signifies a need for life energy. If the whole body produces such a result, reiki energy can be applied anywhere.
- *Cold*—this is probably due to a blockage in energy flow such that an area of the body has been deprived of energy. Such blockages may also require considerable attention and both whole-body and specific treatment will probably be required.
- *Tingling*—an inflamed area will usually produce a tingling in the hands of the therapist. The strength of the stimulus reflects the severity of the problem and additional help from a medical practitioner may be identified as being necessary.

- *Pain*—this usually represents a buildup of energy in some
  form. A sharp pain reflects that the energy is beginning to
  dissipate and in so doing is causing some conflict elsewhere
  in the system. In this case, whole-body therapy is beneficial
  before concentrating upon a particular area.

There are other methods to determine need and identify disruptions in the flow of life energy, but these are, in the main, for the more experienced practitioner. However, details can be found in a variety of publications and involve pendulum dowsing, activity of the chakras and the use of systems such as tarot or I Ching. These latter two, however, are not for novices.

When the need is answered

If reiki is practised regularly, it can have a very positive effect and influence. One of the major problems with modern life is the very pace of life itself—every day seems to be hectic, full of demands and pressure which result in stress, discomfort and ragged emotions.

These emotional ups and downs and stressful pressures are smoothed out by reiki. A more balanced approach to life is developed; a greater inner harmony is achieved which means that the quality of life improves and any illnesses or condition become less of a problem, responds more readily to treatment, or is cleared up seemingly of its own accord. The flow of energy from reiki ensures that there is harmony between the Third Eye (which identifies the ideal path for the individual) and the root chakra (or energy centre). (For an explanation of the chakras *see* below).

The significance of chakras with reiki

Chakras are a common concept in several disciplines of alternative medicine or traditional Asian medicine. A chakra is a centre of energy, subtle energy in reiki, which has several functions. In addition to being 'representative' of a particular organ or group of organs, a chakra also controls our being on different levels and it links these two representative states.

The chakras

In reiki there is considered to be seven major and a number of minor chakras. The seven major chakras are shown in the figure on page 165. These are from the lowest to the highest: the root chakra, the sexual chakra, the personality chakra, the heart chakra, the expressive chakra, the knowledge chakra, the crown chakra.

The number of major chakras does vary in some instances, e.g. Hindu yoga has six centres, but the greatest variation is in the minor chakras. In some regimes of therapy ten minor chakras are identified, and these are interconnected with the major chakras. A typical system could be:

- one in the arch of each foot, connected to the first and third chakras
- one in each knee joint, connected to the fifth and sixth chakras
- one in each palm, connected to the second, third and fourth chakras
- one in each elbow, connected to the second and third chakras
- one below each shoulder, connected to the third and fifth chakras

Brief summaries of the major chakras are given below, followed by an indication of how the chakras interact with reiki.

The root chakra

This is the source of strength and is essential for proper development. The other centres of energy rely upon the root chakra to perform properly. Disorders within the root chakras may result in mental problems (e.g. aggression, confusion) or physical symptoms (e.g. of the intestines, excretory systems, or bones).

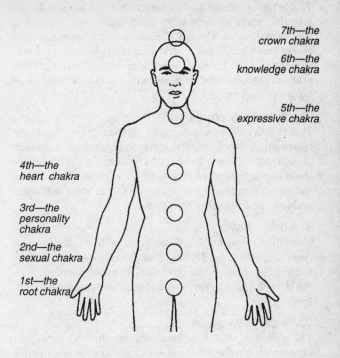

7th—the
crown chakra

6th—the
knowledge chakra

5th—the
expressive chakra

4th—the
heart chakra

3rd—the
personality
chakra

2nd—the
sexual chakra

1st—the
root chakra

The seven major chakras

The sexual chakra

This is highly influential and governs sensual and sexual factors, the means whereby experiences are felt and registered. Blockages result in a variety of phobias or conditions such as a fear of being touched, a general incomprehension or an obsessive cleanliness. Physical manifestations may include being prone to infections, or problems with the kidneys/bladder or lymphatic system.

The personality chakra

This is also called the solar plexus chakra, this is the power centre and focus of personal freedom or, conversely, feelings of guilt. Mental consequences of a blockage might be anxiety about how others perceive you, envy or selfish greed. Physically there could be digestive disorders, liver and gall bladder problems or disorders of the pancreas.

The heart chakra

This effectively controls self-acceptance and by extension everyone else around us. Blockages may result in attitudes such as selfishness or emotional blackmail. Physical manifestations could be disorders of the lungs and heart, and circulatory problems.

The expressive chakra

The expressive chakra (or throat chakra) controls overall self-expression, whether it is language or gesture. An upset in this centre could well result in an individual who becomes dictatorial while the physical signs could be growth problems, or a muscular tension leading to a lack of vocal control.

The knowledge chakra

Otherwise known as the forehead chakra or Third Eye, this is the focus of intuition, the perception of truth which enables a person to find their own course through life. Accordingly, a blockage of this chakra will culminate in a haphazard approach to life, and probably an inability to settle down to any one task for any length of time.

The crown chakra

It is generally felt that the seventh, crown, chakra is appreciated only by experience and it depends upon the other six for its development.

The practicalities of chakras with reiki

This is quite a complicated aspect of reiki and to develop it as an integral part of a programme of reiki, the reader should seek a more extensive treatment of the subject. Some information is, however, presented here by way of introduction.

Some therapists use the technique of balancing chakras to completely attune the energy on the subtle plane. The chakras are paired, first with sixth, second with fifth and third with fourth by placing the hands on the relevant areas. When it feels through the hands as if the energy is balanced with the first and sixth chakras, then the second and fifth can be balanced in the same way. Other combinations may be used if it is felt that these may be beneficial.

The chakras may suffer a number of problems creating an imbalance and although considerable corrective therapy may be required, a balance can be achieved with reiki. Many practitioners recommend sending reiki energy through a problematic chakra. This involves placing one hand at the front of the body above the chakra, and the other hand at the back of the body. The flow of Universal Life Energy eventually corrects any defects. However, it is important to remember that due to the interconnection of the chakras, defects in one affect the whole system. Therefore the healing cannot be undertaken in isolation. It is always good practice to balance the chakras after a session of specific healing.

Higher levels of reiki

Although it is possible to progress beyond the level of proficiency implied so far, second and third degree reiki are really for the experts. This is particularly so with third degree reiki, the details of which are not written down.

Available power is increased with second degree reiki but should only be accessed by someone working with a reiki master. The greater flow of energy means that the effect of reiki therapy is greater and also its effect on a mental and emotional level is enhanced. Further, it is said that reiki at this level can be transmitted over distances, to one or a number of people. This is, of course, highly specialized and advice should be sought from a reiki master by anyone wishing to pursue this goal.

Reiki-do

In Japanese, *do* means path, hence reiki-do is concerned with a way of life in which reiki figures very prominently. Reiki-do is, of course, founded on the reiki therapy described in the preceding pages and it consists of three aspects which enable personal growth. The three categories of reiki-do are:

- *Inner*—based upon meditation as described earlier, and can be augmented by one of the methods outlined, such as the scents of aromatherapy. It adopts a whole-body system of treatment leading to a greater awareness and vitality.
- *Outer*—the application of reiki energy forms the basis of this part of reiki-do, with the chakras, crystals and other subsidiary therapies.
- *Synergistic*—as the word implies, this is the combination of parts which have, when used together, a greater effect than

their combined individual effects; that is a merger of inner and outer reiki-do which exceeds the anticipated combined effect. It is particularly appropriate for anyone who has reasonable experience in this therapy and can appreciate the nonexclusive nature of pleasure and success.

Conclusions

Reiki is a technique of healing available to anyone. It can lead to a more relaxed approach to life and greater harmony with the total environment. It can also be applied to plants and animals, for example your household pets, and for this and further information about the therapy, the reader is advised to seek more detailed treatments.

Shiatsu

Introduction

Origins

Shiatsu originated in China at least 2000 years ago, when the earliest accounts gave the causes of ailments and the remedies that could be effected through a change of diet and way of life. The use of massage and acupuncture was also recommended. The Japanese also practised this massage, after it had been introduced into their country, and it was known as *anma*. The therapy that is known today as *shiatsu* has gradually evolved with time from anma under influences from both East and West. It is only very recently that it has gained recognition and popularity, with people becoming aware of its existence and benefits.

Although East and West have different viewpoints on health and life, these can complement one another. The Eastern belief is of a primary flow of energy throughout the body, which runs along certain channels known as meridians. It is also believed that this energy exists throughout the universe and that all living creatures are dependent upon it as much as on physical nourishment. The energy is known by three similar names, *ki*, *chi* and *prana* in Japan, China and India respectively. (It should be noted that the term 'energy' in this context is not the same as the physical quantity that is measured in joules or calories.) As in acupuncture, there are certain pressure points on the meridians that relate to certain organs, and these points are known as *tsubos*.

The applications of shiatsu

Shiatsu can be used to treat a variety of minor problems such as insomnia, headaches, anxiety, back pain, etc. Western medicine may be unable to find a physical cause for a problem, and although some pain relief may be provided, the underlying cause of the problem may not be cured. It is possible that one session of shiatsu will be sufficient to remedy the problem by stimulating the flow of energy along the channels. A regime of exercise (possibly a specific routine) with a change in diet and/or lifestyle may also be recommended. Shiatsu can encourage a general feeling of good health in the whole person, not just in the physical sense. After some study or practice, shiatsu can be performed on friends and relatives. There are many benefits for both the giver and the receiver of shiatsu, both on a physical and spiritual level.

Energy or ki

Auras

There are believed to be a number of *auras,* or energy layers, that surround the physical body and can be detected or appreciated (*see* the figure on page 172). The first layer, the *etheric body,* is the most dense and is connected with the body and the way it works. An exercise is described later that enables this layer to be detected. The *astral body* is much wider, is affected by people's feelings and, if viewed by a clairvoyant, is said to change in colour and shape depending on the feelings being experienced. The next aura is the *mental body,* which is involved with the thought processes and intelligence of a person. Similarly, this can be viewed by a clairvoyant and is said to contain 'pictures' of ideas emanating from the person. These first three auras comprise the personality of a person. The last

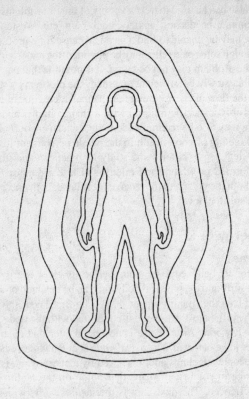

Auras

aura is known as the *causal body*, *soul* or *higher self*. This is concerned more with perceptive feelings and comprehension. It is believed in reincarnation that the first three auras die with the body, but the causal body carries on in its process of development by adopting another personality. As a person grows in maturity and awareness, these different auras are used, and energy is passed from one layer to another. It therefore follows that any alteration in the physical state will, in turn, affect the other layers, and vice versa.

Seven centres of energy, or chakras

It is believed that there are seven main *chakras* (a chakra being a centre of energy) found in a midline down the body, from the top of the head to the bottom of the torso (*see* figure on page 165 of Reiki) . They are situated along the *sushumna*, or spiritual channel, which runs from the crown of the head to the base of the trunk. Energy enters the channel from both ends. Since the flow is most efficient when the back is straight, this is the ideal posture for meditation or when powers of concentration are required. Each chakra has a component of each aura, and it comprises what is known as a centre of consciousness. Each aura is activated as a person develops, and the same occurs with the chakras, beginning with the lowest (the *base* or *root chakra*) and progressing to the others with time. There is also a change of energy between the *auras* of each chakra.

The *crown chakra* is concerned with the pineal gland, which controls the right eye and upper brain and affects spiritual matters. The *ajna* , *brow or forehead chakra* also known as *the Third Eye*, is linked with the pituitary gland, which controls the left eye, lower brain, nose and nervous system. It has an effect on the intellect, perception, intuition and comprehension. The *throat* or *expressive chakra* is concerned with the thyroid gland

and governs the lymphatic system, hands, arms, shoulders, mouth, vocal cords, lungs and throat. It affects communication, creativity and self-expression. The *heart chakra* is concerned with the thymus gland and controls the heart, breasts, vagus nerve and circulatory system, and affects self-awareness, love, humanitarian acts and compassion. The *solar plexus* or *personality chakra* is concerned with the pancreas. It controls the spleen, gall bladder, liver and digestive system and stomach, and has an effect on desire, personal power and the origin of emotions. The *sacral* or *sexual chakra* affects the gonads and controls the lower back, feet, legs and reproductive system. This affects physical, sexual and mental energy, relationships and self-worth. The *base* or *root chakra* is concerned with the adrenal glands. It controls the skeleton, parasympathetic and sympathetic nervous systems, bladder and kidneys, and affects reproduction and the physical will. As an example of this, if a person is suffering from an ailment of the throat, it is possible that he or she may also be unable to voice private thoughts and feelings.

Zang and fu organs

Energy storage and production

According to traditional Eastern therapies, organs have a dual function—their physical one and another that is concerned with the use of energy and might be termed an 'energetic function'. The twelve organs mentioned in the traditional therapies are split into two groups known as *zang* and *fu*, and each is described below.

Zang organs are for energy storage, and the fu organs produce energy from sustenance and drink and also control excretion. The organs can be listed in pairs, each zang matched by a fu with a similar function. Although the pancreas is not specifically mentioned, it is usually included with the spleen. The same applies to the 'triple heater' or 'triple burner', which is connected with the solar plexus, lower abdomen and the thorax. The lungs are a zang organ and are concerned with assimilation of energy, or ki, from the air, which with energy from food ensures the complete body is fed and that mental alertness and a positive attitude are maintained. This is paired with the fu organ of the large intestine, which takes sustenance from the small intestine, absorbs necessary liquids and excretes waste material via the faeces. It is also concerned with self-confidence. The spleen is a zang organ and changes energy or ki from food into energy that is needed by the body. It is concerned with the mental functions of concentration, thinking and analysing. This is paired with the fu organ of the stomach, which prepares food so that nutrients can be extracted and also any energy, or ki, can be taken. It also provides 'food for thought'. The zang organ of the heart assists blood formation from ki and controls the flow of blood and the blood vessels. It is where the mind is housed and therefore affects awareness, belief, long-term memory and feelings. This is paired with the fu organ of the small intestine, which divides food into necessary and unnecessary parts, the latter passing to the large intestine. It is also concerned with the making of decisions. The kidneys are a zang organ and they produce basic energy, or ki, for the other five paired organs and also for reproduction, birth, development and maturity. They also sustain the skeleton and brain and provide willpower and 'get up and go'. They are paired with the fu organ of the bladder, which stores waste fluids until they are passed as urine and also gives strength or courage. The zang organ of the 'heart governor' is concerned with the flow of blood throughout the body. It is a protector and help for the heart and has a bearing on relationships with other people (although there is no organ known as the 'heart governor' it is connected with the heart and its functions). This is paired with the 'triple heater' or 'burner', which passes ki around the body and allows an emotional exchange with others. The liver is the sixth zang organ, and it assists with a regular flow of ki to achieve the most favourable physiological effects and emotional calmness. Positive feelings, humour, planning and creativity are also connected with it. The gall bladder is the sixth fu organ, with which the liver is paired, and this keeps bile from the liver and passes it to the intestines. It concerns decision-making and forward thinking.

The meridian system

The meridians, as previously mentioned, are a system of invisible channels on the back and front of the body along which energy, or ki, flows. There are twelve principal meridians plus two additional ones, which are called *the governing vessel* and the *conception* or *directing vessel*. Each meridian passes partly through the body and partly along the skin, joining various chakras and organs (the organs as recognized in traditional Eastern medicine). One end of every meridian is beneath the skin while the other is on the surface of the skin on the feet or hands. Along each meridian are acupressure or acupuncture points, which in shiatsu are called *tsubos*. These points allow the flow of energy along the meridian to be altered if necessary (*see* the figures on page 177). The meridians receive energy from the chakras and organs (as described previously), from the meridians with ends located on the feet and hands and also via the pressure points, or tsubos. Energy, or ki, can pass from one meridian into another as there is a 'pathway' linking each meridian to two others. The energy passes in a continuous cycle or

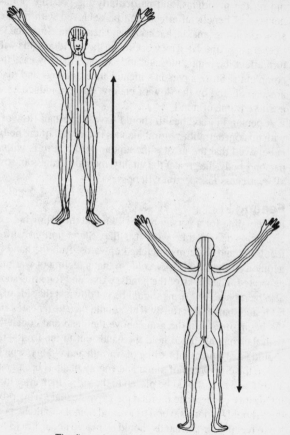

The flow of energy along the meridians

flow and in a set order from one meridian to another. By working on the meridians, and particularly the pressure points, a number of beneficial effects can be achieved with problems such as muscle tension, backache and headache. Since the flow of energy is stimulated by working on the meridians this will in turn affect the joints, muscles and skin and thereby ease these complaints. Since a person's mental state, feelings and moods are also altered by the flow of energy, this can induce a more positive frame of mind.

A person in good health should have a constant flow of ki, with no concentrations or imbalances in any part of the body. It is believed that the greater the amount of ki there is within a person's body, the greater the vitality, mental alertness and overall awareness that person will possess.

Feeling ki

It is possible for a person to 'feel' ki, and the following exercise helps demonstrate what it is like. Stand upright with the feet apart and the arms stretched upwards. Rub the hands together as if they were very cold, so that a feeling of warmth is generated. The backs of the hands, wrists and forearms should also be rubbed. The arms should be put down at the side of the body and shaken vigorously. This should then be repeated from the beginning, with the arms above the head and concluding with the shaking. Then hold the hands out to the front—they should have a pleasant feeling of warmth and vitality, which is due to the circulation of blood and energy that has been generated. The hands should be placed to the sides, then after inhaling deeply concentrate on relaxing as you exhale. This procedure should be done several times, and then it should be possible to feel the ki. The hands should be placed about 1 m (3 feet) apart, with the palms of the hands facing inwards. After relaxa-

Feeling ki

tion, concentrate your thoughts on the gap between your hands and then gradually reduce the space between them—but they must not touch. It is likely that when the hands come quite close, about 15–30 cm (6–12 inches), a feeling of tingling or warmth may be felt, or the sensation that there is something between the hands. This will be when the auras that surround the hands touch. To reinforce the sensation, the hands should be taken apart again and then closed together so that the feeling is experienced again and becomes more familiar.

The following exercise also enables ki to be felt, but this time it is the etheric aura around another person's head and shoulders. The previous procedure to generate ki should be repeated, but this time the hand should be placed near to another person's head, within 60 centimetres–1 metre (2–3 feet). This person should be sitting upright on the floor or on a chair. The hand should be moved gradually nearer to the seated person's head, concentrating attention on the gap between your hand and his or her head. If no sensation is felt, the hand should be moved back to its original position and the process should be repeated. Again, a feeling of tingling or warmth will probably be experienced as the person's aura is felt. When this has been achieved, the hand can progress round the head and down to the shoulders, noting the edge of the aura at the same time. If the person has no success in experiencing the aura, it is likely that the mind is not clear of other thoughts, so relaxation is suggested prior to any further attempt.

It is also possible for a person, by concentrating his or her thoughts and by a slight change of position, to alter the flow of ki in the body. This will have the effect of either making him or her feel a lot heavier or lighter, depending on which is desired. Taken to extremes, someone who is skilled at the control of ki will prove too heavy to be lifted by four people.

Basic rules

There are some basic rules that should be followed before the practice of shiatsu. Clothing should be comfortable, loose-fitting and made of natural fibres since this will help with the flow of energy or ki. The room should be warm, quiet, have adequate space and be neat and clean. If not, this can have an adverse effect on the flow of ki. The person receiving the therapy should ideally lie on a futon (a quilted Japanese mattress) or similar mat on the floor. If necessary, pillows or cushions should be ready to hand if the person does not feel comfortable. Shiatsu should not be given or received by someone who has just eaten a large meal—it is advisable to delay for several hours. No pressure should be exerted on varicose veins or injuries such as cuts or breaks in bones. Although shiatsu can be of benefit to women while pregnant, there are four areas that should be avoided and these are the stomach, any part of the legs from the knees downwards, the fleshy web of skin between the forefinger and thumb, and an area on the shoulders at each side of the neck. Ensure that the person is calm and relaxed. It is generally not advisable to practise shiatsu on people who have serious illnesses such as heart disorders, multiple sclerosis or cancer. An experienced practitioner may be able to help, but a detailed and accurate diagnosis and course of treatment is essential. A verbal check on the person's overall health is important and also to ascertain if a woman is pregnant. If there is any worry or doubt about proceeding, then the safest option is not to go ahead.

Although the general feeling after receiving shiatsu is one of wellbeing and relaxation, there are occasionally unpleasant results, such as coughing, generation of mucus or symptoms of a cold; a feeling of tiredness; a headache or other pains and aches; or feeling emotional. The coughing and production of mucus is due to the body being encouraged to rid itself of its surplus foods (such as sugars and fats) in this form. A cold can sometimes develop when the mucus is produced, usually when the cells of the body are not healthy. Tiredness can occur, frequently with a person who suffers from nervous tension. After therapy has removed this stress or tension, then the body's need for sleep and rest becomes apparent. A short-lived headache or other pain may also develop, for which there are two main reasons. Since shiatsu redresses the balance of ki in the body, this means that blockages in the flow of energy are released and the ki can rush around the body, causing a temporary imbalance in one part and resulting in an ache or pain. It is also possible that too much time or pressure may have been applied to a particular area. The amount needed varies considerably from one person to another. If a pain or headache is still present after a few days, however, it is sensible to obtain qualified medical help. Emotional feelings can occur while the energy is being stimulated to flow and balance is regained. The feelings may be connected with something from the past that has been suppressed and so, when these emotions resurface, it is best for them to be expressed in a way that is beneficial, such as crying. There may, of course, be no reaction at all. Some people are completely 'out of touch' with their bodies and are aware only that all is not well when pain is felt. If this is so, then any beneficial effects from shiatsu may not register. Because of a modern diet that contains an abundance of animal fats, people become overweight through the deposition of fat below the skin and around the internal organs. The body is unable to 'burn off' this fat, and this layer forms a barrier to ki. The flow is stopped, and overweight people do not tend to benefit as much because of the difficulty in stimulating the flow of ki in the body.

Exercises and the three main centres

The body is divided into three main centres—the *head*, the *heart*, and the *abdominal* centres. The head centre is concerned with activities of a mental nature, such as imaginative and intellectual thought processes, and is concerned with the brow chakra. The heart centre is concerned with interactions among people and to the world in general, including the natural world. It is related to the chakra of the throat and heart. The abdominal centre is related to the base, sacral and solar plexus chakras and is concerned with the practical aspects of life and physical activity. Ideally, energy should be divided equally among the three but because of a number of factors, such as activity, education, diet, culture, etc, this is frequently not so. In shiatsu, more importance is attached to the abdominal centre, known as the *hara*. The following exercise uses abdominal breathing and, by so doing, not only is oxygen inhaled but also ki is taken into the hara where it increases a person's vitality. Once the technique is mastered, it can be practised virtually anywhere and will restore composure and calmness.

Sit on the floor with the back straight and, if possible, in the position known in Japan as *seiza* (*see* figure on page 184). The hands should be placed loosely together in the lap and the mind and body should become relaxed after some deep breathing. One hand should be put on the stomach, below the navel, and the other on the chest. When inhaling, this should not be done with the chest but with the abdomen, which should increase in size. As the person exhales the abdomen should contract, and this procedure should be practised for a few minutes. After a rest it should be repeated, inhaling quite deeply but still the chest should not be allowed to rise. Some people may not find this exercise at all difficult while others may need more practice. It may be that there is stress or tension in the diaphragm. Once the technique has been mastered and the hands do not need to be placed on the chest and abdomen, imagine that ki is being inhaled down into the hara. Sit in the same position and inhale slowly via the nose and imagine the ki descending (*see* figure on page 184). (It may aid concentration if the eyes are closed.) The breath should be held for about four seconds and concentration should be centred on the ki. Then exhale gradually through the mouth and repeat the process for a few minutes.

The next exercise is known as a centred movement, which practises movement of the ki, since it is one person's ki that should have an effect on another. After practising shiatsu on a partner, you should not feel tired but refreshed and exhilarated. This is a benefit of the extra ki in the body. The exercise should be begun on hands and knees (a body width apart), and it is most important that you are relaxed and comfortable with no

Seiza

Inhaling through the nose

tension. This position is the basis for other movements that are practised on others. While the position is maintained, begin to move the body backwards and forwards so that you are conscious of the transfer of weight, either on to the hands or knees. The body should then be moved slowly in a circular way, again being aware of the shift of weight from the hands, to hands and knees, to knees, etc, returning to the original position. You should also realize that as the whole body is moved, the abdomen is its 'centre of gravity'. Practise maintaining a position for about five seconds, registering the increase in weight on the hands when you move forwards and the reduction when you rock backwards. Then return to the original position. It is important that the body weight is always used at right angles to the receiver as this will have the maximum effect on the flow of ki. The reason for holding a particular position is that this has the effect of making the person's ki move.

The centred movement previously described can be practised on a partner in exactly the same way, following the same rules. The right hand should be placed on the sacrum, which is between the hips, and the left hand midway between the shoulder blades. As before, you should rock forwards and hold the position for about five seconds and then repeat after rocking backwards on to the knees (*see* figure on page 186). This basic procedure can be repeated about twelve times, and if you are not sure whether too much or too little pressure is being used, check with your partner. You will eventually acquire the skill of knowing what amount is right for a particular person.

To summarize, there are some basic rules to be followed when practising shiatsu. A person should make use of body weight and not muscular strength, and there should be no effort involved. At all times a calm and relaxed state should be maintained, and the weight of the body should be at right angles in

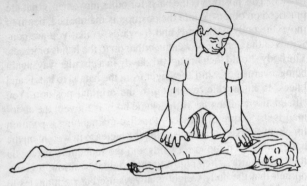

A centred movement

relation to the receiver's body. The person's whole body should
be moved when altering weight on to the receiver, maintaining
the hara as the centre. Any weight or pressure held should be
for a short time only and both hands should be used equally. It
is best to maintain a regular pattern of movement while giving
shiatsu, and always keep in physical contact with the receiver
by keeping a hand on him or her throughout the therapy.

Shiatsu on the face and head

There are a large number of different exercises and techniques,
but at each time the giver must be relaxed and calm to enable
the flow of ki to occur and thus make the shiatsu work to full
effect. As an example, the following exercise on the face and
head begins with the receiver's head being held firmly in one
hand and, using the thumb of the other hand, pressing upwards
in a straight line between the eyebrows towards the hairline.
Each movement should only be quite small, about 12 millime-

tres (0.5 inch). The fingers should then be placed on each side of the head and both thumbs used to press from the inner end of the eyebrows towards the hairline (*see* page 188, figure A). Again, holding the hands at each side of the head, the thumbs should then be used to press from the start of the eyebrows across the brow to the outside (figure B). With the fingers in place at each side of the face, work the thumbs across the bone below the eyes, moving approximately 6 millimetres (0.25 inch) at a time (figure C). Commencing with the thumbs a little to one side of each nostril, press across the face below the cheek-bones (figure D). Press one thumb in the area between the top lip and nose (figure E) and then press with both the thumbs outwards over the upper jaw (figure F). Next, press one thumb in the hollow below the lower lip and then press outwards with both thumbs over the lower part of the jaw (figure G). The giver then puts all fingers of the hands beneath the lower jaw and then leans backwards so that pressure is exerted (figure H).

Kyo and jitsu energy

As a person progresses in the study of shiatsu and comes to understand the needs and requirements of others, he or she will gradually be able to give beneficial therapy. It is believed that energy, as previously defined, is the basis for all life, and it is divided into two types known as *kyo* and *jitsu*. If the energy is low or deficient, it is known as kyo, and if there is an excess or the energy is high, it is known as jitsu. These two factors will therefore affect the type of shiatsu that is given and, with practice, it should be possible to assess visually and also by touch what type a person is. A few general guidelines as to how a person can vary his or her shiatsu to suit either kyo or jitsu types are given below. As the person progresses, however, it is likely that an intuitive awareness will develop of what is most

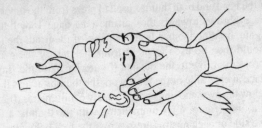

A—press between the eyebrows towards the hairline

B—press from the eyebrows across the brow

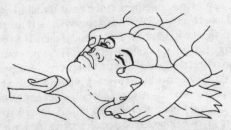

C—work the thumbs across the bones below the eyes

D—press across the face below the cheekbones

E—press the area between the nose and upper lip

F—press with thumbs outwards over the upper jaw

G—press outwards over the lower part of the jaw

H—place fingers beneath the jaw and lean back

suitable for a particular person. For kyo types (low or deficient in energy), a gentle and sensitive touch is required, and any stretched positions can be maintained for a longer time as this will bring more energy to that part of the body. Pressure, held by the thumb or palm, can also be maintained for an increased length of time, approximately 10–15 seconds. For jitsu types (high or excess energy), the stretches can be done quite quickly so that the energy is dispersed, and also shaking or rocking areas of the body can have the same effect. The pressure that is exerted by the thumbs or palms should also be held for a shorter length of time, so that excess energy is dispelled.

Yin and yang

As previously mentioned, a change in diet may also be recommended by a shiatsu practitioner. From the viewpoint of traditional Oriental medicine, food can be defined in an 'energetic' way. This differs from the Western definition of foods consisting of protein, minerals, fats, carbohydrates, fibre and vitamins. It is believed that, according to its 'energetic' definition, food will have differing physical, mental, spiritual and emotional effects. This energy is split into two parts known as *yin* and *yang*. Yin is where energy is expanding and yang where it is contracting. They are thus opposites and, from traditional beliefs, it was thought that interactions between them formed all manner of occurrences in nature and the whole of the world and beyond. All definitions of yin and yang are based on macrobiotic food (a diet intended to prolong life, comprised of pure vegetable foods such as brown rice), this being the most usual reference. Food can be divided into three main types—those that are 'balanced', and some that are yin and some that are yang. Foods that are defined as being yin are milk, alcohol, honey, sugar, oil, fruit juices, spices, stimulants, most drugs (such as aspirin, etc), tropical vegetables and fruits, refined foods, and most food additives of a chemical nature. Yang foods are poultry, seafood, eggs, meat, salt, fish, miso and cheese. Balanced foods are seeds, nuts, vegetables, cereal grains, beans, sea vegetables and temperate fruits (such as apples and pears).

The balance between yin and yang is very important to the body, for example, in the production of hormones such as oestrogen and progesterone, and glycogen and insulin and the expansion and contraction of the lungs, etc. A 'balanced' way of eating, mainly from the grains, beans, seeds, nuts and vegetables, etc, is important as this will help to achieve the energy balance in the meridians, organs and chakras, as defined previ-

A—grasp the left knee with the right hand and the right knee with the left hand

B—inhale, and as you exhale, lean forwards and downwards with the top half of the body

ously. When these two opposing forces of yin and yang are in
harmony and balanced, physical and mental health will result.

Body reading

It is possible for practitioners of shiatsu, as they become increasingly experienced, to assess a person's physical and mental state of health by observing the body and forming accurate
observations. If the traditional ways of Eastern diagnosis are
studied, this can assist greatly. The Eastern methods were based
on the senses of hearing, seeing, smelling and touching and
also by questioning people to obtain information leading to an
overall diagnosis. This is known as body reading.

Makko-ho exercises

Makko-ho exercises are six stretching exercises, each of which
affects one pair of the meridians by stimulating its flow of energy. If the complete set of exercises is performed, all the body's
meridians will have been stimulated in turn, which should result in increased vigour and an absence of tiredness. Before
beginning the exercises, you should feel calm and relaxed. It
may prove beneficial to perform some abdominal breathing first
(as previously described). One example is the triple heater and
heart governor meridian stretch. Sit on the ground with either
the feet together or crossed. The right hand should grasp the
left knee and the left hand the right knee, both quite firmly (*see*
figure A on page 192). Then inhale and, as you exhale, lean
forwards and downwards with the top half of the body so that
the knees are pushed apart (*see* figure B on page 192). Hold
this position for approximately 30 seconds while breathing normally, and then, after inhaling, return to the upright position.
After completion of all exercises, lie flat on the ground for several minutes and relax.

Yoga

Introduction

Origins

From its Indian origins as far back as 4000 years ago, yoga has been continually practised, but it is only in the present century that its use has become more widespread. Yoga has an effect on the whole person, combining the physical, mental and spiritual sides. The word 'yoga' is derived from a Sanskrit word that means 'yoke' or 'union', and thus reflects on the practices of yoga being total in effect. For many hundreds of years in India only a select few, such as philosophers and like-minded people with their disciples, followed the way of life that yoga dictated. The leaders were known as 'yogis' and it was they who taught their followers by passing on their accumulated knowledge. These small groups of people dwelt in caves or woods, or sometimes a yogi would live like a hermit. Yoga has had quite far-reaching effects over many hundreds of years in India.

The basics of yoga were defined by a yogi called Patanjali who lived about 300 BC. He was a very well-respected teacher and commanded great influence at that time, and his classification is one that is used now. He established the fact of yoga being separated into eight different parts. The first two concern a person's lifestyle, which should be serene with the days spent in contemplation, study, maintaining cleanliness, and living very simply and at peace with others. Anything that involves avarice or greed, etc, or is harmful to others has to be avoided. The third and fourth parts are concerned with physical matters and list a number of exercises designed to promote peace and infuse energy into both the mind and body. The remaining four sections are concerned with the advancement of a person's soul or spirit and mental faculties by being able to isolate himself or herself from outside worries and normal life, contemplation and broadening mental faculties with the ultimate knowledge known as *somadhi*. Mentally, this is a complete change that gives final realization of existence. Much more recently, yoga became available in India to everyone, in complete contrast to centuries ago. Doctors and teachers taught yoga, and it is now the rule that all schoolchildren have lessons in some of the exercises.

Modern practice

Nowadays, the practice of yoga is not restricted to India alone, with millions of people worldwide being followers. There are actually five different types of yoga: *raja*, *jnana*, *karma* and *bakti*, and *hatha*. It is this last system that is known in the west, and it involves the use of exercises and positions. The other methods concentrate on matters such as control over the mind, appreciation and intelligence or a morally correct way of life. These other methods are regarded as being of equal importance by the person completely committed to yoga as a way of life. Although people may have little or no spiritual feeling, the basic belief of yoga is the importance of mental attitudes in establishing the physical improvements from exercise. Because of media coverage of a famous violinist receiving successful treatment to a damaged shoulder by yoga, it became very popular throughout the UK. Prior to the 1960s, it was seldom practised, and only then by people who wanted to learn more of eastern therapies or who had worked and travelled in that area.

It is a belief in yoga that the body's essence of life, or *prana*, is contained in the breath. Through a change in the way of breathing there can be a beneficial effect on the general health. If a person is in a heightened emotional condition, or similar state, this will have an effect on the breathing. Therefore, if the breathing is controlled or altered this should promote joint feelings of peace and calm, both mentally and emotionally. There is a variety of exercises, and each promotes different types of breathing, such as the rib cage, shoulder and diaphragm. Some of the movements and stances in use were originally devised from the observation of animals, since they appeared to be adept at relaxation and moved with minimum effort. These stances, which are maintained for one or two minutes, aim to increase freedom of movement and make the person aware of the various parts of the body and any stress that may be present. It is not intended that they be physically tiring or that the person should 'show off' in front of others. The aim is to concentrate on self-knowledge.

The treatment

The benefits

It is recommended to follow some simple rules when practising yoga. Firstly use a fully qualified therapist, and practise daily if at all possible. It is advisable to check with a G.P. first if a person is undergoing a course of treatment or is on permanent medication, has some sort of infirmity or feels generally unwell. It is always best that yoga is undertaken before meal times but if this is not possible then three hours must elapse after a large meal or an hour after a light one. Comfortable clothes are essential and a folded blanket or thick rug should be placed on the ground as the base. Before commencing yoga have a bath or shower and repeat this afterwards to gain the maximum benefit. It is not advisable to do yoga if either the bowels or bladder are full. Should the person have been outside on a hot and sunny day it is not recommended that yoga is practised straight afterwards, as feelings of sickness and dizziness may occur.

Yoga is believed to be of benefit to anyone, providing that they possess determination and patience. If a person has certain physical limitations then these must be taken into account with regard to their expectation, but there is no age barrier. Teachers believe that people suffering from stress and disorder in their lives are in greater need of a time of harmony and peace. Yoga was used in the main to encourage health in the physical and mental states and thereby act as a preventive therapy. Tension or stress was one of the main disorders for which it was used, but nowadays it has been used for differing disorders such as hypertension (high blood pressure), bronchitis, back pain, headaches, asthma, heart disorders, premenstrual tension and an acid stomach. Trials have also been conducted to assess its potential in treating some illnesses such as multiple sclerosis, cerebral palsy, osteoporosis, rheumatoid arthritis and depression experienced after childbirth. Since the effects of tension are often shown by the tightening and contraction of muscles, the stretching exercises performed in yoga are able to release it. Also, being aware of each muscle as it is stretched encourages the person to mentally lose any stress or problems with which they have been beset. Suppleness is developed by the exercises through the use of the bending and twisting actions. This will help to maintain healthy joints, particularly for people who lead rather inactive lives.

There should be no strain felt and after practice some or all of them can be done in order. As mentioned previously, it is best to check with a qualified therapist if the person is an expectant mother, suffers from hypertension, is overweight or is having their monthly period.

The bow

Lie face down on the ground with the knees bent and then raised in the direction of the head. Then hold the ankles and, while inhaling, a pull should be exerted on the ankles so that the chest, head and thighs are raised up away from the floor. To start with it will not be possible to hold the legs together, but this will gradually occur with regular practice. This position should be maintained for up to ten breaths. To complete the bow, exhale and let go of the legs.

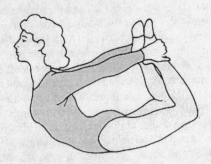

The bow

The bridge

The bridge is carried out on the floor, starting with the person lying on the back, the knees should be bent, with the legs separated a little and the arms at the side of the body. The person should then inhale and lift the torso and legs, thus forming a bridge. The fingers should then be linked under the body and the arms held straight. The person should then incline the body

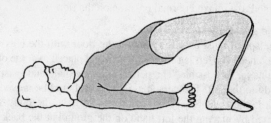

The bridge

The spinal twist

to each side in turn, ensuring that the shoulders stay underneath. To make the bridge a little bigger, pressure can be exerted by the arms and feet. After inhaling, the position should be maintained for a minimum of one minute and the body returned to a relaxed normal position on the floor.

The spinal twist

The spinal twist entails sitting on the floor with the legs outstretched. The left leg should be bent and placed over the other leg as far as possible. The person should exhale and twist the body to the left. The person's right hand should be moved towards the right foot. The person should have the body supported by placing the left hand on the ground at the back but keeping the back straight. Every time the person exhales the body should be further twisted to the left. The position should be maintained for approximately one minute and then the complete action done again, but this time turning to the right. This is a gentle posture that is easy to perform. Relax.

The spinal twist helps to strengthen the spine, improve posture and promote psychological balance.

The triangle

The triangle commences with the person standing upright with the legs apart and the arms held out at shoulder level. Extend the right foot to the side and, upon exhaling, bend over the right-hand side so that the right hand slips downwards in the direction of the ankle. There should be no forward inclination of the body at this time. As the bending action takes place, the left arm should be lifted upright with the palm of the hand to the front. This stretched position should be kept up for the minimum of a minute, with the person trying to extend the stretch as they exhale. After inhaling, the person should then revert to the beginning of the exercise and do it again but leaning in the opposite direction.

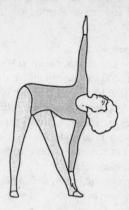

The triangle

The two movements of the cat

The triangle helps to calm the nerves, acts to remove toxins from the body, and promotes good health in general.

The cat

Kneel on all fours with your hands shoulder-distance apart and your knees the same distance apart as your hands. Your elbows should remain straight throughout the entire exercise. Exhale while arching your back up high. Keep your head between your arms, looking at your abdomen. Hold this pose for a few seconds. Inhale, as you slowly hollow your back to a concave position. Raise your head and look up. Hold again. Repeat the sequence five to ten times, creating a slow flowing movement of the two postures. Relax.

The cat helps to strengthen the spine, improve posture and revitalize the whole body.

The tree

Stand with both feet together, arms loosely by your side. Focus your eyes on an imaginary spot directly ahead of you. Bring the right foot up and place the sole against the inside of the left thigh, as high as possible. When balanced, raise both arms simultaneously, placing the palms together over your head. Hold for 30 seconds. Gently lower your arms. Release your foot from your thigh. Repeat the sequence with the other foot. Relax.

The tree promotes concentration, balance and stability of body and mind.

The cobra

Lie face down. Place the palms on the floor under the shoulders, fingers turned slightly inwards. Slowly lift the forehead, the nose, the chin, and the entire upper body, up to the navel. The weight rests on both hands, the pelvis, and the legs. Keep the elbows slightly bent, and do not allow the shoulders to hunch

The tree

The cobra

up towards the ears. Hold for ten seconds, focusing your attention on the lower back. Very slowly lower your trunk to the floor, then the chin, the nose, and the forehead. Relax.

The cobra increases blood supply to the abdominal organs and helps to relieve digestive problems and correct kidney malfunctions.

The plough

Lie on your back, arms by your sides, palms down. Slowly raise your legs and trunk off the floor. Supporting your hips with both hands, bring your legs slightly over your head. Keep your legs as straight as possible. Supporting your back with both hands, continue lifting your legs up and over your head until the toes come to rest on the floor behind your head. Only when you are quite comfortable in the position, release the hold on your back and place your arms flat on the floor. Hold only for ten seconds in the beginning. After your body becomes accustomed to this position, you may hold it longer. Very slowly unroll your body to the starting position. Relax.

The plough helps to reinvigorate the entire nervous system, removing fatigue, listlessness and exhaustion. It is of particular benefit to the pancreas and endocrine glands.

The plough

The forward bend

Make sure you are well warmed up before attempting this posture. Sit with your legs stretched out in front of you, knees very straight. Inhale and stretch your arms above your head. Exhale and very slowly and smoothly bend forward from the hips (*not from the waist*) to grasp your toes. If at first this seems difficult, clasp instead your ankles, calves, or knees. It is important that your legs remain straight. Continue to bend forward and down, aiming to touch your knees with your head. Hold for at least ten seconds and observe your breath. Release your hold and very slowly unroll your spine, returning to a sitting position. Repeat twice.

The forward bend slows the respiratory rate to produce a calm and relaxed state of mind. It also increases the suppleness of the spine and improves blood circulation—which helps to regenerate the abdominal organs and improve digestion.

The forward bend

A salute or greeting to the sun

The following twelve stances, known as *a greeting to the sun*, have the aim of relaxing and invigorating the body and mind. This classic exercise coordinates breathing with variations of six yoga poses in a flowing rhythmic way that stretches and relaxes your body and your mind.

As suggested by its name, it was originally done when the sun rose and when it set. Although these stances are quite safe, they should not be done by pregnant women or those having a monthly period, except with expert tuition. If a person has hypertension (high blood pressure), a hernia, clots in the blood or pain in the lower back they are not recommended. Each exercise should follow on smoothly one after the other.

1 Start by facing east, standing up as straight as you can without forcing it, with your feet together. Inhale and visualize the sun just beginning to rise. Exhale and bring the palms of the hands on to your chest as if you were praying.

2 Then inhale and stretch the arms upright with the palms facing the ceiling and lean backwards, pushing the pelvis forward a little, and look up at your hands.

3 Exhale and, keeping the legs straight, place the fingers or palms on to the ground, ideally, your hands are touching the floor in front of or beside your feet. (Don't force this: if you can't reach the floor, let your hands hold on to the lowest part of your legs they can reach.)

4 Whilst inhaling, bend the knees and place one leg straight out backwards, with the knee touching the ground, in a long, lunging movement. Turn your toes right under and straighten your body.

5 With both hands on the ground, raise the head slightly and push the hips to the front. At the same time as holding the breath, stretch the legs out together backwards, and raise the body off the floor supported by the arms.

6 Exhale and fold the body over bent knees so that the head touches the ground with the arms stretched out in front, toes curled, until you are in the classic push-up position.

7 After inhaling and exhaling once, drop your knees to the floor, with your bottom up. Bend the elbows and bring your chest and chin to the floor. Continue breathing out and lower the whole body to the floor, straightening your legs and keeping your toes curled under with the body being supported by the hands at shoulder level and also by the toes. The stomach and hips should not be on the ground.

8 After taking a deep breath, stretch the arms and push the body upwards pushing down on your hands and slowly lifting your head as you straighten the elbows. Arch your back upwards like a snake before it strikes.

9 Exhale and then raise the hips upwards with the feet and hands being kept on the floor so that the body is in an inverted V-shape. The legs and back should be kept straight .

10 Breathe in and lunge forward by bending your right knee and stepping your right foot forward between your hands. When you breathe out, straighten your right leg and bring the left foot next to the right. Lift your buttocks high until you are touching your toes.

11 Inhale and slowly lift the spine, visualizing it unroll one vertebra at a time. Raise your head and look up, bringing your arms straight overhead, and bring the image of the rising sun back to mind.

12 Place the feet together keeping the
legs straight. Breathe out and slowly
bring your arms back to the sides,
allowing the sun to glow brighter and
brighter in your mind's eye.

Salute the sun six times at first, gradually increasing the
number of repetitions until you are comfortably doing the routine 24 times. This whole sequence of exercises can be performed several times over if wished. If this is the case, it is
suggested to alternate the legs used either forwards or backwards in two of the exercises.

As previously mentioned, yoga has recently been used to treat
some illnesses such as rheumatoid arthritis, and if a person has
such a severe disorder, then a highly skilled and experienced
therapist is essential. Since this form of yoga, known as therapeutic yoga, is so new there is only a limited number of suit-
ably experienced therapists available, although this situation
should be remedied by the introduction of further training. For
those who wish to use yoga to maintain mental and physical
health, joining a class with an instructor is perhaps the best
way to proceed, so that exercises are performed correctly and
any lapses in concentration can be corrected. These classes last
usually in the region of an hour and are separated into sessions
for beginners and those who are more proficient. Proficiency
and progress is achieved by frequent practice, which can be
done at home between lessons. One simple exercise that helps
reduce stress is quite simple to perform and does not take long.
The person should lie on the floor with the arms at the side and
the legs together. After inhaling, all the muscles from the toes

to the thighs should be tightened in turn. As the person exhales, the muscles in the stomach up to the shoulders should then be tightened, including the hands, which should be clenched. After inhaling again, the chest, throat and face muscles should be tightened, as well as screwing up the face and this should be maintained until the next breath has to be taken. All muscles should then be relaxed, the legs parted and the arms spread out comfortably with the palms facing the ceiling. The person should then totally relax with a sensation of falling through the ground.

The majority of doctors regard yoga as a type of exercise that is beneficial, although some do recommend patients to refer to yoga practitioners. However, if a specific disorder is to be treated, it is very important that the ailment should first be seen by a doctor.

Aromatherapy

Healing through aromatherapy

Aromatherapy is a method of healing using very concentrated essential oils that are often highly aromatic and are extracted from plants. Constituents of the oils confer the characteristic perfume or odour given off by a particular plant. Essential oils help the plant in some way to complete its cycle of growth and reproduction. For example, some oils may attract insects for the purpose of pollination; others may render it distasteful as a source of food. Any part of a plant—the stems, leaves, flowers, fruits, seeds, roots or bark—may produce essential oils or essences but often only in minute amounts. Different parts of the same plant may produce their own form of oil. An example of this is the orange, which produces oils with different properties in the flowers, fruits and leaves.

Art and writings from the ancient civilizations of Egypt, China and Persia show that plant essences were used and valued by priests, physicians and healers. Plant essences have been used throughout the ages for healing—in incense for religious rituals, in perfumes and embalming ointments and for culinary purposes. There are many Biblical references that give an insight into the uses of plant oils and the high value that was attached to them. Throughout the course of human history the healing properties of plants and their essential oils has been recognized and most people probably had some knowledge about their use. It was only in more recent times, with the great developments in science and orthodox medicine, particularly the manufacture of antibiotics and synthetic drugs, that knowledge and interest in the older methods of healing declined. However, in the last few years there has been a great rekindling of interest in the practice of aromatherapy with many people turning to this form of treatment.

Extraction of essential oils

Steam distillation, solvent extraction, maceration, defleurage, enfleurage

Since any part of a plant may produce essential oils, the method of extraction depends upon the site and accessibility of the essence in each particular case. The oils are produced by special minute cells or glands and are released naturally by the plant in small amounts over a prolonged period of time when needed. In order to harvest the oils in appreciable amounts, it is usually necessary to collect a large quantity of the part of the plant needed and to subject the material to a process that causes the oil glands to burst. One of the most common methods is *steam distillation*. The plant material is paced tightly into a press or still and steamed at a high temperature. This causes the oil glands to burst and the essential oil vaporises into the steam. This is then cooled to separate the oil from the water. Sometimes water is used for distillation rather than steam. Another method involved dissolving the plant material in a solvent or alcohol and is called *solvent extraction*. This involves placing the material in a centrifuge, which rotates at high speed, and then extracting the essential oils by means of a low temperature distillation process. Substances obtained in this way may be called *resins* or *absolutes*. A further method is called *maceration* in which the plant is soaked in hot oil. The plant cells collapse and release their essential oils, and the whole mixture is then separated and purified by a process called *defleurage*. If fat is used instead of oil, the process is called *enfleurage*. These methods produce a purer oil that is usually more expensive than one obtained by distillation. The essential oils used in aromatherapy tend to be costly as vast quantities of plant material are required to produce them and the methods used are complex and costly.

Storage and use of essential oils

Essential oils are highly concentrated, volatile and aromatic. They readily evaporate and change and deteriorate if exposed to light, heat and air. Hence pure oils need to be stored carefully in brown glass bottles at a moderate temperature away from direct light. They can be stored for one or two years in this way. For most purposes in aromatherapy, essential oils are used in a dilute form, being added either to water or to another oil, called the *base* or *carrier*. The base is often a vegetable oil such as olive or safflower, which both have nutrient and beneficial properties. An essential/carrier oil mixture has a short useful life of two or three months and so they are usually mixed at the time of use and in small amounts.

Techniques used in aromatherapy

Massage

Massage is the most familiar method of treatment associated with aromatherapy. Essential oils are able to penetrate through the skin and are taken into the body, exerting healing and beneficial influences on internal tissues and organs. The oils used for massage are first diluted by being mixed with a base and should never be applied directly to the skin in their pure form in case of an adverse allergic reaction.

An aromatherapist will 'design' an individual whole body

massage based on an accurate history taken from the patient and much experience in the use of essential oils. The oils will be chosen specifically to match the temperament of the patient and also to deal with any particular medical or emotional problems which may be troubling him or her.

Although there is no substitute for a long soothing aromatherapy massage given by an expert, the techniques are not difficult to learn and can be carried out satisfactorily at home.

Bathing
Bathing most people have experienced the benefits of relaxing in a hot bath to which a proprietary perfumed preparation has been added. Most of these preparations contain essential oils used in aromatherapy. The addition of a number of drops of an essential oil to the bath water is soothing and relaxing, easing aches and pains, and can also have a stimulating effect, banishing tiredness and restoring energy. In addition, there is the added benefit of inhaling the vapours of the oil as they evaporate from the hot water.

Inhalation
Inhalation is thought to be the most direct and rapid means of treatment. This is because the molecules of the volatile essential oil act directly on the olfactory organs and are immediately perceived by the brain. A popular method is the time-honoured one of *steam inhalation,* in which a few drops of essential oil are added to hot water in a bowl. The person sits with his or her face above the mixture and covers the head, face and bowl with a towel so that the vapours do not escape. This can be repeated up to three times a day but should not be undertaken by people suffering from asthma. Some essential oils can be applied directly to a handkerchief or onto a pillow and the vapours inhaled in this way.

Steam inhalation with essential oils constitutes a wonderful, time-honoured way of alleviating the symptoms of colds and flu, and can also be beneficial to greasy skins. Steam inhalations should, however, be avoided by asthmatics unless under direction from a medical practitioner, as the steam can occasionally irritate the lungs.

Compresses

Compresses are effective in the treatment of a variety of muscular and rheumatic aches and pains as well as bruises and headaches. To prepare a compress, add 5 drops of oil to a small bowl of water. Soak a piece of flannel or other absorbent material in the solution. Squeeze out excess moisture (although the compress should remain fairly wet) and secure in position with a bandage or cling film. For acute pain, the compress should be renewed when it has reached blood temperature, otherwise it should be left in position for a minimum of two hours and preferably overnight. Cold water should be used wherever fever or acute pain or hot swelling require treatment, whereas the water should be hot if the pain is chronic. If fever is present, the compress should be changed frequently.

Hair treatments/scalp tonics

Many hair conditions such as dryness, excessive grease, or dandruff will respond to aromatherapy using specific recipes of essential oils diluted in a nourishing base oil. For instance, 60 drops of an essential oil diluted in 100 mls of base oil (such as olive or sweet almond) will make a wonderful conditioning treatment. Simply rub the oils thoroughly into the scalp, then wrap the hair in warm towels and allow the oil to penetrate the hair and the scalp for an hour or two. The choice of oil depends of course upon the desired effect: chamomile and rosemary, for instance, will condition and promote healthy hair growth, bergamot and tea tree are helpful in dandruff control whilst lavender has repellent qualities which will deter lice and fleas.

Face creams, oils and lotions

For the face, essential oils should be mixed with base oils in much the same way as for massage, the main difference being that more nourishing oils such as apricot kernel and avocado should be used in preference to ordinary vegetable oils. (It should be noted that avocado is a fairly heavy oil and its use is best reserved for dry skin.) Essential oils can also be added to a non-perfumed cold cream or lotion and used for problem complexions.

Most essential oils have antiseptic properties and can be used to treat infective skin conditions. Certain oils (such as rose and neroli) are anti-inflammatory and have a soothing effect, whereas sandalwood is useful in the treatment of superficial broken veins. Rose and neroli are also excellent for care of mature skins. For dry cracked skin, the addition of wheatgerm and avocado oil (with their high vitamin E content) to preparations will relieve the condition. In general, aromatherapy can improve the skin by encouraging toxin removal, stimulating cell growth and renewal and improving circulation. A gentle circular massage with the tips of the fingers should be used on the face, and special care must be taken not to stretch or drag the delicate skin around the eye area.

Flower waters

Flower waters constitute a refreshing and soothing aid in the treatment and prevention of skin conditions such as eczema and acne, and can be easily prepared at home. Simply add around 20 drops of essential oil to an amber glass bottle containing 100 mls of spring water, then leave it to stand in a dark place for a few days. Filter the water through some coffee or similar filter paper, then apply to the skin as required using a cotton wool pad.

Bathing and showering

Add a few drops (5–10) of essential oil to the bath water after the water has been drawn, then close the door to retain the aromatic vapours. The choice of oils is entirely up to the individual, depending on the desired effect, although those with sensitive skins are advised to have the oils ready diluted in a base oil prior to bathing.

Bathing in essential oils can stimulate and revive or relax and sedate depending on the oils selected: rosemary and pine can have a soothing effect on tired or aching limbs, chamomile and lavender are popular for relieving insomnia and anxiety, etc. A similar effect (although obviously not quite as relaxing) can be achieved whilst showering by soaking a wet sponge in essential oil mix, then rubbing it over the body under the warm spray.

Sitz bath

A sitz, or shallow, bath in the appropriate essential oil can bring enormous relief in conditions such as haemorrhoids, thrush and cystitis.

Foot bath

Tired, swollen feet can be refreshed by bathing in a basin of hot water containing 4–5 drops of lavender, peppermint, rosemary or thyme.

Hands

Dry, chapped hands may be soothed by soaking in a bowl of warm water containing a few drops of essential oil such as patchouli or rose.

Mouthwash and gargles
Used strictly in the correct dilutions, essential oils provide a
natural, gentle way to help clear up mouth ulcers, oral thrush
and infected gums, but it cannot be stressed too much that essential oils should never be swallowed.

Neat application and internal use
Generally, the application of undiluted essential oils directly to
the skin should be avoided as many are highly irritant. However, there are one or two exceptions which have been safely
applied to the skin undiluted for centuries. These include lemon
oil, which can be applied neat to warts (Vaseline can be applied
around the wart to protect the surrounding skin); lavender, which
can be safely applied directly to burns, cuts, bites and stings;
and tea tree, which may be dabbed on spots. Any other oils
must be used in dilution unless under careful direction from a
trained aromatherapist.

Many essential oils are highly toxic when taken orally and
there are *no circumstances* in which they may safely be taken
at home in this way.

Mode of action of essential oils
Although the subject of a great deal of research, there is a lack
of knowledge about how essential oils work in the body to produce their therapeutic effects. It is known that individual essential oils possess antiseptic, antibiotic, sedative, tonic and
stimulating properties, and it is believed that they act in harmony with the natural defences of the body such as the immune system. Some oils, such as eucalyptus and rosemary, act
as natural decongestants whereas others, such as sage, have a
beneficial effect upon the circulation.

Conditions that may benefit from aromatherapy

A wide range of conditions and disorders may benefit from aromatherapy and it is considered to be a gentle treatment suitable for all age groups. It is especially beneficial for long-term chronic conditions, and the use of essential oils is believed by therapists to prevent the development of some illnesses. Conditions that may be relieved by aromatherapy include painful limbs, muscles and joints due to arthritic or rheumatic disorders, respiratory complaints, digestive disorders, skin conditions, throat and mouth infections, urinary tract infections and problems affecting the hair and scalp. Also, period pains, burns, insect bites and stings, headaches, high blood pressure, feverishness, menopausal symptoms, poor circulation and gout can benefit from aromatherapy. Aromatherapy is of great benefit in relieving stress and stress-related symptoms such as anxiety, insomnia and depression.

Many of the essential oils can be safely used at home and the basic techniques of use can soon be mastered. However, some should only be used by a trained aromatherapist and others must be avoided in certain conditions such as pregnancy. In some circumstances, massage is not considered to be advisable. It is wise to seek medical advice in the event of doubt or if the ailment is more than a minor one.

Consulting a professional aromatherapist

Aromatherapy is a holistic approach to healing hence the practitioner endeavours to build up a complete picture of the patient and his or her lifestyle, nature and family circumstances, as well as noting the symptoms which need to be to be treated. Depending upon the picture that is obtained, the aromatherapist decides upon the essential oil or oils that are most suitable and likely to prove most helpful in the circumstances that prevail. The aromatherapist has a wide ranging knowledge and experience upon which to draw. Many oils can be blended together for an enhanced effect and this is called a 'synergistic blend'. Many aromatherapists offer a massage and/or instruction on the use of the selected oils at home.

Base oils

Because essential oils are extremely concentrated and also because of their tendency to evaporate rapidly, they need to be diluted with carrier or base oils. Generally it is not advised that essential oils should be applied undiluted to the skin, although there are one or two specific exceptions. It is very important to use a high quality base oil, as oils such as baby or mineral oil have very poor penetrating qualities which will hamper the passage of the essential oil through the skin. Indeed, it would be better to use a good quality vegetable or nut oil for babies in preference to proprietary baby oils as the vegetable oil is more easily absorbed and contains more nutrients.

Although the choice of base oil is largely a matter of personal preference, it is useful to note that many vegetable oils possess therapeutic properties of their own. Any of sweet almond, soya bean, sunflower, jojoba, olive, grapeseed, hazelnut, avocado, corn or safflower will provide a suitable base for essential oils, although these should preferably be of the cold-pressed variety that has higher nutrient levels.

Pure essential oils should retain their potency for one to two years, but once diluted in a base oil will only last for three months or so before spoiling. They should also be stored at a fairly constant room temperature in corked dark glass bottles or flip-top containers as they will deteriorate quickly when subjected to extremes of light and temperature. Adding some vitamin E or wheatgerm oil to the mixture can help prolong its usefulness. For massage oils, it is best to make up a very small quantity of essential oil in base oil for each application because of its poor keeping qualities.

Below is a very rough guide to the dilution of essential oils. However, you will find many variations and differing opinions on this depending on the preference of individual therapists, and their recipes will differ accordingly.

Base Oil	Essential Oil
100 ml	20-60 drops
25 ml	7-25 drops
1 teaspoon (5 ml)	3-5 drops

Blending essential oils

Essences can be blended to treat specific ailments, and some aromatherapy books contain precise recipes for blends. When two or more essential oils are working together in harmony, this is known as a synergistic blend. Obviously, it takes many years of experience to know which combinations of plant essences will work most effectively together, but as a rough guide, oils extracted from plants of the same botanical family will usually blend and work well together, although it is by no means necessary to stick rigidly to this rule as other combinations may be just as successful. Really, a number of factors need to be taken into account when preparing a blend of oils for a patient, such as the nature of his/her complaint, his personality or frame of mind. For home use, it is not usually beneficial to blend more than three oils for any one preparation.

Around the home

There are a variety of ways in which your home can be enhanced by the use of essential oils. Fragrances, pomanders, ring burners and diffusers can all be used in conjunction with essential oils to impart a wonderful scent to a room. (Essential oils should be put into water and vapourized and not burned as they are inflammable. Follow the instructions on ring burners carefully and never put essential oils directly onto a hot light bulb.) Most essential oils also have antimicrobial properties which make them extremely useful when the occupants of the room are suffering from colds and flu. Oils such as myrtle and eucalyptus also seem to have a soothing effect on coughs and can be used in the bedroom where they will release their aroma throughout the night.

Fragrancers, pomanders, and ring burners can all be purchased quite cheaply from shops and indeed make very welcome gifts, but it is not neccessary to use any extra equipment to benefit from essential oils in the home. By adding a few drops of essential oil to a bowl of water or soaking a cotton ball in the oil and placing it in a warm place the same effect can be achieved. You can also sprinkle logs and twigs before placing them on the fire or barbecue to create a soothing aroma.

In case of colds or flu, a bowl of water is actually preferable as it has a humidifying effect on the air. Three or four drops of an appropriate essential oil such as eucalyptus or cypress sprinkled on a handkerchief can also be inhaled periodically to alleviate the worst symptoms of sinusitis, colds and headaches. Similarly, 2–3 drops of a relaxing essential oil on the pillow at night can help to alleviate insomnia.

How essential oils work

Inhalation, application and bathing are the three main methods used to encourage the entry of essential oils into the body. When inhaled, the extremely volatile oils may enter via the olfactory system, and permeation of the skin occurs when they are diluted and applied externally. By bathing in essential oils, we can inhale and absorb the oils through the skin simultaneously.

Little is known about how essential oils actually affect the mind and the body, although research is currently ongoing in the USA and the UK. However, the effectiveness of aromatherapy has been supported by recent research in central Europe, the USA, the UK and Australia. It appears that most essential oils are antiseptic and bactericidal to some degree, whilst some even seem to be effective in fighting viral infections.

On inhalation, essential oil molecules are received by receptor cells in the lining of the nose, which will transmit signals to the brain. Electrochemical messages received by the olfactory centre in the brain then stimulate the release of powerful neurochemicals into the blood which will then be transported around the body. Molecules inhaled into the lungs may pass into the bloodstream and be disseminated in the same way.

When rubbed or massaged into the skin, essential oils will permeate the pores and hair follicles. From here, they can readily pass into the tiny blood vessels (known as capillaries) by virtue of their molecular structure, and then travel around the body.

Once absorbed, the action of the oil depends upon its chemical constituents. Most essential oils are high in alcohols and esters, although a few contain a high concentration of phenols, aldehydes and ketones. The latter are powerful chemicals and their use should be avoided by all save the skilled professional.

Special care

You may find that your professional aromatherapist will use some of the following oils, but these are generally unsafe for use by the lay person.

Generally
Aniseed, cinamon bark, cinamon leaf, clove bud, clove leaf,
clove stem, fennel (bitter), pine, parsley, nutmeg.

During pregnancy
Basil, cedarwood, clary sage, fennel, juniper, marjoram, myrrh,
rosemary, sage,
thyme, parsley, nutmeg.

Prior to exposure to sun
Bergamot, lemon, mandarin, orange, fennel.

Hypertension
Sage, thyme, cypress.

Aromatherapy massage at home

Before beginning an aromatherapy massage, there are a number
of steps that should be taken in order for the subject of the
massage to derive full benefit from the treatment.

1 It is important to take a brief history from the patient in
   order to be able to select the correct oils. This will involve
   an assessment of his/her emotional state as well as any physical complaints.
2 At least an hour should have elapsed since the last meal
   prior to receiving or giving a massage.
3 Make sure your clothing is loose and will not obstruct your
   movements.
4 Ensure that hands are clean and nails short.
5 Have some tissues ready, and make sure your oil is easily
   accessible.
6 Make sure your hands are warm before touching your subject

The room should be warm so that your subject will be comfortable even though only partly dressed. Lighting should be subdued, and the telephone should be disconnected to avoid interruption. Perhaps music could be played softly in the background, but this is a matter of preference and convenience. It is a good idea to have a compatible essence evaporating in the room prior to commencement. The massage surface needs to be firm, therefore a normal sprung bed is unsuitable—instead, pad the floor or use a futon or similar firm mattress.

First of all the subject may have a warm bath or shower in order that the pores are open and receptive to the essential oil. This, however, is a matter of personal preference on the part of the therapist. The subject should be positioned comfortably and should be covered with towels, exposing only the area that is to be massaged at any one time in order to avoid embarrassment and cold. Hair should be tied out of the way.

Basic techniques

The following constitutes only a very basic guide to massage movements and is no substitute for a comprehensive aromamassage course. However, massage can be used to great benefit at home using the following simple movements and suggestions:

Effleurage

This is the most often used therapy movement, and constitutes a simple, gentle stroking movement. Note that deep pressure should *never* be used by an untrained person. The strokes may be long or short, gentle or firm, but the whole hand should be used, always pushing the blood towards the heart, thus promoting venous return. This stroke promotes muscle relaxation and soothes the nerve endings.

Petrissage
In petrissage, the flesh is gently rolled between the thumbs and fingers in a movement not unlike kneading dough. This technique is best used on the back and on fatty areas. The idea is to stimulate the circulation and lymphatic flow and thereby increase the rate of toxin expulsion.

Head massage
Put a little of the essential massage oil on the fingertips and massage in circular movements over the scalp and temples.

Massage for tension headaches and migraine
Work from the base of the neck and scalp for a few moments, using effleurage strokes firmly, again with the chosen oil(s) on the fingertips

Neck massage
Neck massage should be carried out with the patient sitting on a chair with some support in front. Working around the base of the neck and scalp, use small upward and outward circular movements. Move slowly up, down and around the sides of the neck, alternating firm and gentle movements.

Shoulder massage
Using gentle anticlockwise effleurage movements, stroke firmly from the shoulders to the neck.

Arm massage
Use effleurage and petrissage movements upwards in the direction of the armpit, concentrating on muscular and fatty areas. Avoid bony areas.

Back massage
Avoiding the vertebrae, use gentle or firm petrissage or effleurage movements. Stroke all the way from the lumbar to

the shoulders, move the hands outwards across the shoulders and return slowly down the outer area of the back. Repeat this movement to induce deep relaxation.

Abdomenal massage
Use a clockwise effleurage stroke, taking care not to apply too much pressure.

Leg massage
Always massage the legs in an upward direction. Avoid bony area, and *never* massage varicose veins.

Massage for menstrual or gynaecological problems
Always use gentle effleurage movements and do not exert any pressure on the lower abdomen. Begin at the lower back and slide forwards and downwards across the hips. Repeat several times.

Feet massage
Work in the direction of toe to heel, using the fingers upper-most and the thumb under the foot.

Common ailments

Stress-related disorders
Anxiety	basil, bergamot, geranium, lavender, marjoram (sweet), melissa, neroli, sandalwood, vetiver.
Mild shock	basil, chamomile, melissa, peppermint, rosemary.
Depression	bergamot, chamomile, geranium, jasmine, lavender, neroli, patchouli, rose, rosemary, sage*.
Fatigue	clary sage, eucalyptus, juniper berry, peppermint, rosemary.

Skin complaints/disorders

Dry skin	bergamot, chamomile, geranium, jasmine, lavendar, melissa, neroli, patchouli, sandalwood, ylang ylang.
Oily skin	cypress, lemon, tea tree.
Acne	bergamot, cedarwood, chamomile, cypress, eucalyptus, fennel, geranium, juniper berry, lavender, lemon, myrrh, parsley*, patchouli, petitgrain, rose, rosemary, sandalwood, tea tree.
Eczema	chamomile, geranium, juniper berry, lavender, melissa.
Psoriasis	bergamot, chamomile, eucalyptus, lavender, peppermint.

Feminine/gynaeological disorders

Amenorrhoea	chamomile, clary sage, fennel, geranium, sage*.
Dysmenorrhoea	cypress, geranium, rose.
Hot flushes	chamomile, clary sage, jasmine, lavender, neroli, petitgrain, sandalwood, ylang ylang.
Mastitis	chamomile, clary sage, geranium, lavender, rose.
Period pain	clary sage, lavender, marjoram
PMT	geranium, lavender, neroli, petitgrain, rose.

*Special care should be taken when using the oils marked * . When employed incorrectly they can have adverse effects and are normally recommended to be used only under the guidance of a professional aromatherapist*

A - Z of Essential Oils

The following section is by no means an exhaustive one, but aims to include the most popular oils readily available today. Similarly, whilst therapeutic uses have been suggested, therapists will differ in the choice of oils for particular complaints, just as a general practitioner may prescribe one remedy for a specific complaint, whereas his partner in the same practice may favour another treatment for the same complaint.

Aniseed
Pimpinella anisum
Aniseed seems to have a carminative (flatulence-expelling) effect on the alimentary canal and is therefore useful in the treatment of flatulence and indigestion. It has a strong antiseptic effect, and its antispasmodic properties can be effective against period pains. It also seems to stimulate lactation post-natally and is used in lozenges and cough sweets for its decongestant effect. Its anti-parasitic effect makes it useful in the treatment of lice and scabies.
CAUTION: Can be irritant to sensitive skins and narcotic in large doses. It is not suitable for home use and should only be used by a qualified aromatherapist.

Basil
Ociymum basilicum
Basil is now grown in many countries of the world although it originates from Africa. The herb has a long history of medici-

nal and culinary use, and was familiar to the Ancient Egyptian and Greek civilizations. Basil is sacred in the Hindu religion and has many medicinal uses in India and other Eastern countries. The whole plant is subjected to a process of steam distillation to obtain the essential oil used in aromatherapy. Basil is valued for its soothing and uplifting effects—its sweet, liquorice-like fragrance alleviates fatigue and depression and has a general tonic effect. Basil has a refreshing, invigorating effect and also has antiseptic properties. It can be effective in treating respiratory infections such as colds, bronchitis, asthma and sinusitis. It can also alleviate the symptoms of fever, gout and indigestion. It seems to be equally effective in relieving tired and over-worked muscles and is widely used in baths, inhalation and massage. Its strongly antiseptic effect sooths skin abrasions and assists the healing process. It also has insect repellent qualities. As a digestive aid, basil's antispasmodic effect has made it a favoured herb in cookery throughout the ages.

CAUTION: Basil should be avoided during pregnancy. It can also have a depressant effect, so it should be used in moderation. It is relatively non-toxic, but should be well diluted to avoid possible skin irritation.

Bay
Laurus nobilis

Both *Laurus nobilis* and its West Indian cousin *Pimenta racemosa* are valuable in the treatment of colds, flu and bronchitis. As discovered by the ancients, it also promotes digestion, and combats dyspepsia and flatulence. The West Indian oil is favoured in the treatment of rheumatic pain because of its anti-inflammatory properties and is widely used as a general tonic. Both can be used in inhalation, baths and massage.

CAUTION: Avoid application to sensitive skins.

Benzoin
Styrax benzoin

For skin complaints, benzoin is indicated in the treatment of chapped, inflamed or irritated skin. Its antiseptic properties make it a popular choice for urinary, respiratory and throat infections. Benzoin also has uplifting qualities which can relieve stress and nervous tension when used in a massage oil. As an expectorant, many therapists recommend a few drops of benzoin in a pint of hot water as an inhalation.

CAUTION: Compound tincture of benzoin (which contains other substances including aloe, tolu balsam and storax) occasionally causes sensitivity, but benzoin itself is generally non-toxic and non-irritant.

Bergamot
Citrus bergamia

Oil of bergamot is obtained from a plant that is a native species of some Asian and Eastern countries. The oil was first used and traded in Italy and derives its name from the northern city of Bergamo. In Italian medicine, it was popular as a remedy for feverish illnesses and to expel intestinal worms. It has also been used in cosmetics and perfumes, as the flavouring of Earl Grey tea, and in other foods. Recent research carried out in Italy indicates a wide variety of therapeutic applications for bergamot, including urinary tract and respiratory infections.

Its strong antiseptic effect makes it a good choice for the treatment of skin, throat and mouth infections.

In particular, scalp and skin conditions such as psoriasis, acne and ulcers will often respond to treatment with bergamot, especially where stress and depression may have played a part in lowering resistance to infection. When combined with eucalyptus, its soothing effect will afford relief to sufferers of cold sores and shingles. Insomnia, anxiety and depression can be alleviated by the uplifting and refreshing nature of this oil. It also has a natural deodorizing effect and can be used both as a breath freshener and as a personal deodorant.

CAUTION: Bergamot can irritate the skin if used in concentrations in excess of one per cent. It is phototoxic and should not be used in home-made suntan oil.

Cajeput
Melaleuca cajeputi

In addition to the above, therapists have found cajeput helpful for relief of a wide variety of complaints. Used in baths, diffusers, inhalation and massage, cajeput can bring relief from asthma, bronchitis, sinusitis and throat infections. Occasionally it has been used to treat diarrhoea and indigestion.

CAUTION: It may be irritant to the skin if used in high concentrations.

Cedarwood
Juniperus virginiana

Cedarwood seems to be beneficial in skin and scalp conditions such as alopecia, acne, dandruff and eczema. It also helps the body to fight respiratory infections and problems and has a mild diuretic effect which can be useful in the treatment of urinary tract infections. Cedarwood has been credited with aphrodisiac qualities.

CAUTION: High concentrations may irritate the skin, and on **no account** must cedarwood be used during pregnancy as it is a powerful abortifacient.

Chamomile (Roman)
Chamaemelum nobile

There are several varieties, but Roman chamomile is the essential oil of choice for home use. It is used by therapists to treat many skin complaints and promotes the healing of burns, cuts, bites and inflammations. It is also effective in allergic conditions and can have a beneficial effect on menstrual problems when used regularly in the bath. It seems to be effective in reducing stress and anxiety and problems such as headache, migraine and insomnia. As an analgesic, it is used in the treatment of earache, toothache, neuralgia and abscesses, and is popular for treating childhood illnesses.

CAUTION: Chamomile is generally non-toxic and non-irritant, but may cause dermatitis in very sensitive individuals.

Cinnamon
Cinnamomum zeylanicum

This oil possesses a warm, spicy aroma and has been favoured in the treatment of nausea, dyspepsia, flatulence and other digestive disturbances. Its warm, soothing qualities can be beneficial to rheumatism when used in massage oil on the affected parts.

These soothing, relaxing qualities also impart a strong stress-relieving effect.

CAUTION: Cinnamon can be irritant to the mucous membranes in large doses. Oil distilled from the bark is especially irritant to skin and mucous membranes and should never be directly applied. It is unsafe for home use and must only be used by a trained aromatherapist.

Clary Sage
Salvia sclarea

Clary sage is possessed of antispasmodic, antidepressant, balsamic, carminative, tonic, aperitive, astringent, anti-inflammatory, bactericidal and antiseptic qualities. It is valuable in stress-related conditions and has an anti-hypertensive effect. A thick mucilage can be made from the seeds, which was traditionally used for removing particles of dust from the eyes. Clary sage is also indicated in the treatment of colds and throat infections. It is also good for regulating menstrual problems and for soothing problem skin, particularly if dry or sensitive.

CAUTION: It should be avoided during pregnancy and also in conjunction with alcohol consumption. However, in general, clary sage has very low toxicity levels and is therefore preferable to garden sage for use in aromatherapy.

Clove
Eugenia aromatica

Clove is a useful antiemetic and should also be used for dyspepsia. It has a powerful antiseptic and a mild analgesic action which make it popular in the relief of gum infections and aching teeth. Its expectorant effect is valuable in the treatment of bronchitis and catarrh. It is widely used as an antihistamine and an antirheumatic and to treat skin conditions such as scabies and athlete's foot. It is also good for treating infections, especially colds and flu, and is often an ingredient of commercially available digestive tonics and mouthwashes.

CAUTION: It can cause mucous membrane irritation and is therefore best used in small doses. It can be dangerous and is best used only by a trained aromatherapist.

Cypress
Cupressus sempervirens

Cypress is thought to be beneficial to the urinary system and seems to help in conditions involving a loss of fluid. These include excessive perspiration, diarrhoea and menorrhagia. Used in the bath, cypress brings great relief to tired aching legs and feet. On the skin, or in a massage oil, its antiseptic and astringent actions can have a balancing effect on oily skin and provide an aid to healing. Cypress is often used by therapists to reduce swellings and nasal congestion, and it is useful in the treatment of colds and flu.

CAUTION: Not to be used by those suffering from hypertension, otherwise non-irritant and non-toxic.

Eucalyptus
Eucalyptus globulus

Eucalyptus is a native species of Australia and Tasmania but is now grown in many countries throughout the world. The plant has a characteristic pungent odour, and the oil obtained from it has disinfectant and antiseptic properties, clears the nasal passages and acts as a painkiller. The leaves and twigs are subjected to a process of steam distillation in order to obtain the essential oil used in aromatherapy. The diluted oil is used for muscular and rheumatic aches and pains, skin disorders such as ringworm, insect bites, headaches and neuralgia, shingles, respiratory and bronchitic infections and fevers. Eucalyptus is used in many household products and in remedies for coughs and colds. Its analgesic properties are often used to ease the discomfort of shingles, chicken pox and herpes as well as to soothe muscular aches and sprains.

CAUTION: When diluted, eucalyptus is safe to use externally, but can be fatal if taken internally.

Fennel (Sweet)
Foeniculum vulgare

Fennel has properties similar to those of aniseed, so that it is frequently used to treat colic and flatulence. It is also a mild natural laxative. It is credited with an action similar to oestrogen and is thought to stimulate milk production in nursing mothers. This action also indicates fennel in the treatment of menopausal symptoms. As a mild diuretic, it slows the build-up of toxic waste, which is a causative factor in gout and liver problems. Fennel is also suitable for children's complaints.

CAUTION: Avoid use on sensitive skin or prior to exposure to sun. It should not be used by epileptics or pregnant women. Bitter fennel oil can be dangerous and is best used only by a trained aromatherapist.

Frankincense
Boswellia carteri

The inhalation of frankincense is used to relieve the symptoms of bronchitis and laryngitis, and its soothing effect is useful in the treatment of asthma, attacks of which may be brought on by anxiety or emotional stress. It is also indicated in urinary tract problems such as cystitis and is sometimes used as a uterine tonic. Its healing properties have long been valued in the treatment of wounds, and it is often used in skin preparations for mature skins. It has an extremely relaxing aroma and is ideal in the bath for soothing away the day's stress.

Geranium
Pelargonium graveolens

Geranium is an excellent 'all-round' oil, with a wide range of uses, particularly for menopausal problems and pre-menstrual tension. Its diuretic quality makes it a wise choice for fluid retention, and cellulitis and mastitis often respond well to it. For skin conditions and emotional disorders, it is a popular choice in the bath and in massage oil. Serious skin conditions often respond to its antiseptic and anti-fungal qualities.

CAUTION: Generally non-toxic and non-irritant, it may cause contact dermatitis in hypersensitive individuals.

Jasmine
Jasminum officinalis

Because jasmine is so costly, it is not much used in home aromatherapy, but like all essential oils it does have therapeutic uses. Its heady, uplifting scent makes it useful in the treatment of stress-related illnesses. It also has a smoothing effect on skin and is a valuable component in skin care preparations. It also seems to have a regulating effect on the menstrual cycle, and has been successfully used for throat problems, coughs and catarrh. However, as there are many less expensive oils that will perform these functions, jasmine's main use is as a fragrance ingredient in perfumes.

CAUTION: Although non-toxic and non-irritant, it has, on occasion, caused an allergic reaction

Juniper Berry

Juniperus communis

Juniper is a native species of many northern countries and has a long history of medicinal use. It has stimulant, tonic and antiseptic properties. It is beneficial in the treatment of stress and sleeplessness. In cases of debility, it helps by acting as a tonic for the digestion and boosting the appetite.

Juniper seems to be beneficial to the digestive system, the female reproductive system and the menstrual cycle. It also helps regulate problem skin and is favoured by therapists in the treatment of acne, eczema, dermatitis and haemorrhoids. It helps disperse uric acid build-up and is therefore useful in the treatment of gout and other joint problems. It is a good stress-reliever, especially when used in the bath, and has a mild diuretic action which indicates its use in cystitis. Juniper also acts as an appetite stimulant, and is often used to get rid of intestinal parasites. It can be used in massage and baths.

CAUTION: Juniper stimulates uterine contractions and therefore should not be used in pregnancy. It should also be avoided by those with kidney disease. Generally non-toxic, but it may be slightly irritant.

Lavender
Lavendula vera

The highly perfumed lavender is a native species of the Mediterranean but has long been popular as a garden plant in Britain and many other countries. It has antiseptic, tonic and relaxing properties, and the essential oil used in aromatherapy is obtained by subjecting the flowers to a process of steam distillation. It is considered to be one of the safest preparations and is used in the treatment of a wide range of disorders.

Lavender is an appetite stimulant, a tonic and an antispasmodic. It is particularly effective in the treatment of minor burns and scalds, wounds, sores and varicose ulcers, and is generally one of the most versatile and widely used oils for healing. It also has a strong antiseptic effect and is employed in many cosmetic preparations and as an insect repellent. It is also used in the treatment of muscular aches and pains, respiratory problems, influenza, digestive problems, and genito-urinary problems such as cystitis and dysmenorrhoea. Its soothing effect is recommended for headaches and pre-menstrual tension. Lavender is a very safe oil and can even be applied undiluted to the skin.

Lemon
Citrus limonium

As a massage oil lemon can have a very stimulating effect on the circulation, and seems to have the ability to stimulate the body's own immune system. Therefore, it is frequently used to treat circulatory problems and respiratory ailments such as asthma, bronchitis and catarrh. As a digestive aid, lemon can have a calming effect on dyspepsia. As a natural cosmetic, lemon has an astringent and toning effect.

CAUTION: It is generally safe but should not be used prior to exposure to sunlight.

Lemongrass
Cymbopogon citratus

Combined with neroli in a massage oil, lemongrass brings relief to muscular aches and pains. It also has a sedative effect on the central nervous system, inducing a deep sense of relaxation when used in the bath. Lemongrass has an extremely strong bactericidal and fungicidal effect, which indicates its use in a variety of infections such as athlete's foot and thrush. It is also helpful in digestive disturbances such as colitis and indigestion, especially where stress or anxiety is a factor.

CAUTION: It is generally non-toxic, but occasionally dermatitis has been reported in sensitive individuals. Use under the guidance of a trained therapist.

Mandarin
Citrus nobilis

Mandarin is still a popular oil in the treatment of digestive weaknesses and liver disturbances and is especially preferred for children and the elderly because of its gentle nature. For stress, anxiety, insomnia and nervousness, its use is recommended in conjunction with other citrus oils. Like neroli, it is also a wonderful skin tonic, particularly for acne and oily skins. It is also indicated in the treatment of fluid retention.

CAUTION: Generally very safe, although its use on the skin is not recommended prior to exposure to sunlight.

Marjoram (Sweet)
Origanum marjorana

Marjoram can be extremely effective in reducing the pain and swelling of muscular damage, bruises and sprains, and arthritis. It has an extremely hypnotic effect, which is useful in inducing sleep and calming emotions, especially when used in the bath. It can also be effective in menstrual problems. Marjoram is also a popular treatment for colds and coughs, bronchitis and asthma, and has a carminative and antispasmodic action on colic, constipation and flatulence.

CAUTION: It should be avoided by pregnant women as it has a strong emmenagogic effect.

Melissa True
Melissa officinalis

Melissa is used in the treatment of respiratory disorders, nausea, indigestion and skin disorders. It is said to regulate menstruation and fertility, and is helpful in the treatment of anxiety and depression because of its revitalising properties. It also relieves wasp and bee stings and aids their healing. *The British Herbal Pharmacopoeia* recommends it for flatulent dyspepsia, neurasthenia and depressive illness.

CAUTION: It has caused occasional sensitization and dermal irritations and is therefore best used in low concentrations. Rarely stocked commercially, most melissa oils are blends and should be labelled so.

Myrrh
Commiphora myrrha

Myrrh has a stimulant effect on the mucous membranes and is therefore a useful expectorant. It is still used in Chinese medicine to treat menstrual disturbances and complaints, haemorrhoids and sores. It is also indicated for dental problems and is an effective antiseptic gargle for throat infections. It has long been known as an appetite stimulant and is a valuable ingredient in beauty treatments for mature skin.

CAUTION: Myrrh has an emmenagogic action and therefore should not be used by pregnant women.

Niaouli
Melaleuca viridiflora

Niaouli has a sweet, fresh fragrance and is strongly antiseptic and non-irritant, making it popular in the treatment of acne, boils and other skin irritations. It also makes a very stimulating chest rub and is good when vaporized.

Neroli
Citrus aurantium

Neroli is an extremely expensive oil to produce because of the volume of flowers required, but it is very much in demand because of its wonderful aroma. This is frequently harnessed in massage oil because of its power to uplift, calm and relax. It is also believed to have qualities that are beneficial to the skin, and is widely used to prevent stretch marks and scarring, to reduce thread veins and as an aid for dry, sensitive skin. Neroli's stress-relieving qualities indicate its use in a wide variety of complaints, ranging from colitis and diarrhoea to palpitations, insomnia and pre-menstrual tension.

Nutmeg
Myristica fragrans

Nutmeg is recommended in *The British Herbal Pharmacopoeia* for a variety of digestive complaints such as dysentery, nausea, dyspepsia, flatulence and diarrhoea. It has powerful stimulant properties that lend it to the treatment of poor circulation, poor appetite and menstrual irregularities. It can also be applied locally in massage to soothe aches and pains and to relieve rheumatism. Its warming effects are particularly welcome in the winter, and it has strong stimulant properties that lend it to the treatment of poor circulation.

CAUTION: It must not be used in high doses or for extended periods of time, as essential oil of nutmeg can induce hallucinations and hypnosis. Avoid its use during pregnancy. Nutmeg should always be well diluted, even for bathing purposes, as it can cause skin irritation. It can be dangerous and should be used only under the supervision of a trained aromatherapist.

Orange (Sweet)
Citrus sinensis

Sweet orange essential oil is very useful in the treatment of respiratory infections such as colds, bronchitis and influenza, and is thought to increase bronchial secretions. It can also help oily and dull complexions when used as part of a skin care routine. Having similar stress-relieving qualities to neroli, it is also helpful in the alleviation of stress-related complaints. As a gentle aid to digestion, it is often used to ease dyspepsia and constipation.

CAUTION: It is generally safe but should not be applied to the skin prior to exposure to sunlight.

Parsley
Petroselinum Crispum

Parsley has a diuretic and emmenagogic effect, which makes it useful for menstrual problems. It also has the power to reduce fever and has a soothing effect on colic, flatulence and indigestion. It is used for treating bladder and kidney problems, and is also indicated in the treatment of arthritis, rheumatism and sciatica, cystitis and urinary tract infections.

CAUTION: Oil of parsley is moderately toxic, therefore it is wise to use it in moderation and to avoid it completely in pregnancy. It should be used only under the supervision of a trained aromatherapist.

Patchouli
Pogostemon patchouli
Patchouli possesses a soothing, calming earthy scent. It is a good antiseptic with anti-inflammatory properties, which makes it a sensible choice in the treatment of minor burns. Patchouli has also been credited with aphrodisiac powers, and is excellent for relieving a variety of skin disorders including acne, athlete's foot, eczema and dry and cracked skin. It is also used for treating poisonous snakebites in Japan and Malaysia.

Peppermint
Mentha piperita
Peppermint is a native plant of Europe with a long history of medicinal use dating back to the ancient civilizations of Egypt, Greece and Rome. Oil of peppermint is obtained by subjecting the flowering parts of the plant to a process of steam distillation. The essential oil of peppermint has a calming effect on the digestive tract and is excellent for the relief of indigestion, colic-type pains, nausea, travel and morning sickness. It is also an extremely gentle inhalation for asthma. It is cooling and refreshing, and useful in the treatment of colds, respiratory symptoms and headaches.

Peppermint is widely used in remedies for colds and indigestion, as a food flavouring, especially in confectionery, and in toothpaste.

CAUTION: Possibly irritant to sensitive skin—use in moderation always.

Petitgrain
Citrus bigordia
Petitgrain can be used as a mild antidepressant substitute for neroli, and is effective in the alleviation of anxiety and insomnia. It is also valuable in skin care, having a balancing and ton-

ing effect on greasy skin conditions. In the digestive system, it reduces the symptoms of dyspepsia and flatulence.

Pine
Pinus sylvestris
Pine has a strong antiseptic quality, valued for its effectiveness in treating respiratory conditions and relieving asthma, blocked sinuses and catarrh when used as an inhalation. Its stimulating effect also makes it a good choice as a warming massage oil for muscular pains and strains. It has a multitude of other applications for cuts and sores, arthritis and rheumatism, cystitis and urinary tract infections, fatigue, stress, anxiety and neuralgia. CAUTION: Those with a tendency towards sensitive skin should avoid bathing in pine oil. Pine oil should only be used under the direction of a trained aromatherapist and is unsafe for home use.

Rose
Rosa centifola
Rose has a supremely feminine and deeply sensual aroma, which is the traditional mainstay of the perfume industry. Rose oil has a wonderful antidepressant effect that may be harnessed in body and face massages, baths or vaporizers to treat anxiety, stress and depression. It also has a gentle balancing effect on gynae-cological disorders and is said to have aphrodisiac properties.

Rosemary
Rosemarinus officinalis
Rosemary has a wide application and is effective in the treatment of numerous complaints. Possessing a powerful aroma, rosemary is favoured as a decongestant in inhalation and an invigorating muscle-strengthening massage oil. Skin and hair problems can respond well to rosemary, and gargling with it

will freshen the breath. Above all, rosemary seems to possess remarkable memory and concentration-enhancing properties. Other therapeutic uses are in digestive disorders, headaches and stress.

CAUTION: It should be avoided during pregnancy and should not be used by epileptics.

Sage
Salvia officinalis

Sage is a native plant of the northern coastal regions of the Mediterranean and has a long history of medicinal and culinary use dating back to the ancient civilizations of Greece and Rome. The essential oil used in aromatherapy is obtained by subjecting the dried leaves to a process of steam distillation. Sage has an expectorant effect when used in inhalations, and its astringent and cooling properties make it a popular choice as a tonic, an appetite stimulant and as a fever reducer. Its antiseptic effects are beneficial to sore throats and mouth problems if used in a gargle or mouthwash. It is also used to improve poor circulation, sore throats, colds and viral infections, bronchitic and catarrhal complaints, rheumatism, arthritic pains, joint sprains and strains, mouth infections and headaches. Sage is widely used as a flavouring in foods and in some household preparations and toiletries.

CAUTION: It should be avoided during pregnancy and if epileptic. Sage is toxic if ingested and is best substituted with clary sage for home use.

Sandalwood
Santalum album

Its preservative powers are often employed to lengthen the life of creams and potions. Sandalwood is a wonderful facial oil, with a soothing emollient effect on dry or sensitive skin. This oil also has a powerful relaxing effect and can alleviate upset stomachs, especially where nervous tension or stress has been a causative factor. Sandalwood also seems to have a powerful antiseptic effect that is particularly useful in the treatment of cystitis and urinary tract infections. It is also favoured for menstrual problems, as a sedative and for catarrh.

Tea Tree
Melaleuca alternifolia

Tea tree contains four substances that do not occur anywhere else in nature and, next to thyme, is the most antiseptic of all oils. It is also strongly disinfectant, antibacterial, anti-fungal, and antiviral—all qualities that make tea tree an invaluable weapon in the treatment of a multitude of infections. Similarly, it also seems to offer a boost to the body's own immune system whenever threat of infection occurs. Tea tree should be considered when treating any of the following problems: colds, influenza, bronchitis and asthma, warts and verrucas, burns and inflammation, thrush and similar fungal infections, mild shock and hysteria. It can be used undiluted on facial spots and, in a cream, on sunburn.

CAUTION: It is generally very safe, but may cause sensitization in some people.

Thyme (Sweet)
Thymus vulgaris

Thyme is a strong antiseptic, perhaps the strongest of any oil, and is also a powerful stimulant to the appetite, the immune system, and the central nervous system. Respiratory infections, coughs and asthma all seem to respond well to thyme oil, especially if used in inhalations and gargles. Note, however, that gargles must not be swallowed and care must be taken to use the thyme in low dilutions. Its use is indicated in a wide variety of fungal, bacterial and viral infections, in the treatment of wounds and sores and as an aid to the immune system. CAUTION: It should not be applied undiluted to the skin or used during pregnancy, or on children's skin. Always dilute prior to use in the bath. In fact, generally it is best used in low concentrations. There are several types of thyme, some of which can be dangerous. Only sweet thyme is safe for home use.

Ylang ylang
Cananga odorata

Ylang ylang is a native species of the Far Eastern islands of Indonesia, the Philippines, Java and Madagascar. To obtain the essential oil used in aromatherapy, the flowers are subjected to a process of steam distillation.Like most essential oils ylang ylang has a strong antiseptic effect, but it is best known for its euphoric and aphrodisiac properties. The nervous system can also benefit greatly from its relaxing powers, and its antidepressant powers can also be harnessed to treat mild shock, anger and stress. It has a calming effect on the heart-beat rate and can be used to relieve palpitations, tachycardia, hypertension (raised blood pressure), depression and shock.

It is used widely as an ingredient in skin care, having a wonderful tonic effect and gentle action.

CAUTION: It is generally very safe, although sensitization has been reported in a small number of cases. Used excessively, it can cause nausea or headache.

Herbal Remedies

History of the use of herbal remedies

Herbalism is sometimes maligned as a collection of home-made remedies to be applied in a placebo fashion to one symptom or another, provided the ailment is not too serious and provided there is a powerful chemical wonder-drug at the ready to suppress any 'real' symptoms. We often forget, however, that botanical medicine provides a complete system of healing and disease prevention. It is the oldest and most natural form of medicine. Its record of efficacy and safety spans centuries and covers every country worldwide. Because herbal medicine is holistic medicine, it is, in fact, able to look beyond the symptoms to the underlying systemic imbalance; when skillfully applied by a trained practitioner, herbal medicine offers very real and permanent solutions to concrete problems, many of them seemingly intractable to pharmaceutical intervention.

Early civilizations

The medicinal use of herbs is said to be as old as mankind itself. In early civilizations, food and medicine were linked and many plants were eaten for their health-giving properties. In ancient Egypt, the slave workers were given a daily ration of garlic to help fight off the many fevers and infections that were common at that time. The first written records of herbs and their beneficial properties were compiled by the ancient Egyptians. Most of our knowledge and use of herbs can be traced back to the Egyptian priests who also practised herbal medicine. Records dating back to 1500 BC listed medicinal herbs, including caraway and cinnamon.

The ancient Greeks and Romans also carried out herbal medicine, and as they invaded new lands their doctors encountered new herbs and introduced herbs such as rosemary or lavender into new areas. Other cultures with a history of herbal medicine are the Chinese and the Indians. In Britain, the use of herbs developed along with the establishment of monasteries around the country, each of which had its own herb garden for use in treating both the monks and the local people. In some areas, particularly Wales and Scotland, Druids and other Celtic healers are thought to have had an oral tradition of herbalism, where medicine was mixed with religion and ritual.

The first publications

Over time, these healers and their knowledge led to the writing of the first 'herbals', which rapidly rose in importance and distribution upon the advent of the printing press in the 15th century. John Parkinson of London wrote a herbal around 1630, listing useful plants. Many herbalists set up their own apothecary shops, including the famous Nicholas Culpepper (1616–1654) whose most famous work is *The Complete Herbal and English Physician, Enlarged,* published in 1649. Then in 1812, Henry Potter started a business supplying herbs and dealing in leeches. By this time a huge amount of traditional knowledge and folklore on medicinal herbs was available from Britain, Europe, the Middle East, Asia and the Americas. This promoted Potter to write *Potter's Encyclopaedia of Botanical Drugs and Preparations*, which is still published today.

The decline of herbal medicine

It was in this period that scientifically inspired conventional medicine rose in popularity, sending herbal medicine into a decline. In rural areas, herbal medicine continued to thrive in local folklore, traditions and practices. In 1864 the National Association (later Institute) of Medical Herbalists was established, to organize training of herbal medicine practitioners and to maintain standards of practice. From 1864 until the early part of this century, the Institute fought attempts to ban herbal medicine and over time public interest in herbal medicine has increased, particularly over the last 20 years. This move away from synthetic drugs is partly due to possible side effects, bad publicity, and, in some instances, a mistrust of the medical and pharmacological industries. The more natural appearance of herbal remedies has led to its growing support and popularity. Herbs from America have been incorporated with common remedies and scientific research into herbs and their active ingredients has confirmed their healing power and enlarged the range of medicinal herbs used today.

Its rise and relevance today

Herbal medicine can be viewed as the precursor of modern pharmacology, but today it continues as an effective and more natural method of treating and preventing illness. Globally, herbal medicine is three to four times more commonly practised than conventional medicine.

Nowhere is the efficacy of herbalism more evident than in problems related to the nervous system. Stress, anxiety, tension and depression are intimately connected with most illness. Few health practitioners would argue with the influence of nervous anxiety in pathology. Nervous tension is generally acknowledged by doctors to contribute to duodenal and gastric ulceration, ulcerative colitis, irritable bowel syndrome and many other gut-related pathologies.

We know also, from physiology, that when a person is depressed, the secretion of hydrochloric acid—one of the main digestive juices—is also reduced so that digestion and absorption are rendered less efficient. Anxiety, on the other hand, can lead to the release of adrenaline and stimulate the over-production of hydrochloric acid and result in a state of acidity that may exacerbate the pain of an inflamed ulcer. In fact, whenever the voluntary nervous system (our conscious anxiety) interferes with the autonomic processes (the automatic nervous regulation that in health is never made conscious), illness is the result.

Herbalists rely on their knowledge of botanical remedies to rectify this type of human malfunction. The medical herbalist will treat a stubborn dermatological problem using 'alternatives' specific to the skin problem, and then apply circulatory stimulants to aid in the removal of toxins from the area, with remedies to reinforce other organs of elimination, such as the liver and kidneys. Under such natural treatment, free of any discomforting side effects, the patient can feel confident and relaxed—perhaps for the first time in many months.

Curiously, this is an approach that has never been taken up by orthodox medicine. There, the usual treatment of skin problems involves suppression of symptoms with steroids. However, the use of conventional antihistamines or benzodiazepines often achieves less lasting benefit to the patient because of the additional burden of side effects, such as drowsiness, increased toxicity, and long-term drug dependence.

Herbs, on the other hand, are free from toxicity and habituation. Because they are organic substances and not manmade synthetic molecules, they possess an affinity for the human organism. They are extremely efficient in balancing the nervous system. Restoring a sense of wellbeing and relaxation is necessary for optimum health and for the process of self-healing.

Naturally, the choice of a treatment should be based upon a thorough health assessment and the experience and training of a qualified herbal practitioner. The herbalist will then prepare and prescribe herbal remedies in a variety of different forms, such as infusions, loose teas, suppositories, inhalants, lotions, tinctures, tablets and pills. Many of these preparations are available for home use from chemists, health shops and mail-order suppliers.

Herbs for stress management

Chamomile
This has a relaxing effect on the mind and body. It is an excellent sedative for anxiety and muscle tenseness. Many people enjoy its benefits in the form of chamomile tea.

Valerian
This is the ideal tranquillizer. The rhizomes of this plant contain a volatile oil (which includes valerianic acid), volatile alkaloids (including chatinine), and iridoids (valepotriates), which have been shown to reduce anxiety and aggression. So effective is Valerian in relieving anxiety while maintaining normal mental awareness, that it enables us to continue the most complicated mental exercise without drowsiness, loss of consciousness or depression. Valerian has been usefully taken before an examination or a driving test!

Peppermint
This is effective for treating digestive discomfort: it relieves indigestion, flatulence, constipation and nausea. Peppermint is also a good mind tonic, helping to clarify ideas and focus concentration. It is also helpful in alleviating the symptoms of colds and influenza. peppermint and chamomile tea is thought to be

effective in reducing the pain of tension headaches and migraines.

St John's Wort

Also called *Hypericum perforatum*, St John's wort has analgesic and anti-inflammatory properties, with important local applications to neuralgia and sciatica. Systemically, its sedative properties are based on the glycoside hypericin (a red pigment), which makes it applicable to neurosis and irritability. Many herbalists use it extensively as a background remedy.

Lemon balm

This herb is both carminative and antispasmodic, and is active specifically on that part of the vagus nerve that may interfere with the harmonious functioning of the heart and the stomach. Recent research has indicated that the action of the volatile oil begins within the limbic system of the brain and subsequently operates directly upon the vagus nerve and all the organs that are innervated by it. Accordingly, neurasthenia (complete nervous prostration), migraine, and nervous gastropathy are amenable to its healing power.

Lime flowers

These are thought to be helpful in controlling anxiety and hyperactivity. They are also effective for treating insomnia, high blood pressure and for soothing muscles and nerves.

Borage

This is an effective mind tonic, which helps to alleviate headaches, migraine and depression.

Oats

Oats is one of the great herbal restoratives of the nervous system. The plant contains a nervine alkaloid that is helpful in angina and in cardiac insufficiency. It has also been used in the treatment of addiction to morphine, narcotics, tobacco and alcohol.

Soothing herbal drinks

Warm milk and honey
Perhaps with a dash of cinnamon, this is an ideal drink to take at bedtime. It will help you relax and ward off insomnia.

Hop tea
Three hop cones, or heads, infused in a cup of boiling water whenever you begin to feel excessively tense, is a marvellous remedy for anxiety and insomnia.

A soothing herb tea to sustain a feeling of equilibrium

> 25g (1 oz) each dried chamomile flowers, lime flowers,
>   hibiscus blossoms and marigold flowers
> 15g ($^1/_2$ oz) each dried peppermint leaves and vervain
> 1 teaspoon whole fenugreek seeds
> 100g (4 oz) Lapsang Souchong tea

Mix all the ingredients together and store in a dark airtight container. Use 1 teaspoon to 300 ml ($^1/_2$ pint) of boiling water in a tea pot and leave to infuse for five minutes before straining and serving with a slice of lemon and a teaspoon of honey if desired. This is a very calming tea that soothes feelings of anxiety. It also helps to clear your head and settle an upset tummy. One cup taken morning and night will promote a feeling of wellbeing.

Another calming tea, especially good for the nerves

> 1 teaspoon each grated valerian root and dried mint
> $^1/_2$ teaspoon each dried chamomile and lavender flowers
> 600 ml (1 pint) boiling water

Infuse the dry ingredients in the water for 15 minutes then strain and take a glass three times a day for one week only.

Two tonic teas to sip when feeling depressed

Sip either 2 teaspoons of dandelion and 1 of basil infused in 600 ml (1 pint) of boiling water, or 2 teaspoons each of nettle, basil and melissa infused in 600 ml (1 pint) of boiling water.

A tonic tea to relieve stress and anxiety

1 tablespoon each fresh dandelion and nettle tops
1 teaspoon each fresh blackcurrant and borage leaves
600 ml (1 pint) boiling water

Steep the greenery in the water for five minutes. Strain and drink with lemon and honey.

Dock wine

Dock is one of the great tonic herbs because it is extremely high in iron. Here is a recipe for an old-fashioned dock wine.

175g (7 oz) dock root
15g ($^1/_2$ oz) liquorice wood
7g ($^1/_4$ oz) juniper berries
100g (4 oz) raw cane sugar
2 litres ($3^1/_2$ pints) organic red wine

Put the ingredients in a china container, cover and place either in a very slow oven or in a bain marie. Continue to heat gently until the mixture is reduced by half. Strain, bottle and seal tightly. Drink a sherry glass of the wine every morning for two weeks.

Rosemary in wine

Steep 6 sprigs of rosemary in a well-sealed bottle of sweet white wine for 14 days. Take 1 wineglass as a daily tonic.

Sage tonic

Take 100g (4 oz) of fresh sage leaves and put them in a bottle of organic white wine for two weeks. Sweeten to taste with honey and leave for another day. Press and strain through muslin. Bottle, and take 1 sherry glass before lunch and dinner.

You can also infuse sage leaves in boiling water, strain and sweeten with honey for an uplifting sage tea.

Examples of Herbs

Agrimony *Agrimonia eupatoria.*
COMMON NAME: Church steeples, cockeburr, sticklewort.
OCCURRENCE: field borders, ditches and hedges throughout England. Found locally in Scotland.
PARTS USED: the herb. Contains a particular volatile oil, tannin and a bitter principle.
MEDICINAL USES: mild astringent, tonic, diuretic, deobstruent. It has a reputation for curing liver complaints and is very good for skin eruptions and blood diseases. Also recommended to treat the sting and bite of snakes.
ADMINISTERED AS: liquid extract.

Aloes *Aloe perryi, Aloe vera.*
OCCURRENCE: indigenous to East and South Africa and introduced into the West Indies.
PARTS USED: the drug aloes is described as "the liquid evaporated to dryness which drains from the leaves." It contains two aloin compounds, barbaloin and isobarbaloin, as well as amorphous aloin, resin and aloe-emodin in differing proportions.
MEDICINAL USES: emmenagogue, purgative, vermifuge, anthelmintic. It is generally administered along with carminative and anodyne drugs, and acts on the lower bowel. The liquid form may be used externally to ease skin irritation.
ADMINISTERED AS: fluid extract, powdered extract, decoction, tincture.

Allspice *Pimento officinalis.*

COMMON NAME: Pimento, jamaica pepper, clove pepper.

OCCURRENCE: indigenous to the West Indies and South America; cultivated in jamaica and central America.

PARTS USED: the fruit, which contains a volatile oil made up of eugenol, a sesquiterpene and other unknown chemicals.

MEDICINAL USES: aromatic, stimulant, carminative. Allspice acts on the gastro-intestinal tract and is usually added to drinks tonics and purgatives for flavouring. The spice may also be used for flatulent indigestion and hysteria. Allspice is frequently used as a spice and condiment in food or drinks.

ADMINISTERED AS: essential oil, distilled water, powdered fruit, fluid extract.

Anemone, Wood *Anemone nemorosa.*

COMMON NAME: crowfoot, windflower, smell fox.

OCCURRENCE: found in woods and thickets across Great Britain.

PARTS USED: the root, leaves and juice.

MEDICINAL USES: this species of plant is much less widely used than it has been previously. It used to be good for leprosy, lethargy, eye inflammation and headaches. An ointment made of the leaves is said to be effective in cleansing malignant ulcers.

ADMINISTERED AS: decoction, fresh leaves and root, ointment.

Anemone, Pulsatilla *Anemone pulsatilla.*

COMMON NAME: Pasqueflower, meadow anemone, wind flower.

OCCURRENCE: found locally in chalk downs and limestone areas of England.

PARTS USED: the whole herb. It produces oil of anemone upon distillation with water.

MEDICINAL USES: nervine, antispasmodic, alterative and diaphoretic. It is beneficial in disorders of mucous membranes and of the respiratory and digestive passages. Can be used to treat asthma, whooping cough and bronchitis.

ADMINISTERED AS: fluid extract.

Angelica *Angelica archangelica.*

COMMON NAME: Garden Angelica, *Archangelica officinalis.*

OCCURRENCE: found native to some sites in Scotland although more abundant in Lapland and is a common garden plant in England.

PARTS USED: the root, leaves and seeds. The leaves contain volatile oil, valeric acid, angelic acid, a bitter principle and a resin called angelicin. The roots contain terebangelene and other terpenes while the seeds also yield two acid compounds.

MEDICINAL USES: Angelica has carminative, stimulant, diaphoretic, diuretic, aromatic, stomachic, tonic and expectorant properties and is good for colds, coughs, pleurisy, wind, colic and rheumatism. It is used as a stimulating expectorant and is good for digestion.

ADMINISTERED AS: powdered root, liquid extract, infusion or as a poultice.

Angostura *Galipea officinalis.*

COMMON NAME: Cusparia bark, *Cusparia febrifuga, Bonplandia trifoliata, Galipea cusparia.*

OCCURRENCE: a small tree native to tropical South America.

PARTS USED: the dried bark, which has the active ingredients angosturin, the alkaloids galipine, cusparine, galipidine, cusparidine and cuspareine, as well as a volatile oil and an unidentified glucoside.

MEDICINAL USES: aromatic, bitter, tonic, stimulant, purgative. There is a long history of usage by native South Americans as a stimulant tonic. It is useful in bilious diarrhoea and dysentery, but in large doses it has a purgative and cathartic effect on the body.

ADMINISTERED AS: infusion, powdered bark, tincture, fluid extract.

Anise *Pimpinella anisum.*

COMMON NAME: Aniseed.

OCCURRENCE: native to Egypt, Greece, Crete and western Asia, its cultivation spread to central Europe and North Africa.

PARTS USED: the fruit. Upon distillation, the fruit yields a fragrant volatile oil that is made up of anethol, choline, a fixed oil, sugar and mucilage.

MEDICINAL USES: carminative and pectoral. It is very useful against coughs and chest infections and is made into lozenges or smoked to clear the chest. Aniseed tea is good for infant catarrh, and aids digestion in adults. Anise seed is an ingredient of cathartic and aperient pills, to relieve flatulence and lessen the griping caused by purgative herbs. It can also be given in convulsions quite safely.

ADMINISTERED AS: essence, essential oil, tincture, powdered seeds, tea and pills.

Arrowroot *Maranta arundinacea.*

COMMON NAME: *Maranta indica, M. ramosissima,* maranta starch or arrowroot, araruta, Bermuda arrowroot, Indian arrowroot.

OCCURRENCE: indigenous to the West Indies and central America. It is cultivated in Bengal, Java, the Philippines, mauritius and West Africa.

PARTS USED: the dried, powdered starch from the rhizome.

MEDICINAL USES: nutritive, demulcent, non-irritating. Well suited for infants and convalescents, particularly after bowel complaints. The jelly made of water or milk may be flavoured with sugar, lemon juice or fruit. The fresh rhizomes are mashed and applied to wounds from poisoned arrows, scorpion or spider bites and to stop gangrene. The freshly expressed juice of the rhizome, when mixed with water, is said to be a good antidote against vegetable poisons.

ADMINISTERED AS: fresh root, expressed juice, dietary item.

Balm *Melissa officinalis.*

COMMON NAME: Sweet balm, lemon balm, honey plant, cure-all.

OCCURRENCE: a common garden plant in Great Britain, which was naturalized into southern England at a very early period.

PARTS USED: the herb.

MEDICINAL USES: as a carminative, diaphoretic, or febrifuge. It can be made into a cooling tea for fever patients and balm is often used in combination with other herbs to treat colds and fever.

ADMINISTERED AS: an infusion.

Barley *Hordeum distichon* and *Hordeum vulgare.*

COMMON NAME: Pearl barley, *Perlatum*

OCCURRENCE: throughout Britain.

PARTS USED: decorticated seeds; composed of eighty per cent starch and six per cent proteins, cellulose, etc.

MEDICINAL USES: Barley is used to prepare a nutritive and demulcent drink for ill and fevered patients. Barley water is given to sick children suffering from diarrhoea or bowel inflammation etc. malt extract is also used medicinally.

ADMINISTERED AS: an infusion and beverage.

Basil *Ocimum basilicum.*

COMMON NAME: Sweet basil, garden basil.

OCCURRENCE: as a garden plant throughout Britain.

PARTS USED: the herb, which contains a volatile, camphoraceous oil.

MEDICINAL USES: aromatic with carminative and cooling properties. It is used to treat mild nervous disorders and an infusion of basil is said to be good for obstructions of the internal organs and in stopping vomiting and nausea.

ADMINISTERED AS: a flavouring in food, dried leaves or an infusion.

Belladonna *Atropa belladonna.*

COMMON NAME: Deadly nightshade, devil's cherries, dwale, black cherry, devil's herb, great morel.

OCCURRENCE: native to central and southern Europe but commonly grows in England.

PARTS USED: the roots and leaves. The root contains several alkaloid compounds including hyoscyamine, atropine and belladonnine. The same alkaloids are present in the leaves but the amount of each compound varies according to plant type and methods of storing and drying leaves.

MEDICINAL USES: as a narcotic, diuretic, sedative, mydriatic, antispasmodic. The drug is used as an anodyne in febrile conditions, night-sweats and coughs. It is valuable in treating eye diseases and is used as a pain-relieving lotion to treat neuralgia, gout, rheumatism and sciatica. Belladonna is an extremely poisonous plant and should always be used under medical supervision. cases of accidental poisoning and death are well-known. despite this, it is a valuable drug used to treat a wide range of disease.

ADMINISTERED AS: a liquid extract which is used to produce alcoholic extracts, plasters, liniment, suppositories, tincture and ointment.

Bergamot *Monarda didyma.*

COMMON NAME: Scarlet monarda, oswego tea, bee balm.

OCCURRENCE: a plant which is indigenous to North America.

PARTS USED: the oil extracted from the whole plant, and the leaves.

MEDICINAL USES: used in a similar manner to other plants containing thymol as an active chemical. Oil of bergamot has antiseptic, aromatic, carminative, tonic and antispasmodic properties. An infusion of the young leaves was a common beverage in the USA before tea became more common. The infusion is also good for coughs, sore throats, fevers and colds.

ADMINISTERED AS: essential oil, infusion, fluid extract.

Bluebell *Scilla nutans, Hyacinthus nonscriptus.*

COMMON NAME: Calverkeys, culverkeys, auld man's bell, ring-o' bells, jacinth, wood bells, *Agraphis nutans.*

OCCURRENCE: abundant in western Europe, Great Britain and Italy.

PARTS USED: the bulb, dried and powdered.

MEDICINAL USES: diuretic, styptic. This medicine is little used today but it was considered a very powerful remedy for leucorrhoea. It may also have been used to cure snake bite. The fresh bulbs are poisonous, so the plant is always used when dried.

ADMINISTERED AS: powdered bulb.

Borage *Borago officinalis.*

COMMON NAME: Burrage.

OCCURRENCE: naturalized in Britain and Europe and is found in gardens, rubbish heaps and near houses.

PARTS USED: the leaves and flowers consist of potassium, calcium, mineral acids along with nitrogen salts.

MEDICINAL USES: diuretic, demulcent, emollient, refrigerant. It is effective in treating fevers and pulmonary complaints as it activates the kidneys. It is applied externally as a poultice against inflammation and swelling and has been developed into a cream which treats itch and skin complaints, e.g. eczema and psoriasis. The flowers may be eaten raw, candied or made into a conserve to strengthen people weakened by prolonged illness.

ADMINISTERED AS: an infusion, poultice or lotion.

Broom *Cytisus scoparius.*

COMMON NAME: Broom tops, Irish tops, basam, bizzom, browne, brum, bream, green broom.

OCCURRENCE: indigenous to England and commonly found on heathland throughout Britain, Europe and northern Asia.

PARTS USED: the young herbaceous tops which contain sparteine and scoparin as the active components.

MEDICINAL USES: diuretic and cathartic. The broom tops may be used as a decoction or infusion to aid dropsy while if the tops are pressed and treated broom juice is obtained. This fluid extract is generally used in combination with other diuretic compounds. An infusion of broom, AGRIMONY and DANDELION root is excellent in remedying bladder, kidney and liver trouble. *Cytisus* should be used carefully as the sparteine has a strong effect on the heart and, depending upon dose, can cause weakness of the heart similar to that caused by HEMLOCK (*Conium maculatum*). Death can occur in extreme cases if the respiratory organ's activity is impaired.

ADMINISTERED AS: fluid extract and infusion.

Burdock *Artium lappa.*

COMMON NAME: Lappa, fox's clote, thorny burr, beggar's buttons, cockle buttons, love leaves, philanthropium, personata, happy major, clot-bur.

OCCURRENCE: freely found in ditches and hedgerows throughout England and Europe but rare in Scotland

PARTS USED: the root, herb and seeds (fruits). They contain the chemicals inulin, mucilage, sugar and tannic acid along with a crystalline glucoside, lappin.

MEDICINAL USES: alterative, diuretic and diaphoretic. It is an excellent blood purifier and very effective in remedying all skin diseases. The root is most powerful and has anti-scorbutic prop-

erties which make it very useful for boils, scurvy and rheumatism. Also used as a wash for ulcers, a poultice for tumours,
gouty swellings and bruises. An infusion of the leaves aids the
stomach and eases indigestion. The tincture obtained from the
seeds is relaxant, demulcent and a tonic for the skin.

ADMINISTERED AS: a fluid extract, infusion, tincture and solid
extract.

Butterbur *Petasites vulgaris.*

COMMON NAME: Langwort, umbrella plant, bog rhubarb,
plapperdock, blatterdock, capdockin, bogshorns, butterdock.

OCCURRENCE: in low wet grounds, marshy meadows and
riversides in Great Britain.

PARTS USED: the rhizome or root-stock.

MEDICINAL USES: as a cardiac tonic, stimulant, and diuretic. It is
good as a remedy for fevers, asthma, colds, urinary complaints,
gravel and plague. It is also taken as a homoeopathic remedy
for severe neuralgia in the back and loins. Recently, the use of
butterbur has been recommended in easing the pain of migraine and painful menstruation. One of the most important
developments is the treatment of cancer with *petasites* where
the drug attacks tumours and abnormal cell changes very
strongly and, in clinical tests, it has been shown to slow or
stop the cancer spreading through the body. It has also become an effective remedy for severe asthma.

ADMINISTERED AS: a decoction and tincture.

Cacao *Theobroma cacao.*

COMMON NAME: Cocoa, chocolate tree.

OCCURRENCE: found in tropical America and cultivated in most
tropical countries, e.g. Sri Lanka and Java

PARTS USED: the seed which contain about two per cent of the
chemical theobromine and forty to sixty per cent solid fat.

MEDICINAL USES: emollient, diuretic, stimulant and nutritive. The seeds are ground into a paste between hot rollers, with sugar and starch being added to produce cocoa. The cocoa butter (or oil of theobroma) produced forms a hard solid which is used in cosmetics, suppositories and coating pills. It has very good emollient qualities and is used to soften chapped hands and lips. The alkaloid, theobromine, which is contained in the beans is similar to caffeine in action on the central nervous system, but less powerful. It acts on the heart, kidneys and muscle and is used as a diuretic and stimulant of the kidneys. This is useful after fluid has accumulated in the body after heart failure and it is given in conjunction with digitalis (FOXGLOVE). The drug is also of benefit in high blood pressure.

ADMINISTERED AS: expressed oil, theobromine.

Camphor *Cinnamonum camphora.*

COMMON NAME: gum Camphor, laurel camphor, camphire, *Laurus camphora, Camphora officinarum.*

OCCURRENCE: found in China, Japan and parts of East Asia.

PARTS USED: the gum and distilled oil.

MEDICINAL USES: sedative, anodyne, antispasmodic, diaphoretic, anthelmintic, aromatic. It is mainly used in colds, chills, fevers, inflammatory complaints and for severe diarrhoea. It is taken internally for hysteria, nervousness, neuralgia and is used as an excitant in cases of heart failure due to infections, fevers and pneumonia. Camphor is highly valued in all irritations of the sexual organs. Large doses of camphor should be avoided as they can cause vomiting, palpitations and convulsions due to the effects it has on the human brain.

ADMINISTERED AS: tincture, distilled oil, injection, capsules.

Caraway *Carum Carvi.*

COMMON NAME: Caraway seed, caraway fruit, alcaravea.

OCCURRENCE: common in Europe and Asia and naturalized in Britain.

PARTS USED: the fruit, which produces a volatile oil containing a hydrocarbon, carvene and an oxygenated oil, carvol.

MEDICINAL USES: aromatic, stimulant and carminative. It was widely used as a cordial to ease dyspepsia and hysteria. The oil is applied to treat flatulence and stomach disorders. Distilled caraway water is used to ease flatulent colic in infants and is an excellent children's medicine. The bruised fruits were used to remove pain from bad earache and was also used as a poultice to take away bruises. Caraway is widely as a flavouring for cheeses and seed-cakes.

ADMINISTERED AS: a liquid extract and poultice.

Cardamom *Elettaria cardamomum.*

COMMON NAME: Mysore cardamon seeds, malabar cardamom, ebil, kakelah seghar, capalaga, gujalatti elachi, ilachi, ailum, *Amomum cardamomum, A. repens, Alpina cardamom, matonia Cardamomum, Cardamomum minus, Cardamomi Semina.*

OCCURRENCE: native to southern India and cultivated in Sri Lanka.

PARTS USED: the dried ripe seed containing volatile and fixed oil, starch, mucilage, potassium salts, resin and lignin.

MEDICINAL USES: carminative, stimulant, aromatic. They have a warming aromatic effect which is useful in indigestion and flatulence. If chewed, they are said to be good for colic and headaches. Cardamom is used chiefly as a flavouring for cakes, liqueurs, etc. and forms part of curry powder mixtures used in cookery.

ADMINISTERED AS: powdered seeds, tincture and fluid extract.

Castor oil plant *Ricinus communis.*

COMMON NAME: palma Christi, castor oil bush.

OCCURRENCE: a native of India, but has been cultivated in many tropical, sub-tropical and temperate countries around the globe.

PARTS USED: the oil expressed from the seeds.

MEDICINAL USES: cathartic, purgative, laxative, vermifuge, galactogogue. Castor oil is regarded as one of the best laxative and purgative preparations available. It is of particular benefit for children and pregnant women due to its mild action in easing constipation, colic and diarrhoea due to slow digestion. The oil expels worms from the body, after other suitable remedies have been given. When applied externally, Castor oil eases cutaneous complaints such as ringworm, itch and leprosy, while it is used as a carrier oil for solutions of pure alkaloids, e.g. atropine or cocaine, from BELLADONNA (*Atropa belladonna*), that these drugs can be used in eye surgery. Castor oil is used for a range of industrial purposes from soap-making to varnishes.

ADMINISTERED AS: expressed oil.

Catmint *Nepeta cataria.*

COMMON NAME: Catnep, nep.

OCCURRENCE: a wild English plant in hedges, field borders and waste ground. It is found on a localized basis in Scotland.

PARTS USED: the herb.

MEDICINAL USES: carminative, tonic, diaphoretic, refrigerant, mildly stimulating and slightly emmenagogue. This herb is good in treating colds, fevers, restlessness and colic. It is also used in nervousness and insanity and to calm children and soothe nightmares when taken as an infusion or conserve. Catmint can be applied to swellings and bruises as a poultice.

ADMINISTERED AS: an infusion, injection or poultice.

Cayenne *Capsicum minimum, Capsicum frutescens.*

COMMON NAME: African pepper, chillies, bird pepper.

OCCURRENCE: native to Zanzibar but is now cultivated in most tropical and sub-tropical countries, e.g. Sierra Leone, Japan and Madagascar

PARTS USED: the fruit, both fresh and dried.

MEDICINAL USES: stimulant, tonic, carminative, rubefacient. It is possibly the purest and best stimulant in herbal medicine. It produces natural warmth and helps the blood circulation, and eases weakness of the stomach and intestines. Cayenne is added to tonics and is said to ward off disease and can prevent development of colds and fevers.

ADMINISTERED AS: powdered fruit, tincture, capsules, dietary item.

Celery *Apium graveolens*.

COMMON NAME: Smallage, wild celery.

OCCURRENCE: native to southern Europe and cultivated in Britain.

PARTS USED: the ripe seeds, herb and root of which the seeds contain two oils and apiol.

MEDICINAL USES: carminative, stimulant, diuretic, tonic, nervine and aphrodisiac. It is utilised as a tonic in combination with other herbs, promoting restfulness, sleep and lack of hysteria and is excellent in relieving rheumatism.

ADMINISTERED AS: fluid extract, essential oil and powdered seeds.

Chamomile *Anthemis nobilis*.

COMMON NAME: Roman chamomile, double chamomile, manzanilla (Spanish), maythen (Saxon).

OCCURRENCE: a low growing plant found wild in the British Isles.

PARTS USED: the flowers and herb. The active principles therein are a volatile oil, anthemic acid, tannic acid and a glucoside.

MEDICINAL USES: tonic, stomachic, anodyne and anti-spasmodic. An infusion of chamomile tea is an extremely effective remedy for hysterical and nervous afflictions in women, as well as an emmenagogue. Chamomile has a powerful soothing and sedative effect which is harmless. A tincture is used to cure diarrhoea in children and it is used with purgatives to prevent griping, and as a tonic it helps dropsy. Externally, it can be applied alone or with other herbs as a poultice to relieve pain, swellings, inflammation and neuralgia. Its strong antiseptic properties make it invaluable for reducing swelling of the face due to abscess or injury. As a lotion, the flowers are good for resolving toothache and earache. The herb itself is an ingredient in herb beers. The use of chamomile can be dated back to ancient Egyptian times when they dedicated the plant to the sun because of its extensive healing properties.

ADMINISTERED AS: decoction, infusion, fluid extract and essential oil.

Chickweed *Stellania media.*

COMMON NAME: Starweed, star chickweed, *Alsine media*, passerina.

OCCURRENCE: native to all temperate and North Arctic regions and is naturalized wherever Man has settled. A common weed.

PARTS USED: the whole herb, both fresh and dried.

MEDICINAL USES: demulcent, refrigerant. It is good as a poultice to reduce inflammation and heal indolent ulcers, but is most important as an ointment in treating eye problems and cutaneous diseases. It will also benefit scurvy and kidney disorders as an infusion.

ADMINISTERED AS: an infusion, poultice and ointment.

Chicory *Cichonium intybus.*

COMMON NAME: Succory, wild succory, hendibeh, barbe de capucin.

OCCURRENCE: common in England and Ireland but rarer in Scotland.

PARTS USED: the root.

MEDICINAL USES: tonic, diuretic and laxative. A decoction of the root has benefit in jaundice, liver problems, gout and rheumatic complaints. The root, when dried, roasted and ground, may be added to coffee or may be drunk on its own as a beverage.

ADMINISTERED AS: a decoction, poultice, syrup or distilled water.

Chives *Allium schoenoprasum.*

COMMON NAME: Cives.

OCCURRENCE: native to temperate and northern Europe and Great Britain and has been cultivated over a large area of the northern hemisphere.

PARTS USED: the herb.

MEDICINAL USES: this herb stimulates the appetite and helps digestion during convalescence. It is also said to be effective against infections and prevent anaemia. They are also widely used in food dishes and add vitamins and colour to many meals.

ADMINISTERED AS: fresh herbs.

Cinnamon *Cinnamomum zeylanicum.*

COMMON NAME: Lauris cinnamomum.

OCCURRENCE: native to Sri Lanka but is cultivated in other Eastern countries.

PARTS USED: the bark.

MEDICINAL USES: carminative, astringent, stimulant, antiseptic, aromatic. It is used as a local stimulant as a powder and infusion, generally combined with other herbs. Cinnamon stops vomiting and nausea, relieves flatulence and diarrhoea and can also be employed to stop haemorrhage of the womb.

ADMINISTERED AS: powder, distilled water, tincture or an essential oil.

Clover, Red *Trifolium pratense.*

COMMON NAME: Trefoil, purple clover.

OCCURRENCE: widely distributed in Britain and Europe.

PARTS USED: the flowers.

MEDICINAL USES: alterative, sedative, antispasmodic. The fluid extract or infusion are excellent in treating bronchial and whooping coughs. External applications of the herb in a poultice has been used on cancerous growths.

ADMINISTERED AS: fluid extract and infusion.

Cloves *Eugenia caryophyllata.*

COMMON NAME: *Eugenia aromatica*, *Eugenia caryophyllus*, clavos.

OCCURRENCE: grows on the Molucca Islands in the southern Philippines.

PARTS USED: the underdeveloped flowers.

MEDICINAL USES: stimulating, carminative, aromatic. It is given as powder or an infusion for nausea, vomiting, flatulence, languid indigestion and dyspepsia. The volatile oil contains the medicinal properties and it is a strong germicide, antiseptic and a local irritant. It has been used as an expectorant to aid bronchial troubles. Clove oil is often used in association with other medicines.

ADMINISTERED AS: powdered cloves, infusion, essential oil, fluid extract.

Coffee *Coffea arabica.*

COMMON NAME: Caffea.

OCCURRENCE: native to a province of Abyssinia and cultivated throughout the tropics.

PARTS USED: the seed and leaves. When roasted, coffee contains oil, wax, caffeine, aromatic oil, tannic acid, caffetannic acid, gum, sugar and protein.

MEDICINAL USES: stimulant, diuretic, anti-narcotic, anti-emetic. Coffee is commonly used as a beverage but it can also be applied as a medicine. It is a brain stimulant, causing sleeplessness and hence is useful in cases of narcotic poisoning. For this reason it is very good against snake bite in that it helps stop people falling into a coma. Caffeine can be valuable for heart disease, fluid retention and it is used against drunkenness. As a powerful diuretic, it can help ease gout, rheumatism, gravel and dropsy.

ADMINISTERED AS: beverage, caffeine preparation.

Coriander *Coriandrum sativum*

OCCURRENCE: indigenous to southern Europe and found occasionally in Britain, at riversides, fields and waste ground.

PARTS USED: the fruit and leaves.

MEDICINAL USES: stimulant, aromatic and carminative. It is generally used with active purgatives as flavouring and to lessen their griping tendencies. Coriander water was formerly used for windy colic.

ADMINISTERED AS: powdered fruit, fluid extract.

Cornflower *Centaurea cyanus.*

COMMON NAME: bluebottle, bluebow, hurtsickle, blue cap, bluet.

OCCURRENCE: common in cultivated fields and roadsides in Britain.

PARTS USED: the flowers.

MEDICINAL USES: tonic, stimulant and emmenagogue properties. A water distilled from cornflower petals was said to be a remedy for eye inflammation and weak eyesight.

ADMINISTERED AS: distilled water and infusion.

Couchgrass *Agropyrum repens.*

COMMON NAME: Twitchgrass, Scotch quelch, quickgrass, dog's grass, *Triticum repens*.

OCCURRENCE: abundant in fields and waste ground in Britain, Europe, northern Asia and North and South America

PARTS USED: the rhizome, which contains triticin (a carbohydrate).

MEDICINAL USES: diuretic, demulcent, aperient. Widely used in complaints of the urinary organs and bladder. Also recommended for gout and rheumatism.

ADMINISTERED AS: an infusion, decoction and liquid extract.

Cowslip *Primula veris.*

COMMON NAME: Herb peter, paigle, peggle, key flower, key of heaven, fairy cups, petty mulleins, patsywort, plumrocks, mayflower, Our Lady's keys, arthritica.

OCCURRENCE: a common wild flower in all parts of Great Britain.

PARTS USED: the flower.

MEDICINAL USES: sedative, antispasmodic. It is very good in relieving restlessness and insomnia. Commonly brewed into a wine which was a good children's medicine in small doses.

ADMINISTERED AS: an infusion or wine.

Crowfoot, Upright meadow *Ranunculus acris.*

COMMON NAME: gold cup, grenouillette.

OCCURRENCE: native in meadows, pastures and fields in all parts of northern Europe and Great Britain.

PARTS USED: the whole herb.

MEDICINAL USES: the expressed juice is used to remove warts. A poultice of the fresh herb is good at removing violent, painful headaches or in relieving gout. The fresh herb once formed part of a famous cure for cancer practised in 1794.

ADMINISTERED AS: fresh leaves, expressed juice.

Cumin *Cuminum cyminum.*

common name: Cummin, *Cumino aigro.*

OCCURRENCE indigenous to upper Egypt and is cultivated in Arabia, India, China and Mediterranean countries since early times.

PARTS USED: the fruit. The chief constituents are a volatile oil, a fatty oil with resin, mucilage, gum, malates and albuminous matter.

MEDICINAL USES: stimulant, carminative, antispasmodic. This herb has similar effects to FENNEL and CARAWAY but its use has declined due to its disagreeable taste. It had a considerable reputation in helping correct flatulence due to languid digestion and as a remedy for colic and dyspeptic headache. Applied externally as a plaster, it eased stitches and pains in the side and has been combined with other herbs to form a stimulating liniment.

ADMINISTERED AS: dried, powdered fruit, whole fruit.

Daffodil *Narcissus pseudo-narcissus.*

COMMON NAME: Narcissus, porillion, daffy-down-dilly, fleur de coucou, Lent lily.

OCCURRENCE: found wild in most European countries including the British Isles.

PARTS USED: the bulb, leaves and flowers. The bulbs contain an alkaloid called lyconine.

MEDICINAL USES: the flowers, when powdered, have emetic properties and as an infusion are used in pulmonary catarrh. The bulbs are also emetic and, indeed, can cause people to collapse and die due to paralysis of the central nervous system due to the action of lyconine, which acts quickly. Accidents have resulted from daffodil bulbs being mistaken for ONIONS and eaten. Since high temperatures and cooking does not break down the poisonous alkaloid, considerable care should be taken to avoid problems. The bulbs are used externally as an astringent poultice to dissolve hard swellings and aid wound healing.

ADMINISTERED AS: powder and extract.

Daisy, Ox-eye *Chrysanthemum leuconthemum.*

COMMON NAME: great ox-eye, goldens, marguerite, moon daisy, horse gowan, maudlin daisy, field daisy, dun daisy, butter daisy, horse daisy, maudlinwort, white weed, gowan.

OCCURRENCE: found in fields throughout Europe and northern Asia.

PARTS USED: the whole herb, flowers and root.

MEDICINAL USES: antispasmodic, diuretic, tonic. This herb's main use has been in whooping cough, asthma and nervous excitability. When taken as a tonic, it acts in a similar way to chamomile flowers and calms night-sweats and nightmares. An infusion of ox-eye daisy flowers is good at relieving bronchial coughs and catarrh. It is also used as a lotion for wounds, bruises and ulcers.

ADMINISTERED AS: an infusion and lotion.

Dandelion *Taraxacum officinale.*

COMMON NAME: priest's crown, swine's snout.

OCCURRENCE: widely found across the northern temperate zone in pastures, meadows and waste ground.

PARTS USED: the root and leaves. The main constituents of the root are taraxacin, a bitter substance, and taraxacerin, an acid resin, along with the sugar inulin.

MEDICINAL USES: diuretic, tonic and slightly aperient. It acts as a general body stimulant, but chiefly acts on the liver and kidneys. Dandelion is used as a bitter tonic in atonic dyspepsia as a mild laxative and to promote increased appetite and digestion. The herb is best used in combination with other herbs and is used in many patent medicines. Roasted dandelion root is also used as a coffee substitute and helps ease dyspepsia, gout and rheumatism.

ADMINISTERED AS: fluid and solid extract, decoction, infusion and tincture.

Dill *Peucedanum graveolus, Fructus anethi.*

COMMON NAME: Dill seed, dill fruit, *Anethum graveolus, Fructus anethi.*

OCCURRENCE: indigenous to Mediterranean districts and South Russia and is cultivated in England and Europe.

PARTS USED: the dried ripe fruit. An oil obtained from the fruit is almost identical to oil of CARAWAY, both containing limonene and carvone.

MEDICINAL USES: stimulant, aromatic, carminative and stomachic. It is usually given as dillwater which is very good for children's flatulence or disordered digestion.

ADMINISTERED AS: distilled water, essential oil.

Dock, Yellow *Rumex crispus.*

COMMON NAME: Curled dock.

OCCURRENCE: normally found on roadside ditches and waste ground, all over Great Britain.

PARTS USED: the root and whole herb.

MEDICINAL USES: the root has laxative, alterative and a mildly tonic action and is used in rheumatism, bilious complaints and haemorrhoids. It is very useful in treating jaundice, diseases of the blood, scurvy, chronic skin diseases and as a tonic on the digestive system. Yellow dock is said to have a positive effect on slowing the development of cancer, due to its alterative and tonic properties. It has similar effects to that of rhubarb and has been used in treating diphtheria.

ADMINISTERED AS: dried extract, syrup, infusion, tincture, ointment, fluid extract and solid extract.

Dog-rose *Rosa canina.*

COMMON NAME: Wild briar, hip tree, cynosbatos.

OCCURRENCE: indigenous to Great Britain.

PARTS USED: the ripe fruit which contain invert fruit sugars, a range of mineral salts and a large proportion of vitamin C or ascorbic acid.

MEDICINAL USES: astringent, refrigerant and pectoral. The fruit is used in strengthening the stomach and digestion, as well as easing coughs. It is made into an uncooked preserve, a syrup which is excellent for infants and children and rose-hip tea has very beneficial effects. An infusion of dog-rose leaves has been used as a tea substitute and has a pleasant aroma.

ADMINISTERED AS: an infusion, syrup or dietary item.

Elecampane *Inula helenium.*

COMMON NAME: Scabwort, elf dock, wild sunflower, horseheal, velvet dock.

OCCURRENCE: a true native of southern England, temperate Europe and Asia, but cultivated in northern Britain.

PARTS USED: the root. This plant is a rich source of the drug inulin.

MEDICINAL USES: diuretic, tonic, diaphoretic, expectorant, antiseptic, astringent, and gently stimulant. It is used principally in coughs, consumption and pulmonary complaints, e.g. bronchitis. It is also used in acute catarrhal afflictions, dyspepsia ans asthma. Internally, it is normally combined with other herbs, as a decoction. Applied externally, it is rubefacient, and used in treating sciatica and facial neuralgia. The active bitter principle in the herb, helenin, is a very powerful antiseptic and bacterial chemical. This has meant elecampane has been used against the Tubercle bacteria and in surgical dressings.

ADMINISTERED AS: powdered root, fluid extract, tincture, poultice, infusion.

Eucalyptus *Eucalyptus globulus.*

COMMON NAME: Blue gum tree, stringy bark tree.

OCCURRENCE: native to Australia and Tasmania; now introduced into North and South Africa, India and southern Europe.

PARTS USED: the oil distilled from the leaves. The oil contains
  eucalyptol, which is the important medically-active chemical.
MEDICINAL USES: antiseptic, antispasmodic, stimulant, aromatic.
  The oil is used as an antiseptic and stimulant gargle; it increases the action of the heart and is said to have some anti-
  malarial properties. It is taken internally in pulmonary tuberculosis, scarlet fever, typhoid and intermittent fevers. The
  oil is used as an inhalant to clear catarrh and used externally
  to ease croup and throat troubles. However, in large doses it
  can irritate the kidneys, depress the nervous system and possibly stop respiration and breathing. Despite its harmless appearance, care should be used when administering the drug
  internally.
ADMINISTERED AS: distilled oil, emulsion.

Evening primrose *Oenothera biennis.*

COMMON NAME: Tree primrose, sun drop.
OCCURRENCE: native to North America but has been naturalized
  to British and European gardens.
PARTS USED: the bark and leaves.
MEDICINAL USES: astringent, sedative. The drug from this herb is
  not extensively used but has been of benefit in treating gastro-
  intestinal disorders, dyspepsia, liver torpor and in female problems in association with pelvic illness. It has also been successfully used in whooping cough and spasmodic asthma.
ADMINISTERED AS: liquid extract.

Fennel *Foeniculum vulgare.*

COMMON NAME: Hinojo, fenkel, sweet fennel, wild fennel.
OCCURRENCE: found wild in most areas of temperate Europe and
  generally considered indigenous to the shores of the Mediterranean. It is cultivated for medicinal benefit in France, Russia, India and Persia.

PARTS USED: the seeds, leaves and roots. The roots are rarely used in herbal medicine today. The essential oil is separated by distillation with water. Fennel oil varies widely in quality and composition dependent upon where and under what conditions the fennel was grown.

MEDICINAL USES: aromatic, stimulant, carminative and stomachic. The herb is principally used with purgatives to allay their tendency to griping, and the seeds form an ingredient of the compound liquorice powder. Fennel water also acts in a similar manner to DILL water in correcting infant flatulence.

ADMINISTERED AS: fluid extract, distilled water, essential oil.

Fenugreek *Trigonella foenum-graecum.*

COMMON NAME: Bird's foot, Greek hay-seed.

OCCURRENCE: indigenous to eastern Mediterranean countries, but is cultivated in India, Africa and England.

PARTS USED: the seeds. These contain mucilage, two alkaloids trigonelline and choline—phosphates, lecithin and nucleoalbumin.

MEDICINAL USES: a preparation where seeds are soaked in water until they swell and form a thick paste is used to prevent fevers, is comforting to the stomach and has been utilized for diabetes. Alcoholic tinctures are used to prepare emollient cream, ointments and plasters while the mucilage is used externally as a poultice for skin infections such as abscesses, boils and carbuncles. It is also good at relieving rickets, anaemia and scrofula, while, combined with the normal dosage of conventional medicine e.g insulin, it is helpful in gout, diabetes and neurasthenia. It is widely used as a flavouring for both human and cattle feed.

ADMINISTERED AS: poultice, ointment, infusion or tincture.

Feverfew *Chrysanthemum parthenium.*

COMMON NAME: Featherfew, featherfoil, flirtwort, bachelor's buttons, pyrethrum parthenium.

OCCURRENCE: a wild hedgerow plant found in many areas of Europe and Great Britain.

PARTS USED: the herb.

MEDICINAL USES: aperient, carminative, bitter, stimulant, emmenagogue. It is employed in hysterical complaints, nervousness and low spirits as a general tonic. A decoction is made and is useful in easing coughs, wheezing and difficult breathing. Earache was relieved by a cold infusion while a tincture of feverfew eased the pain and swelling caused after insect or vermin bites. The herb was planted around dwellings to purify the atmosphere and ward off disease. Today, it is used to prevent or ease migraines or headaches.

ADMINISTERED AS: warm or cold infusion, poultice, tincture, decoction.

Foxglove *Digitalis purpurea.*

COMMON NAME: Witch's gloves, dead men's bells, fairy's glove, gloves of Our Lady, bloody fingers, virgin's glove, fairy caps, folk's glove, fairy thimbles, fair women's plant.

OCCURRENCE: indigenous and widely distributed throughout Great Britain and Europe.

PARTS USED: the leaves, which contain four important glucosides—digitoxin, digitalin, digitalein and digitonin—of which the first three listed are cardiac stimulants.

MEDICINAL USES: cardiac tonic, sedative, diuretic. Administering digitalis increases the activity of all forms of muscle tissue, particularly the heart and arterioles. It causes a very high rise in blood pressure and the pulse is slowed and becomes regular. Digitalis causes the heart to contract in size, allowing in-

creased blood flow and nutrient delivery to the organ. It also
acts on the kidneys and is a good remedy for dropsy, particularly when it is connected with cardiac problems. The drug
has benefits in treating internal haemorrhage, epilepsy, inflammatory diseases and delirium tremens. Digitalis has a cumu-
lative action whereby it is liable to accumulate in the body
and then have poisonous effects. It should only be used under
medical advice. Digitalis is an excellent antidote in aconite
poisoning when given as a hypodermic injection.

ADMINISTERED AS: tincture, infusion, powdered leaves, solid extract, injection.

Garlic *Allium sativum.*

COMMON NAME: Poor man's treacle.

OCCURRENCE: cultivated throughout Europe since antiquity.

PARTS USED: the bulb.

MEDICINAL USES: antiseptic, diaphoretic, diuretic, expectorant,
stimulant. It may be externally applied as ointment, lotion,
antiseptic or as a poultice. Syrup of garlic is very good for
asthma, coughs, difficulty in breathing and chronic bronchitis, while fresh juice has been used to ease tubercular consumption. The essential oil is commonly taken as a supple-
ment in the form of gelatine capsules. Several species of wild
garlic are utilized for both medicinal and dietary purposes.

ADMINISTERED AS: expressed juice, syrup, tincture, essential oil,
poultice, lotion and ointment.

Ginger *Zingiber officinale.*

OCCURRENCE: a native of Asia, it is now cultivated in the West
Indies, Jamaica and Africa.

PARTS USED: the root, which contains volatile oil, two resins,
gum, starch, lignin, acetic acid and asmazone as well as several unidentified compounds.

MEDICINAL USES: stimulant, carminative, expectorant. A valuable herb in dyspepsia, flatulent colic, alcoholic gastritis and diarrhoea. Ginger tea is taken to relieve the effects of cold temperatures including triggering normal menstruation patterns in women. Ginger is also used to flavour bitter infusions, cough mixtures or syrups.

ADMINISTERED AS: infusion, fluid extract, tincture and syrup.

Ginseng *Panax quinquefolium.*

COMMON NAME: *Aralia quinquefolia*, five fingers, tartar root, red berry, man's health, panax, pannag.

OCCURRENCE: native to certain areas of China, eastern Asia and North America. It is largely cultivated in China, Korea and Japan.

PARTS USED: the root which contains a large quantity of gum, resin, volatile oil and the peculiar sweetish compound, panaquilon.

MEDICINAL USES: mild stomachic, tonic, stimulant. The generic name, *panax*, is derived from the Greek for panacea meaning "all-healing." The name ginseng is said to mean "the wonder of the world" and the Chinese consider this herb a sovereign remedy in all diseases. It is good in dyspepsia, vomiting and nervous disorders, consumption and exhaustion. In the West, it is used to treat loss of appetite, stomach and digestive problems, possibly arising from nervous and mental exhaustion. Ginseng is considered to work well against fatigue, old age and its infirmities and to help convalescents recover their health. In healthy people, the drug is said to increase vitality, cure pulmonary complaints and tumours and increase life expectancy. It was also used by the native American Indians for similar problems.

ADMINISTERED AS: tincture, decoction, capsules.

Golden rod *Solidago virgaurea.*

COMMON NAME: Verge d'or, solidago, goldruthe, woundwort, Aaron's rod.

OCCURRENCE: normally found wild in woods in Britain, Europe, central Asia and North America but it is also a common garden plant.

PARTS USED: the leaves contain tannin, with some bitter and astringent chemicals which are unknown.

MEDICINAL USES: aromatic, stimulant, carminative. This herb is astringent and diuretic and is highly effective in curing gravel and urinary stones. It aids weak digestion, stops sickness and is very good against diphtheria. As a warm infusion it is a good diaphoretic drug and is used as such to help painful menstruation and amenorrhoea (absence or stopping of menstrual periods).

ADMINISTERED AS: fluid extract, infusion, spray.

Guarana *Paullinia cupara.*

COMMON NAME: Paullina, guarana bread, Brazilian cocoa, uabano, uaranzeiro, *Paullina sorbilis*.

OCCURRENCE: native to Brazil and Uruguay.

PARTS USED: the prepared seed, crushed. The seeds are shelled, roasted for six hours and shaken until their outer shell comes off. They are ground to a fine powder, made into a dough with water and formed into cylinders which are dried in the sun or over a fire. The seed preparation is eaten with water by the native people. The roasted seeds contain caffeine, tannic acid, catechutannic acid, starch and a fixed oil.

MEDICINAL USES: nervine, tonic, stimulant, aphrodisiac, febrifuge, slightly narcotic. It is used in mild forms of diarrhoea or leucorrhoea and also for headaches, in particular those linked to the menstrual cycle. Guarana stimulates the brain after mental exertion, or after fatigue or exhaustion due to hot temperatures. It may also have diuretic effects where it can help rheumatism, lumbago and bowel complaints. The drug is similar to that of coca or COFFEE.

ADMINISTERED AS: powder, fluid extract, tincture.

Hemlock *Conium maculatum.*

COMMON NAME: Herb bennet, spotted conebane, musquash root, beaver poison, poison hemlock, poison parsley, spotted hemlock, vex, vecksies.

OCCURRENCE: common in hedges, meadows, waste ground and stream banks throughout Europe and is also found in temperate Asia and North Africa.

PARTS USED: the leaves, fruits and seeds. The most important constituent of hemlock leaves is the alkaloid coniine, which is poisonous, with a disagreeable odour. Other alkaloids in the plant include methyl-coniine, conhydrine, pseudoconhydrine, ethyl piperidine.

MEDICINAL USES: sedative, antispasmodic, anodyne. The drug acts on the centres of motion and causes paralysis and so it is used to remedy undue nervous motor excitability, e.g. teething, cramp and muscle spasms of the larynx and gullet. When inhaled, hemlock is said to be good in relieving coughs, bronchitis, whooping cough and asthma. The method of action of *Conium* means it is directly antagonistic to the effects of strychnine, from NUX VOMICA (*Strychnos nux-vomica*), and hence it is used as an antidote to strychnine poisoning and similar poisons. Hemlock has to be administered with care as narcotic poisoning may result from internal application and overdoses induce paralysis, with loss of speech and depression of respiratory function leading to death. Antidotes to hemlock poisoning are tannic acid, stimulants, e.g. COFFEE, mustard and CASTOR OIL.

ADMINISTERED AS: powdered leaves, fluid extract, tincture, expressed juice of the leaves and solid extract.

Hops *Humulus lupulus.*

OCCURRENCE: a native British plant, found wild in hedges and woods from Yorkshire southward. It is considered an introduced species to Scotland but is also found in most countries of the northern temperate zone.

PARTS USED: the flowers, which contain a volatile oil, two bitter principles—lupamaric acid, lupalinic acid- and tannin.

MEDICINAL USES: tonic, nervine, diuretic, anodyne, aromatic. The volatile oil has sedative and soporific effects while the bitter principles are stomachic and tonic. Hops are used to promote the appetite and enhance sleep. An infusion is very effective in heart disease, fits, neuralgia, indigestion, jaundice, nervous disorders and stomach or liver problems. Hop juice is a blood cleanser and is very effective in remedying calculus problems. As an external application, hops are used with CHAMOMILE heads as an infusion to reduce painful swellings or inflammation and bruises. This combination may also be used as a poultice.

ADMINISTERED AS: an infusion, tincture, poultice, expressed juice or tea.

Horseradish *Cochlearia armoracia.*

COMMON NAME: Mountain radish, great raifort, red cole, *Armoracia rusticara.*

OCCURRENCE: cultivated in the British Isles for centuries. The place of origin is unknown.

PARTS USED: the root which contains the glucoside sinigrin, vitamin C, aspargin and resin.

MEDICINAL USES: stimulant, aperient, rubefacient, diuretic, antiseptic, diaphoretic. Horseradish is a powerful stimulant of the digestive organs, and it acts on lung and urinary infections clearing them away. The herb is a very strong diuretic and as such is used to ease dropsy, gravel and calculus, as well as being taken internally for gout and rheumatism. A poultice can be made from the fresh root and applied to rheumatic joints, chilblains and to ease facial neuralgia. Horseradish juice, when diluted with vinegar and glycerine, was used in children's whooping cough and to relieve hoarseness of the throat. An infusion of the root in urine was stimulating to the entire nervous system and promoted perspiration, while it was also used to expel worms in children. Care should be taken when using this herb because over-use of horseradish can blister the skin and is not suitable for people with thyroid troubles.

ADMINISTERED AS: infusion, syrup, expressed juice, fluid extract.

Ipecacuanha *Cephaelis ipecacuanha.*

COMMON NAME: *Psychotria ipecacuanha.*

OCCURRENCE: native to Brazil, Bolivia and parts of South America and was introduced into Europe in the seventeenth century.

PARTS USED: the chief constituents of the root are the alkaloids emetrine, cephaelin and psychotrine, as well as two glucosides, choline, resin, calcium oxalate and a volatile oil among other compounds.

MEDICINAL USES: diaphoretic, emetic, expectorant, stimulant. The effects of the drug on the body are entirely dependent on the dose given. In very small doses, ipecacuanha stimulates the stomach, liver and intestine aiding digestion and increasing appetite while in slightly larger doses it has diaphoretic and expectorant properties which is good for colds, coughs and dysentery. Large doses of the drug are emetic. There is a lot of historical use of this drug against amoebic (or tropical) dysentery where rapid cures can occur. Care should be taken in utilizing this drug as emetine can have a toxic effect on the heart, blood vessels, lungs and intestines and cause severe illness.

ADMINISTERED AS: powdered root, fluid extract, tincture, syrup.

Ivy *Hedera helix.*

COMMON NAME: Common ivy.

OCCURRENCE: native to many parts of Europe and northern and central Asia.

PARTS USED: the leaves and berries.

MEDICINAL USES: stimulating, diaphoretic, cathartic. The leaves have been used as poultices on enlarged glands, ulcers and abscesses and the berries ease fevers and were used extensively during the Great Plague of London.

ADMINISTERED AS: poultice, infusion.

Ivy, Poison *Rhus toxicodendron.*

COMMON NAME: Poison oak, poison vine.

OCCURRENCE: native to the United States of America.

PARTS USED: the fresh leaves which contain a resin called toxicodendron as the active principle.

MEDICINAL USES: irritant, rubefacient, stimulant, narcotic. This herb is successful in treating obstinate skin eruptions, palsy, paralysis, acute rheumatism and joint stiffness. It has also been good in treating ringworm, allergic rashes and urinary incontinence. In small doses, poison ivy is a very good sedative for the nervous system, but care must be taken in its use as it can trigger gastric and intestinal irritation, drowsiness, stupor and delirium.

ADMINISTERED AS: tincture, fluid extract, infusion.

Juniper *Juniperus communis*

OCCURRENCE: a common shrub native to Great Britain and widely distributed through many parts of the world.

PARTS USED: the berry and leaves.

MEDICINAL USES: the oil of juniper obtained from the ripe berries
is stomachic, diuretic and carminative and is used to treat indigestion, flatulence as well as kidney and bladder diseases.
The main use of juniper is in dropsy, and aiding other diuretic
herbs to ease the disease.

ADMINISTERED AS: essential oil from berries, essential oil from
wood, fluid extract, liquid extract, solid extract.

Kamala *Mallotus philippinensis.*

COMMON NAME: Glandulae rottelerde, kamcela, spoonwood,
Röttlera tinctoria, kameela.

occurrence: native to India, Abyssinia, southern Arabia, China
and Australia.

parts used: the powder removed from the capsular fruit, composed of hairs and glands.

MEDICINAL USES: taeniafuge, purgative. The powder kills and
expels tapeworms from the body. The worm is usually removed
whole. It is a quick and active purgative drug, causing griping
and nausea. It is used externally for cutaneous complaints including scabies and herpetic ringworm.

ADMINISTERED AS: powdered kamala, fluid extract.

Kola nuts *Kola vera.*

COMMON NAME: Guru nut, cola, kola seeds, gurru nuts, bissy nuts,
cola seeds, *Cola acuminata*, *Sterculia acuminata*.

OCCURRENCE: native to Sierra Leone and North Ashanti and cultivated in tropical western Africa, West Indies, Brazil and Java.

PARTS USED: the seeds.

MEDICINAL USES: nerve stimulant, diuretic, cardiac tonic. This
drug is a good overall tonic, largely due to the caffeine it contains. It has been used as a remedy for diarrhoea and for those
with an alcoholic habit.

ADMINISTERED AS: powdered seeds, tincture, fluid and solid extract.

Laburnum *Cytisus laburnam.*

COMMON NAME: Yellow laburnum.

OCCURRENCE: indigenous to high mountain regions of Europe and widely cultivated across the globe as a garden plant.

PARTS USED: the alkaloid, obtained from the plant, called cytisine.

MEDICINAL USES: all parts of the laburnum are thought to be poisonous, particularly the seeds. The alkaloid has been recommended in whooping cough and asthma, and also as an insecticide, but it has not been used due to the very poisonous nature of the compound. Laburnum poisoning symptoms include intense sleepiness, vomiting, convulsive movements, coma and unequally dilated pupils. Laburnum is also poisonous to cattle and horses and deaths of both livestock and humans have resulted from ingestion of this plant.

Lavender, English *Lavandula vera*

OCCURRENCE: indigenous to mountainous regions in the western Mediterranean and is cultivated extensively in France, Italy, England and Norway.

PARTS USED: the flowers and the essential oil which contains linalool, linalyl acetate, cineol, pinene, limonene and tannin

MEDICINAL USES: aromatic, carminative, stimulant, nervine. It is mainly used as a flavouring agent for disagreeable odours in ointments or syrups. The essential oil when taken internally is restorative and a tonic against faintness, heart palpitations, giddiness and colic. It raises the spirits, promotes the appetite and dispels flatulence. When applied externally, the oil relieves toothache, neuralgia, sprains and rheumatism. The oil is utilized widely in aromatherapy, often to very beneficial effects.

ADMINISTERED AS: fluid extract, tincture, essential oil, spirit, infusion, tea, poultice, distilled water.

Lemon *Citrus limonica.*

COMMON NAME: Limon, *Citrus medica*, *Citrus Limonum*,
citronnier, neemoo, leemoo, limoun, limone.

OCCURRENCE: indigenous to northern India and widely cultivated
in Mediterranean countries.

PARTS USED: the fruit, rind, juice and oil. Lemon peel contains an
essential oil and a bitter principle, while lemon juice is rich in
citric acid, sugar and gum. Oil of lemon contains the aldehyde, citral and the oils pinene and citronella.

MEDICINAL USES: antiscorbutic, tonic, refrigerant, cooling. Lemon
juice is the best preventative drug for scurvy and is also very
valuable in fevers and allaying thirst. It is recommended in
acute rheumatism and may be given to counteract narcotic
poisons such as opium. It is used as an astringent gargle in
sore throats, for uterine haemorrhage after childbirth, as a lotion in sunburn and as a cure for severe hiccoughs. The juice
is also good for jaundice and heart palpitations. A decoction
of lemon is a good antiperiodic drug and can be used to replace quinine in malarial injections, or to reduce the temperature in typhoid fever. Lemon oil is a strong external rubefacient
and also has stomachic and carminative qualities.

ADMINISTERED AS: syrup, decoction, fresh juice, tincture, essential oil, dietary item.

Lily of the valley *Convallaria magalis.*

COMMON NAME: May lily, convarraria, Our Lady's tears, conval-
lily, lily constancy, ladder to heaven, Jacob's ladder.

OCCURRENCE: native to Europe and distributed over North
America and northern Asia. It is a very localized plant in England and Scotland.

PARTS USED: the flowers, leaves and whole herb. The chief constituents are two glucosides—convallamarin (the active principle) and convallarin, as well as tannin and mineral salts.

MEDICINAL USES: cardiac tonic, diuretic. A similar drug to digitalis, from the FOXGLOVE, although it is less powerful. Strongly recommended in valvular heart disease, cardiac debility, dropsy and it slows the action of a weak, irritated heart. Lily of the valley does not have accumulatory effects and can be taken in full and frequent doses without harm. A decoction of the flowers is good at removing obstructions in the urinary canal.

ADMINISTERED AS: fluid extracts, decoction tincture, powdered flowers.

Lily, Madonna *Lilium candidum.*

COMMON NAME: White lily, meadow lily.

OCCURRENCE: a southern European native which has been cultivated in Great Britain and America for centuries.

PARTS USED: the bulb.

MEDICINAL USES: demulcent, astringent, mucilaginous. The bulb is mainly used as an emollient poultice for ulcers, tumours and external inflammation. When made into an ointment, Madonna lily removes corns and eliminates pain and inflammation from burns and scalds, reducing scarring. When used in combination with life root (*Senecio aureus*), Madonnna lily is of great value in treating leucorrhoea, prolapse of the womb and other female complaints. The bulb is very often eaten as food in Japan.

ADMINISTERED AS: poultice, ointment, decoction.

Lime fruit *Citrus medica* var. *acida.*

COMMON NAME: *Citrus acris*, *Citrus acida*, limettae fructus.

OCCURRENCE: a native Asian tree which is cultivated in many warm countries including the West Indies and Italy.

PARTS USED: the fruit and juice.

MEDICINAL USES: refrigerant, antiscorbutic. The juice of the lime contains citric acid and is a popular beverage, sweetened as a syrup. It is used to treat dyspepsia.

ADMINISTERED AS: fresh juice, syrup

Lime tree *Tilia europoea.*

COMMON NAME: Linden flowers, linn flowers, common lime, tilleul, flores tiliae, *Tilia vulgaris, T. intermedia, T. cordata, T. platyphylla.*

OCCURRENCE: native to the British Isles and the northern temperate zone.

PARTS USED: the lime flowers, bark, powdered charcoal. The flowers contain volatile oil, flavonid glucosides, saponins, condensed tannins and mucilage.

MEDICINAL USES: nervine, stimulant, tonic. An infusion of the flowers is good for indigestion, hysteria, nervous vomiting, colds, 'flu and catarrh. They can also help calm overactive children and relax the nervous system. Lime flower tea eases headaches and insomnia. The flowers are said to lower blood pressure (possibly due to the bioflavonoids they contain) and are said to remedy arteriosclerosis. The inner bark of the lime has a diuretic effect and is utilized for gout and kidney stones as well as treating coronary artery disease by dilating the coronary arteries. The powdered charcoal was used in gastric and dyspeptic disorders and applied to burnt or sore areas.

ADMINISTERED AS: infusion, powdered charcoal, dried inner bark, tea.

Liquorice *Glycyrrhiza glabra.*

COMMON NAME: Licorice, lycorys, *Liquiriha officinalis.*

OCCURRENCE: a shrub native to south-east Europe and south-west Asia and cultivated in the British Isles

PARTS USED: the root. The chief compound in the root is

glycyrrhizin along with sugar, starch, gum, asparagus, tannin and resin.

MEDICINAL USES: demulcent, pectoral, emollient. A very popular and well-known remedy for coughs, consumption and chest complaints. Liquorice extract is included in cough lozenges and pastilles, with sedatives and expectorants. An infusion of bruised root and flax (linseed) is good for irritable coughs, sore throats and laryngitis. Liquorice is used to a greater extent as a medicine in China and other eastern countries. The herb is used by brewers to give colour to porter and stout and is employed in the manufacture of chewing or smoking tobacco.

ADMINISTERED AS: powdered root, fluid extract, infusion, solid extract.

Male fern *Dryopteris felix-mas.*

COMMON NAME: *Aspidium felix-mas*, male shield fern.

OCCURRENCE: grows in all areas of Europe, temperate Asia, North India, North and South Africa, the temperate areas of the United States and the South American Andes.

PARTS USED: the root and the oil extracted from it. The oil is extracted using ether and contains the acid, filmaron, filicic acid, tannin, resin and sugar.

MEDICINAL USES: anthelmintic, vermifuge, taeniafuge. It is probably the best drug against tapeworm, it is normally given at night after several hours of fasting. When followed by a purgative drug in the morning, e.g. CASTOR OIL very good results are obtained. The size of the dose administered must be carefully assessed as male fern is an irritant poison in too large a dose, causing muscle weakness, coma and possible damage to the eyesight.

ADMINISTERED AS: powdered root, fluid extract; oil of male fern.

Marigold *Calendula officinalis.*

COMMON NAME: *Caltha officinalis*, golds, ruddes, marg gowles, oculus Christi, marygold, garden marigold, solis sponsa.

OCCURRENCE: a native of southern Europe and a common garden plant in Great Britain.

PARTS USED: the petals and herb. Only the deep orange-flowered variety is of medicinal use.

MEDICINAL USES: stimulant, diaphoretic. Mainly used as a local remedy. Taken internally, an infusion of the herb prevents pus formation and externally is good in cleaning chronic ulcers and varicose veins. Formerly considered to be of benefit as an aperient and detergent to clear visceral obstructions and jaundice. A marigold flower, when rubbed onto a bee or wasp sting, was known to relieve pain and reduce swelling, while a lotion from the flowers was good for inflamed and sore eyes. The expressed juice of the plant was used to clear headaches and remove warts.

ADMINISTERED AS: infusion, distilled water and lotion.

Marjoram *Origanum vulgare*

OCCURRENCE: generally distributed over Asia, Europe and North Africa and also found freely in England.

PARTS USED: the herb and volatile oil.

MEDICINAL USES: the oil has stimulant, carminative, diaphoretic, mildly tonic and emmenagogue qualities. As a warm infusion, it is used to produce perspiration and bring out the spots of measles as well as giving relief from spasms, colic and dyspeptic pain. The oil has been used externally as a rubefacient and liniment, and on cotton wool placed next to an aching tooth it relieves the pain. The dried herb may be utilized as a hot poultice for swellings, rheumatism and colic, while an infusion of the fresh plant will ease a nervous headache.

ADMINISTERED AS: essential oil, poultice and infusion.

Marshmallow *Althaea officinalis.*

COMMON NAME: Mallards, mauls, schloss tea, cheeses, mortification, root, guimauve.

OCCURRENCE: a native of Europe, found in salt marshes, meadows, ditches and riverbanks. It is locally distributed in England and has been introduced to Scotland.

PARTS USED: the leaves, root and flowers. Marshmallow contains starch, mucilage, pectin, oil, sugar, asparagin, glutinous matter and cellulose.

MEDICINAL USES: demulcent, emollient. Very useful in inflammation and irritation of the alimentary canal and the urinary and respiratory organs. A decoction of the root is effective against sprains, bruises of any muscle aches. When boiled in milk or wine marshmallow relieves diseases of the chest, e.g. coughs, bronchitis or whooping cough and it eases the bowels after dysentery without any astringent effects. It is frequently given as a syrup to infants and children.

ADMINISTERED AS: infusion, decoction, syrup, fluid extract.

Meadowsweet *Spiraea ulmaria.*

COMMON NAME: Meadsweet, dolloff, queen of the meadow, bridewort, lady of the meadow.

OCCURRENCE: common in the British Isles in meadows or woods

PARTS USED: the herb

MEDICINAL USES: aromatic, astringent, diuretic, alterative. This herb is good against diarrhoea, stomach complaints and blood disorders. It is highly recommended for children's diarrhoea and dropsy and was used as a decoction ir wine to reduce fevers. Meadowsweet makes a pleasant everyday drink when infused and sweetened with honey. It is also included in many herb beers.

ADMINISTERED AS: infusion, decoction.

Mescal buttons *Anhalonicum lewinii.*

COMMON NAME: *Lopophora lewinii, Analonium williamsii, Echinacactus lewinii, Echinocactus williamsii*, pellote, muscal buttons.

OCCURRENCE: Mexico and Texas.

PARTS USED: the tops of the cacti plant. The drug contains four alkaloids—anhalonine, mescaline, anhalonidine and lophophorine—as well as the chemicals pellotine and anhalamine.

MEDICINAL USES: cardiac, tonic, narcotic, emetic. The drug is useful in head injuries, hysteria, asthma, gout, neuralgia and rheumatism. The extracted compound pellotine has been used to induce sleep in people with insanity as it has no undesirable reactions. Large doses of mescal buttons produce an odd cerebral excitement, with visual disturbances. The physical effects include muscular relaxation, wakefulness, nausea, vomiting and dilation of the pupil. The ancient Aztec Indians believed mescal buttons to have divine properties and included its use to produce exaltation in their religious ceremonies.

ADMINISTERED AS: fluid extract, tincture, extracted alkaloid.

Mistletoe *Viscum album.*

COMMON NAME: European mistletoe, bird lime mistletoe, herbe de la croix, mystyldene, lignum crucis.

OCCURRENCE: an evergreen, true parasitic plant found on several tree species including fruit and oak trees. It is found throughout Europe and Britain except in Scotland, where it is very rare.

PARTS USED: the leaves and young twigs. They contain mucilage, sugar, fixed oil, tannin and viscin, the active part of the plant.

MEDICINAL USES: nervine, antispasmodic, tonic and narcotic. It is highly recommended for epilepsy and other convulsive disorders, along with stopping internal haemorrhage. It has also been used in delirium, hysteria, neuralgia, nervous debility, urinary disorders and many other complaints arising from a weakened state of the nervous system. The berries are taken to cure severe stitches in the side, and the plant produces a sticky substance called bird-lime which is applied to ulcers and sores. Mistletoe is excellent for reducing blood pressure and has been indicated to be a successful cure for chronic arthritis and in treating malignant tumours in the body.

ADMINISTERED AS: tincture, powdered leaves, infusion, fluid extract.

Myrrh *Commiphora molmol.*

COMMON NAME: *Balsamodendron myrrha, Commiphora myrrha* var. *molmol,* mira, morr.

OCCURRENCE: obtained from bushes in North-East Africa and in ARABIA.

PARTS USED: the oleo-gum-resin which contains volatile oil, resins and gum.

MEDICINAL USES: stimulant, tonic, healing, antiseptic, astringent, expectorant, emmenagogue. Myrrh has a long history of use incountering poisons and putrid tissues throughout the body. It is used in leucorrhoea, chronic catarrh, thrush, athlete's foot, absence of menstrual periods, ulcers and as a vermifuge. The resin acts as a tonic in dyspepsia, stimulates the circulation, appetite and the production of gastric juices. It makes a very good gargle or mouthwash for an inflamed sore throat, spongy gums and mouth ulcers.

ADMINISTERED AS: fluid extract, tincture, pills.

Nettle *Urtica dioica, Urtica urens.*
COMMON NAME: Common nettle, stinging nettle.
OCCURRENCE: widely distributed throughout temperate Europe and Asia, Japan, South Africa and Australia.
PARTS USED: the whole herb, which contains formic acid, mucilage, mineral salts, ammonia and carbonic acid.
MEDICINAL USES: astringent, stimulating, diuretic, tonic. The herb is anti-asthmatic and the juice of the nettle will relieve bronchial and asthmatic troubles, as will the dried leaves when burnt and inhaled. The seeds are taken as an infusion or in wine to ease consumption or ague. Nettles are used widely as a food source. A hair tonic or lotion can also be made from the nettle. In the Highlands of Scotland, they were chopped, added to egg white and applied to the temples as a cure for insomnia.
ADMINISTERED AS: expressed juice, infusion, decoction, seeds, dried herb, dietary item.

Nightshade, Black *Solarum nignum.*
COMMON NAME: garden nightshade, petty morel.
OCCURRENCE: a common plant in south England, seen less frequently in northern England and Scotland.
PARTS USED: the whole plant, fresh leaves. Both contain the active principle, solanine which is found in variable quantities within the plant, throughout the year.
MEDICINAL USES: the bruised fresh leaves are used external to the body to ease pain and reduce inflammation. Juice of the leaves has been used for ringworm, gout and earache and is supposed to make a good gargle or mouthwash when mixed with vinegar. This species of plant is reputed to be very poisonous, narcotic and sudorific, so is only utilized in very small doses, under careful supervision.
ADMINISTERED AS: infusion, expressed juice and fresh leaves.

Nux vomica *Strychnos Nux-vomica.*

COMMON NAME: Poison nut, semen strychnox, Quaker buttons.

OCCURRENCE: a tree indigenous to India and now cultvated for medicinal purposes in Burma, China, Australia and the Malay Archipelago.

PARTS USED: the dried ripe seeds. They contain the alkaloids, strychnine, brucine and strychnicine, fatty matter, caffeotannic acid and the glucoside, loganin.

MEDICINAL USES: tonic, bitter, stimulant. Nux vomica is utilized as a general tonic, mainly when combined with other herbal remedies, to treat neuralgia, dyspepsia, impotence, constipation and general debility. This drug can also be of benefit in cardiac failure, surgical shock or poisoning by chloroform where it raises blood pressure and increases pulse rate, but it can also cause violent convulsions. Nux vomica should only be used under strict control as strychnine is very poisonous.

ADMINISTERED AS: fluid extract, tincture.

Oats *Avena sativa.*

COMMON NAME: Groats, oatmeal.

OCCURRENCE: distributed across Europe, Britain and the USA.

PARTS USED: the seeds which are made up of starch, gluten, albumen and other proteins, sugar, gum oil and salts.

MEDICINAL USES: nervine, stimulant, antispasmodic, *Avena* forms a nutritious and easily digested food for convalescent patients. It can be made into a demulcent enema, or an emollient poultice. Oat extract or tincture is useful as a nerve and uterine tonic.

ADMINISTERED AS: fluid extract, tincture, enema, dietary item.

Olive *Olea Europea.*

COMMON NAME: *Olea oleaster, Olea larcifolia, Olea gallica,* oliver.

OCCURRENCE: native to the Mediterranean countries, Syria and Turkey. Now cultivated in Chile, Peru and Australia.

PARTS USED: the oil expressed from the ripe fruit, the leaves.

MEDICINAL USES: the oil is emollient, demulcent, laxative and aperient. It is a good substitute for castor oil when given to children, but its value in clearing parasitic worms or gallstones is unsure. The oil is a good ingredient in liniments or ointment and is used for bruises, sprains, cutaneous injuries and rheumatic problems. It is also utilized externally in joint, kidney and chest complaints or for chills, typhoid and scarlet fevers, plague and dropsy. When combined with alcohol, the oil is good as a hair tonic. Olive leaves have astringent and antiseptic properties, and an infusion of these leaves has proved beneficial in obstinate fevers.

ADMINISTERED AS: expressed oil, infusion, ointment.

Orris *Iris florentina* (and other species).

COMMON NAME: Florentine orris, orris root.

OCCURRENCE: grown in Italy and Morocco and to a smaller extent in England.

PARTS USED: the root contains oil of orris, fat, resin, starch, mucilage, a glucoside called iridin and a bitter extractive substance.

MEDICINAL USES: Orris root is rarely used in medicine today. The fresh root has emetic, diuretic and cathartic properties and was formerly used against congested headache, dropsy, bronchitis and chronic diarrhoea. It is more generally used in perfumery, as it strengthens the odour of other fragrant herbs and acts as a fixative in perfumes and pot pourri. It is also part of dusting powders, toilet powders and tooth powders.

Parsley *Carum petroselinum*.

COMMON NAME: *Apium petroselinum*, *Petroselinum lativum*, petersylinge, persely, persele.

OCCURRENCE: this was first cultivated in Britain in 1548, now completely naturalized through England and Scotland.

PARTS USED: the root, seeds and leaves. The root is slightly aromatic and contains starch mucilage, sugar, volatile oil and apiin. Parsley seeds contain more volatile oil, which consists of terpenes and apiol, an allyl compound.

MEDICINAL USES: carminative, tonic, aperient, diuretic. A strong decoction of the root is used in gravel, stone, kidney congestion, jaundice and dropsy. Bruised parsley seeds used to be given against plague and intermittent fevers, while the external application of the leaves may help to dispel tumours. A poultice of the leaves is effective against bites and stings of poisonous insects.

ADMINISTERED AS: fluid extract, essential oil, infusion, ointment and poultice.

Pepper *Piper nigrum.*

COMMON NAME: Black pepper, piper.

OCCURRENCE: grows wild in South India and Cechin-China; now cultivated in the East and West Indies, Malay Archipelago, the Philippines, Java, Sumatra and Borneo.

PARTS USED: the dried unripe fruits. White pepper comes from the same plant, except that the pericarp of the fruit has been removed prior to drying. The active chemicals in black or white pepper are piperine, volatile oil, starch, cellulose and a resin called chavicin.

MEDICINAL USES: aromatic, stimulant, carminative, febrifuge. The herb is useful in treating constipation, gonorrhoea, prolapsed rectum, paralysis of the tongue and acts on the urinary organs. The stimulant properties of pepper work on the gastro-intestinal system to aid digestion, ease dyspepsia, torbid stomach conditions, and relieve flatulence and nausea. Pepper has also been recommended in diarrhoea, cholera, scarlatina, vertigo and paralytic and arthritic disorders. Peppercorns, as the dried fruit is known, are used both whole and ground in many culinary dishes and are used as a condiment. In the Siege of Rome in 408 AD, pepper was so highly priced that it was used as a form of currency.

ADMINISTERED AS: powdered dried fruits, gargle.

Peppermint *Mentha piperita.*

COMMON NAME: Brandy mint, curled mint, balm mint.

OCCURRENCE: found across Europe, was introduced into Britain and grows widely in damp places and waste ground.

PARTS USED: the herb and distilled oil. The plant contains peppermint oil, which is composed of menthol, menthyl acetate and isovalerate, menthone, cineol, pinene and limonene. The medicinal qualities are found in the alcoholic chemicals.

MEDICINAL USES: stimulant, antispasmodic, carminative, stomachic, oil of peppermint is extensively used in both medicine and commerce. It is good in dyspepsia, flatulence, colic and abdominal cramps. The oil allays sickness and nausea, is used for chorea and diarrhoea but is normally used with other medicines to disguise unpalatable tastes and effects. Peppermint water is in most general use and is used to raise body temperature and induce perspiration. Peppermint tea can help ward off colds and influenza at an early stage, can calm heart palpitations and is used to reduce the appetite.

ADMINISTERED AS: infusion, distilled water, spirit, essential oil and fluid extract.

Pine oils there are several kinds: **Siberian pine oil**, from *Abies Sibirica*; **Pumilio pine oil**, from *Pinus muge*; **Sylvestris pine oil**, from *Pinus sylvestris*.

PARTS USED: the oil produced from when pine wood is distilled using steam under pressure.

MEDICINAL USES: rubefacient, aromatic. These oils are mainly used as inhalants for bronchitis or laryngitis or as liniment plasters.

ADMINISTERED AS: distilled oil.

Poppy, Red *Papaver rhoeas.*

COMMON NAME: Headache, corn poppy, corn rose, flores rhoeados.

OCCURRENCE: a common flowering plant in fields and waste ground across Europe and Great Britain.

PARTS USED: flowers and petals. the fresh petals contain rhoeadic and papaveric acids, which give the flowers their colour, and the alkaloid rhoeadine. The amount and quantity of active ingredients in the plant is uncertain so its action is open to debate.

MEDICINAL USES: very slightly narcotic, anodyne, expectorant. The petals can be made into a syrup which is used to ease pain. It may be used for chest complaints, e.g. pleurisy.

ADMINISTERED AS: syrup, infusion, distilled water.

Poppy, White *Papaver somniferum.*

COMMON NAME: Opium poppy, mawseed.

OCCURRENCE: indigenous to Turkey and Asia, cultivated in Europe, Great Britain, Persia, India and China for opium production.

PARTS USED: the capsules and flowers. The white poppy contains twenty one different alkaloids of which morphine, narcotine, codeine, codamine and thebaine are the most important.

MEDICINAL USES: hypnotic, sedative, astringent, expectorant, diaphoretic, antispasmodic, anodyne. The use of this drug dates back to Greek and Roman times. It is the best possible hypnotic and sedative drug, frequently used to relieve pain and calm excitement. It has also been used in diarrhoea, dysentery and some forms of cough. The tincture of opium is commonly called laudanum, and when applied externally with soap liniment it provides quick pain relief.

ADMINISTERED AS: syrup, tincture, decoction and poultice.

Primrose *Primula vulgaris.*

OCCURRENCE: a common wild flower found in woods, hedgerows and pastures throughout Great Britain.

PARTS USED: the root and whole herb. Both parts of the plant contain a fragrant oil called primulin and the active principle saponin.

MEDICINAL USES: astringent, antispasmodic, vermifuge, emetic. It was formerly considered to be an important remedy in muscular rheumatism, paralysis and gout. A tincture of the whole plant has sedative effects and is used successfully in extreme sensitivity, restlessness and insomnia. Nervous headaches can be eased by treatment with an infusion of the root, while the powdered dry root serves as an emetic. An infusion of primrose flowers is excellent in nervous headaches and an ointment can be made out of the leaves to heal and salve wounds and cuts.

ADMINISTERED AS: infusion, tincture, powdered root and ointment.

Quince *Cydonia oblongata.*

COMMON NAME: Quince seed, *Cydonica vulgaris.*

OCCURRENCE: grown in England for its fruit but is native to Persia.

PARTS USED: the fruit and seeds.

MEDICINAL USES: astringent, mucilaginous, demulcent. The fruit is used to prepare a syrup which is added to drinks when ill, as it restrains looseness of the bowels and helps relieve dysentery and diarrhoea. The soaked seeds form a mucilaginous mass similar to that produced by flax. A decoction of the seeds is used against gonorrhoea, thrush and in irritable conditions of the mucous membranes. The liquid is also used as a skin lotion or cream and administered in eye diseases as a soothing lotion.

ADMINISTERED AS: syrup, decoction or lotion.

Rosemary *Rosmarinus officinalis.*

COMMON NAME: Polar plant, compass-weed, compass plant, romero, *Rosmarinus coronarium.*

OCCURRENCE: native to the dry hills of the Mediterranean, from Spain westward to Turkey. A common garden plant in Britain, having been cultivated prior to the Norman Conquest.

PARTS USED: the herb and root. Oil of rosemary is distilled from the plant tops and used medicinally. Rosemary contains tannic acid, a bitter principle, resin and a volatile oil.

MEDICINAL USES: tonic, astringent, diaphoretic, stimulant. The essential oil is also stomachic, nervine and carminative and cures many types of headache. It is mainly applied externally as a hair lotion which is said to prevent baldness and the formation of dandruff. The oil is used externally as a rubefacient and is added to liniments for fragrance and stimulant properties. Rosemary tea can remove headache, colic, colds and nervous diseases and may also lift nervous depression.

ADMINISTERED AS: infusion, essential oil and lotion.

Rowan tree *Pyrus aucuparia.*

COMMON NAME: Mountain ash, *Sorbus aucuparia, Mespilus aucuparia.*

OCCURRENCE: generally distributed over Great Britain and Europe, especially at high altitudes.

PARTS USED: the bark and fruit. The fruit may contain tartaric, citric or malic acids dependent upon its stage of ripeness. It also contains sorbitol, sorbin, sorbit, parascorbic acid and bitter, acrid colouring matters. The bark contains amygdalin.

MEDICINAL USES: astringent, antiscorbutic. A decoction of Rowan bark is given for diarrhoea and as a vaginal injection for leucorrhoea. The berries are made into an acid gargle to ease sore throats and inflamed tonsils. An infusion of the fruit is administered to ease haemorrhoids. The berries may also be made into jelly, flour, cider, ale or an alcoholic spirit. The rowan tree planted next to a house was said to protect the house against witchcraft.

ADMINISTERED AS: decoction, injection, infusion and dietary item.

Rue *Ruta graveolens.*

COMMON NAME: Herb of grace, garden rue, herbygrass, ave-grace.
OCCURRENCE: indigenous to southern Europe and was introduced into Great Britain by the Romans.
PARTS USED: the herb. The herb is covered by glands which contain a volatile oil. The oil is composed of methylnonylketone, limonene, cineole, a crystalline substance called rutin and several acids. The plant also contains several alkaloids including fagarine and arborinine as well as coumarins.
MEDICINAL USES: stimulant, antispasmodic, emmenagogue, irritant, rubefacient. This is a very powerful herb and the dose administered should be kept low. It is useful in treating coughs, croup, colic, flatulence, hysteria and it is particularly good against strained eyes and headaches caused by eyestrain. An infusion of the herb is good for nervous indigestion, heart palpitations, nervous headaches and to expel worms. The chemical, rutin, strengthens weak blood vessels and aids varicose veins. In Chinese medicine, rue is a specific for insect and snake bites. When made into an ointment, rue is effective in gouty and rheumatic pains, sprained and bruised tendons and chilblains. The bruised leaves irritate and blister the skin and so can ease sciatica. This herb should not be used in preg-

nancy as the volatile oil, alkaloids and coumarins in the plant all stimulate the uterus and strongly promote menstrual bleeding. When a fresh leaf is chewed, it flavours the mouth and relieves headache, giddiness or any hysterical spasms quickly.

ADMINISTERED AS: fresh leaf, volatile oil, ointment, infusion, decoction, tea, expressed juice.

Saffron *Crocus sativus*.

COMMON NAME: Croccus, karcom, Alicante saffron, valencia saffron, krokos, gatinais, saffron, hay saffron, saffron crocus.

OCCURRENCE: grown from Persia and Kurdistan in the east to most European countries including Great Britain.

PARTS USED: the dried flower pistils. These parts contain an essential oil composed of terpenes, terepene alcohols and esters, a coloured glycoside called crocin and a bitter glucoside, called picrocrocin.

MEDICINAL USES: carminative, diaphoretic, emmenagogue. This herb is used as a diaphoretic drug for children and can also absent or painful menstruation and stop chronic haemorrhage of the uterus in adults.

ADMINISTERED AS: tincture, powdered saffron.

Sage, Common *Salvia officinalis*.

COMMON NAME: garden sage, red sage, saurge, broad-leaved white sage, *Salvia salvatrix*.

OCCURRENCE: native to the northern Mediterranean and cultivated through Britain, France and Germany.

PARTS USED: the leaves, whole herb. The herb contains a volatile oil, tannin and resin and is distilled to produce sage oil. This is made up of salvene, pinene, cineol, vorneol, thujone and some esters.

MEDICINAL USES: stimulant, astringent, tonic, carminative, aromatic. Sage makes an excellent gargle for relaxed throat and tonsils, bleeding gums, laryngitis and ulcerated throat. Sage tea is valuable against delirium of fevers, nervous excitement and accompanying brain and nervous diseases; as a stimulant tonic in stomach and nervous system complaints and in weak digestion. It also works as an emmenagogue, in treating typhoid fever, bilious and liver problems, kidney troubles and lung or stomach haemorrhages. The infusion is used in head colds, quinsy, measles, painful joints, lethargy, palsy and nervous headaches. Fresh leaves are rubbed on the teeth to cleanse them and strengthen gums—even today sage is included in toothpowders. The oil of sage was used to remove mucus collections from the respiratory organs and is included in embrocations for rheumatism. The herb is also applied warm as a poultice.

ADMINISTERED AS: infusion, essential oil, tea and poultice.

Salep: early purple orchid, *Orchis mascula*; spotted orchid, *Orchis maculata*; marsh orchid, *Orchis latifolia*.

COMMON NAME: Saloop, schlep, satrion, Levant salep.

OCCURRENCE: *Orchis mascula* is found in woods throughout England. *O. maculata* grows wild on heaths and commons; *O. latifolia* is found growing in marshes and damp pastures across Great Britain.

PARTS USED: the tuberous root, which contains mucilage, sugar, starch and volatile oil.

MEDICINAL USES: very nutritive, demulcent. This herb is used as a food item for convalescent people and children, made with milk or water and flavoured. It is prepared in a similar way to arrowroot. A decoction with sugar, spice or wine was given to invalids to build them up. The root is used to stop irritation of the gastro-intestinal canal and for invalids suffering from bilious fevers or chronic diarrhoea. In the old sailing ships, salep was carried and used as an emergency food source. It was

sold on street corners in London as a hot drink, before COFFEE
replaced its use as a beverage.

ADMINISTERED AS: decoction, dietary item.

Sandalwood *Santalum album.*

COMMON NAME: Santalwood, sanders-wood.

OCCURRENCE: a tree native to India and the Malay Archipelago.

PARTS USED: the wood oil.

MEDICINAL USES: aromatic, antiseptic, diuretic. The oil is given
internally for chronic mucous conditions, e.g. bronchitis, inflammation of the bladder. It is also used in chronic cystitis,
gleet and gonorrhoea. The oil is used in aromatherapy to lessen
tension and anxiety and it was also considered a sexual stimulant in folk traditions. The fluid extract of sandalwood may be
better tolerated by some people than the oil.

ADMINISTERED AS: wood oil, fluid extract.

Savory, Summer *Saturcia hortensis.*

COMMON NAME: Garden savory.

OCCURRENCE: a shrub native to the Mediterranean region and
introduced into Great Britain.

PARTS USED: the herb.

MEDICINAL USES: aromatic, carminative. This herb is mainly used
in cookery, as a pot-herb or flavouring. In medicine, it is added
to remedies to flavour and add warmth. It was formerly used
for colic, flatulence and was considered a good expectorant.
A sprig of summer savory rubbed on a wasp or bee sting relieves the pain quickly.

ADMINISTERED AS: fresh or dried herb.

Senna, Alexandrian *Cassia acutifolia*; **Senna, East Indian** *Cassia angustifolia.*

COMMON NAME: Nubian senna, Egyptian senna, tinnevelly senna,

Cassia senna, Cassia lenitiva, Cassia lanceolata, Cassia officinalis, Cassia aethiopica, Senna acutifolia.

OCCURRENCE: *C. acutifolia* is native to the upper and middle Nile in Egypt and Sudan. *C. angustifolia* is indigenous to southern Arabia and is cultivated in southern and eastern India.

PARTS USED: the dried leaflets and pods. The active principles of senna can be extracted using water or dilute alcohol. The drug contains anthraquinone derivatives and their glucosides, as well as cathartic acid as its active chemicals.

MEDICINAL USES: laxative, purgative, cathartic. This drug acts primarily on the lower bowel, acts locally upon the intestinal wall, increasing the peristaltic movements of the colon. The taste is nauseating and prone to cause sickness and griping pains. It is generally combined with aromatics, e.g. GINGER or CINNAMON and stimulants to modify senna's deleterious effects. Generally, senna is a good medicine for children, people of a delicate constitution and elderly people. Senna pods have milder effects than the leaves and lack their griping effects.

ADMINISTERED AS: infusion, powdered leaves, syrup, fluid extract, tincture, dried pods.

Shepherd's purse *Capsella bursa-pastoris.*

COMMON NAME: Shepherd's bag, shepherd's scrip, lady's purse, witches' pouches, case-weed, pick-pocket, blindweed, pepper and salt, sanguinary, mother's heart, poor man's parmacettie, clappedepouch.

OCCURRENCE: native to Europe and found all over the world outside tropical zones.

PARTS USED: the whole plant which contains various chemicals which have not yet been entirely analyzed but they include an organic acid, a volatile oil, a fixed oil, a tannate, an alkaloid and a resin.

MEDICINAL USES: haemostatic, antiscorbutic, diuretic, stimulant. As an infusion of the dried plant, shepherd's purse is one of the best specifics for arresting bleeding of all kinds, particularly from the kidneys, uterus, stomach or lungs. It is said to be as effective as ergot or golden seal. It has been used for diarrhoea, haemorrhoids, dysentery, dropsy and kidney complaints. Shepherd's purse is an important remedy in catarrhal infections of the bladder and ureter and in ulcerated and abscess of the bladder where it increases the flow of urine and provides relief. Externally, the bruised herb is used as a poultice on bruised and strained areas, rheumatic joints and some skin problems. Since the herb tastes slightly unpleasant it is normally taken internally with other herbs to disguise the flavour, e.g. couch grass, juniper, pellitory-of-the-wall.

ADMINISTERED AS: fluid extract, poultice, decoction, infusion.

Solomon's seal *Polygonatum multiflorum.*

COMMON NAME: Lady's seals, St. Mary's seal, sigillum sanctae Mariae.

OCCURRENCE: a native plant of northern Europe and Siberia. It is found wild in some localities in England but naturalized in Scotland and Ireland.

PARTS USED: the rhizome which contains asparagin, gum, sugar, starch, pectin and convallarin, one of the active chemicals in LILY OF THE VALLEY.

MEDICINAL USES: astringent, demulcent, tonic. When combined with other herbs, it is good for bleeding of the lungs and pulmonary complaints. It is used on its own in female complaints and as a poultice for tumours, inflammations, bruises and haemorrhoids. As it is mucilaginous, it makes a very good healing and restorative tonic for inflammation of the bowels and stomach, haemorrhoids and chronic dysentery. A decoction was used to cure erysipelas and was taken by people with broken bones, as Solomon's Seal was supposed to 'encourage the bones to knit'. A distilled water prepared from the root was used as a cosmetic to remove spots, freckles and marks from the skin.

ADMINISTERED AS: decoction, infusion, poultice, distilled water.

Spearmint *Mentha viridis.*

COMMON NAME: Mackerel mint, Our Lady's mint, green mint, spire mint, sage of Bethlehem, fish mint, lamb mint, menthe de Notre Dame, erba Santa Maria, *Mentha spicata*, *Mentha crispa*, yerba buena.

OCCURRENCE: originally a Mediterranean native and was introduced into the British Isles by the Romans.

PARTS USED: the herb and essential oil. The main component of the essential oil is carvone along with phellandrine, limonene and dihydrocarveol acetate. The oil also has the esters of acetic, butyric and caproic acids within it.

MEDICINAL USES: antispasmodic, aromatic, carminative, stimulant. This herb is very similar to peppermint, but it seems to be less powerful. It is more suited to children's remedies. A distilled water from spearmint is used to relieve hiccoughs, flatulence and indigestion while the infusion is good for fevers, inflammatory diseases and all infantile troubles. Spearmint is considered a specific in stopping nausea and vomiting and in easing the pain due to colic. As a homoeopathic remedy, spearmint has been used for strangury, gravel and as a local application for painful haemorrhoids.

ADMINISTERED AS: distilled water, infusion, tincture, fluid extract.

St John's wort *Hypericum perforatum.*

OCCURRENCE: found in woods, hedges, roadsides and meadows across Britain, Europe and Asia.

PARTS USED: the herb and flowers.

MEDICINAL USES: aromatic, astringent, resolvent, expectorant, diuretic and nervine. It is generally utilized in all pulmonary complaints, bladder trouble, suppression of urine, dysentery, diarrhoea and jaundice. It is good against hysteria, nervous depression, haemorrhages, coughing up blood and dispelling worms from the body. If children have a problem with night incontinence, an infusion of St John's wort taken before bed will stop the problem. The herb is used externally to break up hard tissues, e.g. tumours, bruising. and swollen, hard breasts when feeding infants.

ADMINISTERED AS: an infusion and poultice.

Sundew *Drosera rotundifolia.*

COMMON NAME: Roundleaved sundew, dew plant, red rot, youthwort, rosa solis, herba rosellae, rosée du soleil.

OCCURRENCE: an insectivorous plant found in bogs, wet places and river edges throughout Britain, Europe, India, China, North and South America and Russian Asia.

PARTS USED: the air-dried flowering plant.

MEDICINAL USES: pectoral, expectorant, demulcent, anti-asthmatic. In small doses sundew is a specific in dry, spasmodic, tickling coughs and is considered very good in whooping cough, for which it may also be used as a prophylactic drug. The fresh juice is used to remove corns and warts. In America, the sundew has been advocated as a cure for old age and has been used with colloidal silicates in cases of thickening of arteries due to old age, or calcium or fat deposition.

ADMINISTERED AS: fluid extract, expressed juice, solid extract.

Sunflower *Helicanthus annuus.*

COMMON NAME: Helianthus, marigold of Peru, *Sola indianus, Chrysanthemum peruvianum, Corona solis.*

OCCURRENCE: native to Peru and Mexico and was introduced into America, Europe and Great Britain as a garden plant.

PARTS USED: the seeds. These contain a vegetable oil, carbonate of potash, tannin and vitamins B1, B3 and B6. The oil is expressed from the crushed seeds and, according to the range of temperature to which the seeds are heated, several grades of oil are obtained.

MEDICINAL USES: diuretic, expectorant. It has been used successfully in treating pulmonary, bronchial and laryngeal afflictions as well as whooping cough, colds and coughs. The leaves are used, in some parts of the world, to treat malaria and the tincture may replace quinine in easing intermittent fevers and the ague. Sunflowers produce the seed cake which is used as cattle food; the fresh leaves are given to poultry; the plants can be used as a vegetable; the stems are used as bedding for ducks; the plant used for silage, fuel, manure, and textiles.

ADMINISTERED AS: sunflower oil, tincture, decoction, poultice.

Tarragon *Artemisia dracunculus.*

common name: Mugwort, little dragon.

OCCURRENCE: cultivated in kitchen gardens across Europe and Great Britain. Tarragon originally arose from both Siberia and southern Europe to form the French and Russian tarragon we know today.

PARTS USED: the leaves, which contain an essential volatile oil which is lost on drying.

MEDICINAL USES: today there are few medicinal uses for tarragon but it has been used previously to stimulate the appetite and to cure toothache. Tarragon is mostly used in cooking—particularly on the European continent. It is used for dressings, salads, vinegar and pickles.

ADMINISTERED AS: fresh root, fresh herb.

Tea *Camellia thea.*

COMMON NAME: *Camellia theifera*, *Thea sinensis*, *Thea veridis*, *Thea bohea*, *Thea stricta jassamica.*

OCCURRENCE: native to Assam in India, and the plant has spread to Sri Lanka, Java, China and Japan.

PARTS USED: the dried leaves.

MEDICINAL USES: stimulant, astringent. The infusion of the leaves has a stimulating effect on the nervous system, producing a feeling of comfort. It may also act as a nerve sedative where it can relieve headaches. When drunk in excessive quantities, tea can produce unpleasant nervous symptoms, dyspepsia and unnatural wakefulness.

ADMINISTERED AS: infusion.

Thyme *Thymus vulgaris.*

COMMON NAME: Garden or common thyme, tomillo.

OCCURRENCE: cultivated in temperate countries in northern Europe.

PARTS USED: the herb. Thyme gives rise to oil of thyme after distillation of the fresh leaves. This oil contains the phenols, thymol and carvacrol, as well as cymene, pinene and borneol.

MEDICINAL USES: antiseptic, antispasmodic, tonic, carminative. The fresh herb, in syrup, forms a safe cure for whooping cough, as is an infusion of the dried herb. The infusion or tea is beneficial for catarrh, sore throat, wind spasms, colic and in allaying fevers and colds. Thyme is generally used in conjunction with other remedies in herbal medicine.

ADMINISTERED AS: fluid extract, essential oil and infusion.

Turpentine oil distilled from *Pinus palustris, Pinus maritima* and other species.

MEDICINAL USES: rubefacient, irritant, diuretic. When taken internally, turpentine forms a valuable remedy in bladder, kidney, and rheumatic problems and diseases of the mucous membranes. The oil is also used for respiratory complaints and externally as a liniment, an embrocation and an inhalant for rheumatism and chest problems. Turpentine may be combined with other aromatic oils as a remedy.

ADMINISTERED AS: essential oil.

Valerian *Valeriana officinalis.*

COMMON NAME: all-heal, great wild valerian, amantilla, setwall, sete-wale, capon's tail.

OCCURRENCE: found throughout Europe and northern Asia. It is common in England in marshy thickets, riverbanks and ditches.

PARTS USED: the root, which contains a volatile oil, two alkaloids called chatarine and valerianine as well as several unidentified compounds.

MEDICINAL USES: powerful nervine, stimulant, carminative anodyne and antispasmodic herb. It may be given in all cases of nervous debility and irritation as it is not narcotic. The expressed juice of the fresh root has been used as a narcotic in insomnia and as an anticonvulsant in epilepsy. The oil of valerian is of use against cholera and in strengthening the eyesight. A herbal compound containing valerian was given to civilians during the Second World War, to reduce the effects of stress caused by repeated air raids and to minimize damage to health.

ADMINISTERED AS: fluid and solid extract, tincture, oil, expressed juice.

Violet *Viola adorata.*

COMMON NAME: Blue violet, sweet violet, sweet-scented violet.

occurrence: native to Great Britain and found widely over Europe, northern Asia and North America.

parts used: the dried flowers and leaves and whole plant when fresh.

MEDICINAL USES: antiseptic, expectorant, laxative. The herb is
mainly taken as syrup of violets which has been used to cure
the ague, epilepsy, eye inflammation, pleurisy, jaundice and
sleeplessness which are some of the many other complaints
that benefit from treatment with this herb. The flowers possess expectorant properties and have long been used to treat
coughs. The flowers may also be crystallized as a sweetmeat
or added to salads. The rhizome is strongly emetic and purgative and has violent effects when administered. The seeds
also have purgative and diuretic effects and are beneficial in
treating urinary complaints and gravel. In the early part of
this century, violet preparations were used to great effect
against cancer. Fresh violet leaves are made into an infusion
which was drunk regularly, and a poultice of the leaves was
applied to the affected area. The herb has been used successfully to both allay pain and perhaps cure the cancer. It is said
to be particularly good against throat cancer.

ADMINISTERED AS: infusion, poultice, injection, ointment, syrup
and powdered root.

Walnut *Juglans nigra.*

COMMON NAME: Carya, Jupiter's nuts, *Juglans regia.*

OCCURRENCE: cultivated throughout Europe and was probably
native to Persia.

PARTS USED: the bark and leaves. The active principle of the
walnut tree is nucin or juglon, while the kernels also contain
oil, mucilage, albumin, cellulose, mineral matter and water.

MEDICINAL USES: alterative, laxative, detergent, astringent. The
bark and leaves are used in skin problems, e.g. scrofulous diseases, herpes, eczema and for healing indolent ulcers. A strong
infusion of the powdered bark has purgative effects, while the
walnut has various properties dependent upon its stage of ripe-

ness. Green walnuts are anthelminthic and vermifuge in action and are pickled in vinegar, which is then used as a gargle for sore and ulcerated throats. The wood is used for furniture, gun-stocks and for cabinets. Walnut oil expressed from the kernels is used in wood polishing, painting and is used as butter or frying oil.

ADMINISTERED AS: fluid extract, infusion, expressed oil, whole fruit.

Watercress *Nasturtium officinale*

OCCURRENCE: a perennial creeping plant often growing near springs and running water across Great Britain and Europe.

PARTS USED: the stem and leaves, which contain nicotinamide, volatile oil, a glucoside, gluconasturtin and vitamins A, C and E.

MEDICINAL USES: stimulant, expectorant, nutritive, antiscorbutic, diuretic. Watercress was proposed as a specific in tuberculosis and has a very long history of medical use. It is used to treat bronchitis and coughs as well as boosting digestion, lowering blood sugar and helping the body to remove toxic wastes from the blood and tissues. The herb is of value nutritionally as it contains many vitamins and mineral salts which help during convalescence and general debility. It can be bruised and made into a poultice for arthritis and gout, and is chewed raw to strengthen gums.

ADMINISTERED AS: expressed juice, poultice, dietary item.

Water dock *Rumex aquaticus.*

COMMON NAME: Red Dock, bloodwort.

OCCURRENCE: found frequently in fields, meadows, pools and ditches throughout Europe and Great Britain and is particularly common in the northern latitudes.

PARTS USED: the root.

MEDICINAL USES: alterative, deobstruent, detergent. It has a tonic action and is used externally to clean ulcers in afflictions of the mouth. It is applied to eruptive and scorbutic diseases, skin ulcers and sores. As a powder, Water dock has a cleansing and detergent effect upon the teeth.

ADMINISTERED AS: fluid extract and infusion.

Wintergreen *Gaultheria procumbens.*

COMMON NAME: Mountain tea, teaberry, boxberry, thé du Canada, aromatic wintergreen, partridge berry, deerberry, checkerberry.

OCCURRENCE: native to the northern United States and Canada from Georgia northwards.

PARTS USED: the leaves, which produce a volatile oil upon distillation. The oil is made up of methyl salicylate, gaultherilene, an aldehyde, a secondary alcohol and an ester. The aromatic odour of the plant is due to the alcohol and the ester.

MEDICINAL USES: aromatic, tonic, stimulant, diuretic, emmenagogue, astringent, galactogogue. The oil is of great benefit in acute rheumatism, but must be given in the form of capsules so stomach inflammation does not occur. The true distilled oil when applied to the skin can give rise to an eruption and so the synthetic oil of wintergreen is recommended for external use as it still contains methyl salicylate, but with no deleterious effects. The synthetic oil is exceedingly valuable for all chronic joint and muscular troubles, lumbago, sciatica and rheumatism. The oil is also used as a flavouring for toothpowders and mouth washes, particularly when combined with menthol and EUCALYPTUS. The berries are a winter food for many animals and also produce a bitter tonic, after being steeped in brandy. The leaves are either used to flavour tea or as a substitute for tea itself.

ADMINISTERED AS: capsules, synthetic oil, infusion, tincture.

Woodruff *Asperula odorata.*

COMMON NAME: Wuderove, wood-rova, sweet woodruff, woodroof, waldmeister tea.

OCCURRENCE: grows in woods or shaded hedges in England.

PARTS USED: the herb, which contains coumarin, a fragrant crystalline chemical, citric, malic and rubichloric acids and tannic acid.

MEDICINAL USES: diuretic, tonic. The fresh leaves, when applied to wounds, were said to have a strong healing effect. A strong decoction of the fresh herb was used as a cordial and stomachic and is said to be useful in removing biliary obstructions of the liver.

ADMINISTERED AS: a poultice and decoction.

Wormwood *Artemisia absinthium.*

COMMON NAME: Green ginger, old women, ajenjo.

OCCURRENCE: a plant found wild in many parts of the world including Siberia, Europe and the United States of America.

PARTS USED: the whole herb. The herb contains a volatile oil made up of thujone, pinene, cadinene and chamazulene, a bitter principle called absinthum, carotene, tannins and vitamin C.

MEDICINAL USES: bitter tonic, anthelmintic, febrifuge, stomachic. The liqueur, absinthe, was made using this plant as flavouring and it was banned in France in 1915 as excess intake caused irreversible damage to the nervous system. In modern herbal medicine, it is used as a bitter tonic to stimulate the appetite, the liver and gall bladder, production of digestive juices and peristalsis. Wormwood also expels parasitic worms, particularly roundworms and threadworms. The plant contains chemicals which have anti-inflammatory effects and help reduce fevers. Since ancient times this herb has been used by women to encourage menstruation, and it is applied as an external compress during labour to speed up the birth process. After labour, wormwood was taken both internally and externally to expel the afterbirth. This herb should not be used during pregnancy and should only be administered for short time periods.

ADMINISTERED AS: infusion, essential oil, fluid extract.

Woundwort *Stachys palustris.*

COMMON NAME: all-heal, panay, opopanewort, clown's woundwort, rusticum vulna herba, downy woundwort, stinking marsh stachys.

OCCURRENCE: common to marshy meadows, riversides and ditches in most parts of Great Britain.

PARTS USED: the herb.

MEDICINAL USES: antiseptic, antispasmodic. The herb relieves cramp, gout, painful joints and vertigo, while bruised leaves will stop bleeding and encourage healing when applied to a wound. Woundwort had an excellent reputation as a vulnerary among all of the early herbalists. A syrup made of the fresh juice will stop haemorrhages and dysentery when taken internally. The tuberous roots are edible as are the young shoot which resemble asparagus.

ADMINISTERED AS: poultice or syrup.

Yam, wild *dioscorea villosa.*

COMMON NAME: Dioscorea, colic root, rheumatism root, wilde yamwurzel.

OCCURRENCE: native to the southern United States and Canada.

PARTS USED: the roots and rhizome, which contain steroidal saponins, phytosterols, tannins, starch and various alkaloids including dioscorine.

MEDICINAL USES: antispasmodic, diuretic. This plant has a history of traditional use in relieving menstrual cramps and in stopping threatened miscarriage. It brings quick relief for bilious colic and flatulence, particularly in pregnant women. It is prescribed for the inflammatory stage of rheumatoid arthritis and in painful disorders of the urinary tract. Wild Yam is also beneficial for poor circulation, spasmodic hiccoughs, neuralgic complaints and spasmodic asthma. Prior to 1970, the wild yam was the only source of diosgenin, one of the starting materials used in commercial manufacturing of steroid hormones for the contraceptive pill.

ADMINISTERED AS: fluid extract, powdered bark, infusion.

Yew *Taxus baccata.*

OCCURRENCE: found in Europe, North Africa and Western Asia. The tree has been closely associated with the history and legends of Europe.

PARTS USED: the leaves, seeds and fruit. The seeds and fruit are the most poisonous parts of the plant and contain an alkaloid toxine and another principle milrossin.

MEDICINAL USES: it has few medicinal uses due to its poisonous nature but the leaves were once used effectively in treating epilepsy. The wood was used for making longbows.

ADMINISTERED AS: powdered leaves.

Herb Action

alterative a term given to a substance that speeds up the renewal of the tissues so that they can carry out their functions more effectively.

anodyne a drug that eases and soothes pain.

anthelmintic a substance that causes the death or expulsion of parasitic worms.

antiperiodic a drug that prevents the return of recurring diseases, e.g. malaria.

antiscorbutic a substance that prevents scurvy and contains necessary vitamins, e.g. vitamin C.

antiseptic a substance that prevents the growth of disease-causing micro-organisms, e.g. bacteria, without causing damage to living tissue. It is applied to wounds to cleanse them and prevent infection.

antispasmodic a drug that diminishes muscle spasms.

aperient a medicine that produces a natural movement of the bowel.

aphrodisiac a compound that excites the sexual organs.

aromatic a substance that has an aroma.

astringent a substance that causes cells to contract by losing proteins from their surface. This causes localized contraction of blood vessels and tissues.

balsamic a substance that contains resins and benzoic acid and is used to alleviate colds and abrasions.

bitter a drug that is bitter-tasting and is used to stimulate the appetite.

cardiac compounds that have some effect on the heart.

carminative a preparation to relieve flatulence and any resultant griping.

cathartic a compound that produces an evacuation of the bowels.

cholagogue the name given to a substance that produces a flow of bile from the gall bladder.

cooling a substance that reduces the temperature and cools the skin.

demulcent a substance that soothes and protects the alimentary canal.

deobstruent a compound that is said to clear obstructions and open the natural passages of the body.

detergent a substance that has a cleansing action, either internally or on the skin.

diaphoretic a term given to drugs that promote perspiration.

diuretics a substance that stimulates the kidneys and increases urine and solute production.

emetic a drug that induces vomiting.

emmenagogue a compound that is able to excite the menstrual discharge.

emollient a substance that softens or soothes the skin.

expectorant a group of drugs that are taken to help in the removal of secretions from the lungs, bronchi and trachea.

febrifuge a substance that reduces fever.

galactogogue an agent that stimulates the production of breast milk or increases milk flow.

haemostatic a drug used to control bleeding.

hepatic a substance that acts upon the liver.

hydrogogue a substance that has the property of removing accumulations of water or serum.

hypnotic a drug or substance that induces sleep.

insecticide a substance that kills insects.

irritant a general term encompassing any agent that causes irritation of a tissue.

laxative a substance that is taken to evacuate the bowel or soften stools.

mydriatic a compound that causes dilation of the pupil.

nervine a name given to drugs that are used to restore the nerves to their natural state.

narcotic a drug that leads to a stupor and total loss of awareness.

nephritic a drug that has an action on the kidneys.

nutritive a compounds that is nourishing to the body.

parasiticide a substance that destroys parasites internally and externally.

pectoral a term applied to drugs that are remedies in treating chest and lung complaints.

purgative the name given to drugs or other measures that produce evacuation of the bowels. They normally have a more severe effect than aperients or laxatives.

refrigerant a substance that relieves thirst and produces a feeling of coolness.

resolvent a substance that is applied to swellings to reduce them in size.

rubefacient a compound that causes the skin to redden and peel off. It causes blisters and inflammation.

sedative a drug that lessens tension, anxiety and soothes overexcitement of the nervous system.

sternutatory the name given to a substance that irritates the mucous membrane and produces sneezing.

stimulant a drug or other agent that increases the activity of an organ or system within the body.

stomachic name given to drugs that treat stomach disorders.

styptic applications that check bleeding by blood vessel contraction or by causing rapid blood clotting.

sudorific a drug or agent that produces copious perspiration.

taeniacide drugs that are used to expel tapeworms from the body.

tonic substances that are traditionally thought to give strength and vigour to the body and that are said to produce a feeling of wellbeing.

vermifuge a substance that kills, or expels, worms from the intestines.

vesicant similar to a rubefacient, agent that causes blistering when applied to the skin.

vulnerary a drug that is said to be good at healing wounds.

Forms of Herbal Preparations

capsule this is a gelatine container for swallowing and holding oils or balsams that would otherwise be difficult to administer due to their unpleasant taste or smell. It is used for cod liver oil and castor oil.

decoction this is prepared using cut, bruised or ground bark and roots placed into a stainless steel or enamel pan (not aluminium) with cold water poured on. The mixture is boiled for 20–30 minutes, cooled and strained. It is best drunk when warm.

herbal dressing this may be a compress or poultice. A compress is made of cloth or cotton wool soaked in cold or warm herbal decoctions or infusions while a poultice can be made with fresh or dried herbs. Bruised fresh herbs are applied directly to the affected area and dried herbs are made into a paste with water and placed on gauze on the required area. Both dressings are very effective in easing pain, swelling and inflammation of the skin and tissues.

infusion this liquid is made from ground or bruised roots, bark, herbs or seeds, by pouring boiling water onto the herb and leaving it to stand for 10-30 minutes, possibly stirring the mixture occasionally. The resultant liquid is strained and used. Cold infusions may be made if the active principles are yielded from the herb without heat. Today, infusions may be packaged into teabags for convenience.

liquid extract this preparation, if correctly made, is the most concentrated fluid form in which herbal drugs may be obtained and, as such, is very popular and convenient. Each herb is treated by various means dependent upon the individual properties of the herb, e.g. cold percolation, high pressure, evaporation by heat in a vacuum. These extracts are commonly held in a household stock of domestic remedies.

pessary similar to suppositories, but it is used in female complaints to apply a preparation to the walls of the vagina and cervix.

pill probably the best known and most widely used herbal preparation. It is normally composed of concentrated extracts and alkaloids, in combination with active crude drugs. The pill may be coated with sugar or another pleasant-tasting substance that is readily soluble in the stomach.

solid extract this type of preparation is prepared by evaporating the fresh juices or strong infusions of herbal drugs to the consistency of honey. It may also be prepared from an alcoholic tincture base. It is used mainly to produce pills, plasters, ointments and compressed tablets.

suppository this preparation is a small cone of a convenient and easily soluble base with herbal extracts added, which is used to apply medicines to the rectum. It is very effective in the treatment of piles, cancers, etc.

tablet this is made by compressing drugs into a small compass. It is more easily administered and has a quicker action as it dissolves more rapidly in the stomach.

tincture this is the most prescribed form of herbal medicine. It is based on alcohol and, as such, removes certain active principles from herbs that will not dissolve in water, or in the presence of heat. The tincture produced is long-lasting, highly concentrated and only needs to be taken in small doses for beneficial effects. The ground or chopped dried herb is placed in a container with 40 per cent alcohol such as gin or vodka and left for two weeks. The tincture is then decanted into a dark bottle and sealed before use.

Homoeopathy

Introduction

The aim of homoeopathy is to cure an illness or disorder by treating the whole person rather than merely concentrating on a set of symptoms. Hence, in homoeopathy the approach is holistic, and the overall state of health of the patient, especially his or her emotional and psychological wellbeing, is regarded as being significant. A homoeopath notes the symptoms that the person wishes to have cured but also takes time to discover other signs or indications of disorder that the patient may regard as being less important. The reasoning behind this is that illness is a sign of disorder or imbalance within the body. It is believed that the whole 'make-up' of a person determines, to a great extent, the type of disorders to which that individual is prone and the symptoms likely to occur. A homoeopathic remedy must be suitable both for the symptoms and the characteristics and temperament of the patient. Hence, two patients with the same illness may be offered different remedies according to their individual natures. One remedy may also be used to treat different groups of symptoms or ailments.

Like cures like

Homoeopathic remedies are based on the concept that 'like cures like', an ancient philosophy that can be traced back to the 5th century BC, when it was formulated by Hippocrates. In the early 1800s, this idea awakened the interest of a German doctor, Samuel Hahnemann, who believed that the medical practices at the time were too harsh and tended to hinder rather than aid healing. Hahnemann observed that a treatment for malaria, based on an extract of cinchona bark (quinine), actually produced symptoms of this disease when taken in a small dose by a healthy person. Further extensive studies convinced him that the production of symptoms was the body's way of combating illness. Hence, to give a minute dose of a substance that stimulated the symptoms of an illness in a healthy person could be used to fight that illness in someone who was sick. Hahnemann conducted numerous trials (called 'provings'), giving minute doses of substances to healthy people and recording the symptoms produced. Eventually, these very dilute remedies were given to people with illnesses, often with encouraging results.

Modern homoeopathy is based on the work of Hahnemann, and the medicines derived from plant, mineral and animal sources are used in extremely dilute amounts. Indeed, it is believed that the curative properties are enhanced by each dilution because impurities that might cause unwanted side effects are lost. Substances used in homoeopathy are first soaked in alcohol to extract their essential ingredients. This initial solution, called the 'mother tincture', is diluted successively either by factors of ten (called the 'decimal scale' and designated X) or 100 (the 'centesimal scale' and designated C). Each dilution is shaken vigorously before further ones are made, and this is thought to make the properties more powerful by adding energy at each stage while impurities are removed. The thorough shakings of each dilution are said to energize, or 'potentiate', the medicine. The remedies are made into tablets or may be used in the form of ointment, solutions, powders, suppositories, etc. High potency (i.e. more dilute) remedies are used for severe symptoms and lower potency (less dilute) for milder ones.

The homoeopathic view is that during the process of healing, symptoms are redirected from more important to less important body systems. It is also held that healing is from innermost to outermost parts of the body and that more recent symptoms disappear first, this being known as the 'law of direction of cure'. Occasionally, symptoms may worsen initially when a homoeopathic remedy is taken, but this is usually short-lived and is known as a 'healing crisis'. It is taken to indicate a change and that improvement is likely to follow. Usually, with a homoeopathic remedy, an improvement is noticed fairly quickly although this depends upon the nature of the ailment, health, age and wellbeing of the patient and potency of the remedy.

A first homoeopathic consultation is likely to last about one hour so that the specialist can obtain a full picture of the patient's medical history and personal circumstances. On the basis of this information, the homoeopathic doctor decides on an appropriate remedy and potency (which is usually 6C). Subsequent consultations are generally shorter, and full advice is given on how to store and take the medicine. It is widely accepted that homoeopathic remedies are safe and non-addictive, but they are covered by the legal requirements governing all medicines and should be obtained from a recognized source.

Potency table for homoeopathic medicines

The centesimal scale

1C =	1/100	$(1/100^1)$ of mother tincture
2C =	1/10 000	$(1/100^2)$ of mother tincture
3C =	1/1 000 000	$(1/100^3)$ of mother tincture
6C =	1/1 000 000 000 000	$(1/100^6)$ of mother tincture

The decimal scale

$1X =$	$1/10$	$(1/10^1)$ of mother tincture
$2X =$	$1/100$	$(1/10^2)$ of mother tincture
$6X =$	$1/1\ 000\ 000$	$(1/10^6)$ of mother tincture

The development of homoeopathy

The Greek physician Hippocrates, who lived several hundred years before the birth of Christ (460–370 BC), is regarded as the founding father of all medicine. The Hippocratic Oath taken by newly qualified doctors in orthodox medicine binds them to an ethical code of medical practice in honour of Hippocrates. Hippocrates believed that disease resulted from natural elements in the world in which people lived. This contrasted with the view that held sway for centuries that disease was some form of punishment from the gods or God. He believed that it was essential to observe and take account of the course and progress of a disease in each individual, and that any cure should encourage that person's own innate healing power. Hippocrates embraced the idea of 'like being able to cure like' and had many remedies that were based on this principle. Hence, in his practice and study of medicine he laid the foundations of the homoeopathic approach although this was not to be appreciated and developed for many centuries.

During the period of Roman civilization a greater knowledge and insight into the nature of the human body was developed. Many herbs and plants were used for healing by people throughout the world, and much knowledge was gained and handed down from generation to generation. The belief persisted, however, that diseases were caused by supernatural or divine forces. It was not until the early 1500s that a Swiss doctor, Paracelsus (1493–1541), put forward the view that disease resulted from external environmental forces. He also believed that plants and natural substances held the key to healing and embraced the 'like can cure like' principle. One of his ideas, known as the 'doctrine of signatures', was that the appearance of a plant, or the substances it contained, gave an idea of the disorders it could cure.

In the succeeding centuries, increased knowledge was gained about the healing properties of plants and the way the human body worked. In spite of this, the methods of medical practice were extremely harsh, and there is no doubt that many people suffered needlessly and died because of the treatment they received. It was against this background that Samuel Hahnemann (1755–1843), the founding father of modern homoeopathy, began his work as a doctor in the late 1700s. In his early writings, Hahnemann criticized the severe practices of medicine and advocated a healthy diet, clean living conditions and high standards of hygiene as a means of improving health and warding off disease. In 1790, he became interested in quinine, extracted from the bark of the cinchona tree, which was known to be an effective treatment for malaria. He tested the substance first on himself, and later on friends and close family members, and recorded the results. These 'provings' led him to conduct many further investigations and provings of other natural substances, during the course of which he rediscovered and established the principle of like being able to cure like.

By 1812, the principle and practice of homoeopathy had become established, and many other doctors adopted the homoeopathic approach. Hahnemann himself became a teacher in homoeopathy at the University of Leipzig and published many important writings—the results of his years of research. He continued to practise, teach and conduct research throughout his life, especially in producing more dilute remedies that were succussed, or shaken, at each stage and were found to be more potent. Although his work was not without its detractors, Hahnemann had attracted a considerable following by the 1830s. In 1831 there was a widespread cholera epidemic in central Europe for which Hahnemann recommended treatment with camphor. Many people were cured, including Dr Frederick Quin (1799–1878), a medical practitioner at that time. He went on to establish the first homoeopathic hospital in London in 1849. A later resurgence of cholera in Britain enabled the effectiveness of camphor to be established beyond doubt, as the numbers of people cured at the homoeopathic hospital were far greater than those treated at other hospitals.

In the United States of America, homoeopathy became firmly established in the early part of the 19th century, and there were several eminent practitioners who further enhanced knowledge and practice. These included Dr Constantine Hering (1800–80), who formulated the 'laws of cure', explaining how symptoms affect organ systems and move from one part of the body to another as a cure occurs. Dr James Tyler Kent (1849–1916) introduced the idea of constitutional types, which is now the basis of classical homoeopathy, and advocated the use of high potency remedies.

In the later years of the 19th century, a fundamental split occurred in the practice of homoeopathy, which was brought about by Dr Richard Hughes (1836–1902), who worked in London and Brighton. He insisted that physical symptoms and the nature of the disease itself was the important factor rather than the holistic approach based on the make-up of the whole individual person. Hughes rejected the concept of constitutional types and advocated the use of low potency remedies. Although he worked as a homoeopath, his approach was to attempt to make homoeopathy more scientific and to bring it closer to the practices of conventional medicine. Some other homoeopathic doctors followed the approach of Hughes, and the split led to a collapse in faith in the whole practice of homoeopathy during the earlier part of the 20th century. As the 20th century advanced, however, homoeopathy regained its following and respect. Conventional medicine and homoeopathy have continued to advance, and there is now a greater sympathy and understanding between the practitioners in both these important disciplines.

Homoeopathic Remedies in Common Use

Aconitum napellus

Aconite, monkshood, wolfsbane, friar's cap, mousebane

Aconitum is a native plant of Switzerland and other mountainous regions of Europe, where it grows in the damp conditions of alpine meadows. Attractive purple/dark blue flowers are borne on tall, upright stems produced from tubers developed from the root system. Aconite is highly poisonous, and its sap was used by ancient hunters on the ends of their arrows. 'Wolfsbane' refers to this use, and *Aconitum* is derived from the Latin word *acon*, meaning 'dart'. This was one of the homoeopathic remedies extensively tested and proved by Hahnemann. He used it for the acute infections and fevers, accompanied by severe pain, that were usually treated by bloodletting by the physicians of his day. This remains its main use in modern homoeopathy, and the whole plant is used to produce the remedy.

Aconite is a valuable treatment for acute illnesses of rapid onset in people who have previously been healthy and well. These often occur after the person has been out in cold wet weather. It is used especially at the start of feverish respiratory infections, such as colds and influenza and those affecting the eyes and ears. The person usually experiences restlessness, a hot, flushed face and pains and disturbed sleep but may be pale when first getting up. It is also used to treat the menopausal symptoms of hot flushes. It is an effective remedy for some mental symptoms, including extreme anxiety and fear, palpitations and attacks of panic, especially the belief that death is imminent during illness. The remedy encourages sweating and is sometimes used in conjunction with BELLADONNA. Symptoms are made worse by cold, draughts, tobacco smoke, stuffy, airless, warm rooms, listening to music, at midnight and by lying on the painful part. They improve out in the fresh air and with warmth. The people who benefit from Aconite are typically strong, solid or well-built, high-coloured and usually enjoy good health but have a poor opinion of themselves. Because of this, they tend to have a constant need to prove their own worth, to the point of insensitivity or unkindness to others. When in good health, Aconite people have a need for the company of others. However, they also have fears that they keep concealed and may be frightened of going out or of being in a crowd. When ill, they are inclined to be morbid and to believe that death is imminent, and they cope badly with any kind of shock.

Actea racemosa
Actea rac.; cimic, *Cimifuga racemosa*, black snakeroot, rattleroot, bugbane, rattleweed, squawroot.

This plant is a native of woodlands in North America and was used by the American Indian peoples as a remedy for the bite of the rattlesnake. It was also used as a tranquillizer and for pain relief in labour and menstruation. An infusion made from the plant was sprinkled in the home to protect against supernatural forces and evil spirits. The plant has a dark, woody underground stem (rhizome) and roots, and produces feathery, tall stems of white flowers. The fresh rhizomes and roots are used in homoeopathy, being collected, cut and dried in the autumn after the stems and leaves have died down and the fruit has been formed. The rhizome has a faint, unpleasant smell and the taste is acrid and bitter. The remedy was extensively tested and proved by the English homoeopath Dr Richard Hughes, who used it in the treatment of a stiff neck and associated headache. It is used for this purpose in modern homoeopathy and also to treat pain in the lower back and between the shoulder blades. Also for rheumatic pain and swelling of joints or muscles and other sudden, sharp pains. Actea rac. is considered to be of great value in the treatment of menstrual problems with cramps, bloatedness, and pain and symptoms of pregnancy, e.g. morning sickness and abdominal discomfort. It is also of value for postnatal depression and menopausal symptoms. Emotional symptoms that accompany these periods of hormonal change, such as weepiness, anxiety and irritability, are also eased by this remedy. Symptoms are made worse by exposure to cold, wet, draughty conditions, by any sudden change in the weather, on drinking alcohol and with excitement. They improve with keeping warm, with gentle exercise and in the fresh, open air. A person suitable for this remedy is often a woman. She may be a bubbly, extrovert, talkative person or withdrawn, depressed and sad, heaving great sighs. The woman is usually emotionally intense with a fear of dying and madness. These fears are at their height in a woman going through the menopause.

Allium

Allium cepa; Spanish onion

The onion has been cultivated and used for many centuries, both for culinary and medicinal purposes, and was important in the ancient Egyptian civilization. The volatile oil released when an onion is sliced stimulates the tear glands of the eyes and mucous membranes of the nose, throat and air passages. Hence, in homoeopathy the onion is used to treat ailments with symptoms of a streaming nose and watering eyes. The red Spanish onion, which is cultivated throughout the world, is used to make the homoeopathic remedy. It is used to treat allergic conditions, such as hay fever, colds and pains or symptoms that go from one side to the other. It is useful for shooting, stabbing or burning pains associated with neuralgia, which may alternate from side to side, frontal headaches, painful molar teeth and earache in children. The symptoms are made worse by cold, damp conditions and improve in fresh air and cool, dry surroundings.

Apis mellifica
Apis; *Apis mellifera*, the honey bee

The source of the medicine is the entire body of the honey bee, which is crushed or ground to prepare the remedy. It is used particularly to treat inflammation, redness, swelling and itching of the skin, which is sensitive to touch, and with stinging hot pains. There is usually feverishness and thirst and the pains are worsened by heat and relieved by cold. The remedy is used for insect stings, nettle rash, allergic conditions, blisters, whitlow (an abscess on the fingertip) and infections of the urinary tract, including cystitis, with stabbing hot pains. Also for urinary incontinence in elderly persons, fluid retention causing swelling of the eyelids or other areas, allergic conditions that cause sore throat and swallowing difficulty, and tonsillitis. The person often experiences hot, stabbing headaches and has dry skin. Apis is additionally valued as a remedy for swollen, painful inflammation of the joints as in arthritic conditions and for peritonitis and pleurisy. The symptoms are made worse by heat and touch, stuffy airless rooms following sleep and in the early evening. They improve in the fresh, cool open air, after taking a cold bath, or any cold application. A person suitable for the Apis remedy tends to expect high standards and may be rather irritable and hard to please. He (or she) likes to organize others and is jealous of his own domain, tending to be resentful of anyone new. Apis types may seem to be rushing around and working hard but may achieve very little as a result.

Argenticum nitricum
Argent. nit; silver nitrate, devil's stone, lunar caustic, hellstone

Silver nitrate is obtained from the mineral acanthite, which is a natural ore of silver. White silver nitrate crystals are derived from a chemical solution of the mineral ore and these are used to make the homoeopathic remedy. Silver nitrate is poisonous in large doses and has antiseptic and caustic properties. In the past it was used to clean out wounds and prevent infection. In homoeopathy, it is used to treat states of great anxiety, panic, fear or apprehension about a forthcoming event, e.g. taking an examination, having to perform a public role (speech-making, chairing a public meeting, acting, singing), going for an interview, or any activity involving scrutiny and criticism by others. It was also used as a remedy for digestive complaints including indigestion, abdominal pain, wind, nausea and headache. Often, there is a longing for sweet 'comfort' or other types of food. Argent. nit. may be given for laryngitis, sore throat and hoarseness, eye inflammation such as conjunctivitis, and period pains. Other types of pain, asthma and warts may benefit from Argent. nit.

Often, a person experiences symptoms mainly on the left side, and these are worse with heat and at night. Also, they are made worse by anxiety and overwork, emotional tension and resting on the left side. Pains are made worse with talking and movement. Symptoms improve in cold or cool fresh air and are relieved by belching. Pains are helped by applying pressure to the painful part. People suitable for Argent nit. are quick-witted and rapid in thought and action. They may appear outgoing and happy but are prey to worry, anxiety and ungrounded fears that make them tense. All the emotions are quick to surface, and Argent nit. people are able to put on an impressive perform-ance. They enjoy a wide variety of foods, particularly salty and sweet things although these may upset the digestion. They have a fear of heights, crowds, of being burgled and of failure and arriving late for an appointment. Also, of serious illness, dying and madness. Argent. nit. people are generally slim and full of restless energy and tension. They may have deeply etched fea-tures and lines on the skin that make them appear older than their real age.

Arnica montana
Arnica; leopard's bane, sneezewort, mountain tobacco

Arnica is a native plant of woodland and mountainous regions of central Europe and Siberia. It has a dark brown root system from which a central stem arises, producing pairs of elongated green leaves and bright yellow flowers. If the flowers are crushed or bruised and a person then inhales the scent, this causes sneezing. All the fresh parts of the flowering plant are used to prepare the homoeopathic remedy. It is a commonly used first aid remedy for symptoms relating to injury or trauma of any kind, e.g. bruising, swelling, pain and bleeding. It is also used to treat physical and mental shock. It is helpful following surgery, childbirth or tooth extraction, promoting healing, and also for gout, rheumatic joints with pain, heat and inflamma-tion, sore sprained or strained muscles, concussion, and osteoarthritis. Taken internally, it is a remedy for black eyes, eye strain, skin conditions such as eczema and boils. Arnica is helpful in the treatment of whooping cough in children and also wetting the bed when the cause is nightmares. Symptoms are made worse with heat, touch and continued movement, and also with heat and resting for a long period. The symptoms improve when the person first begins to move and with lying down with the head at a lower level than the feet. A person suitable for this remedy tends to be solemn, fatalistic and subject to morbid fears. Arnica types usually deny the existence of any illness, even when obviously not well, and do not seek medical help, preferring to manage on their own.

Arsenicum album
Arsen. alb.; white arsenic trioxide

This is a widely used homoeopathic remedy, the source being white arsenic trioxide derived from arsenopyrite, a metallic mineral ore of arsenic. Arsenic has been known for centuries as a poison and was once used as a treatment for syphilis. White arsenic trioxide used to be given to improve muscles and skin in animals such as horses. It is used to treat acute conditions of the digestive system and chest and mental symptoms of anxiety and fear. Hence it is a remedy for diarrhoea and vomiting caused by eating the wrong kinds of food, or food poisoning or overindulgence in alcohol. Also, for dehydration in children following gastroenteritis or feverish illness. It is a remedy for asthma and breathing difficulty, mouth ulcers, carbuncle (a collection of boils), dry, cracked lips, burning skin, inflamed, watering stinging eyes and psoriasis. Also, for sciatica, shingles, sore throat and painful swallowing, candidiasis (fungal infection) of the mouth and motion sickness. There may be oedema (retention of fluid) showing as a puffiness around the ankles.

An ill person who benefits from Arsen. alb. experiences burning pains but also feels cold. The skin may be either hot or cold to the touch. The symptoms are worse with cold in any form, including cold food and drink, and between midnight and 3 a.m. They are worse on the right side and if the person is near the coast. Symptoms improve with warmth, including warm drinks, gentle movement and lying down with the head raised. People suitable for Arsen. alb. are precise, meticulous and ambitious and loathe any form of disorder. They are always immaculately dressed and everything in their life is neat and tidy. However, they tend to have great worries, especially about their financial security and their own health and that of their family. They fear illness and dying, loss of financial and personal status, being burgled, darkness and the supernatural. Arsen. alb. people have strongly held views and do not readily tolerate contrary opinions or those with a more relaxed or disordered lifestyle. They enjoy a variety of different foods, coffee and alcoholic drinks. They are usually thin, with delicate, fine features and pale skin that may show worry lines. Their movements tend to be rapid and their manner serious and somewhat restless, although always polite.

Atropa belladonna
Belladonna, deadly nightshade, black cherry, devil's cherries, naughty man's cherries, devil's herb

Belladonna is a native plant of most of Europe although it is uncommon in Scotland. The plant is extremely poisonous, and many children have died as a result of being tempted to eat the shiny black berries of deadly nightshade. It is a stout, stocky plant with light brown roots, growing to about four feet high, with green oval leaves and pale purple, bell-shaped flowers. In medieval times, the plant had its place in the potions of witchcraft. Italian women used extracts of the plant as eye drops to widen the pupils of the eye and make them more beautiful (hence *bella donna*, which means 'beautiful woman'). The plant contains atropine, an alkaloid substance that induces paralysis of nerves and is used in orthodox medicine to relieve painful spasms and in ophthalmic (eye) procedures.

In homoeopathy, the remedy is obtained from the pulped leaves and flowers. It was investigated and proved by Hahnemann as a treatment for scarlet fever. Belladonna is used to treat acute conditions that arise suddenly in which there is a throbbing, pulsing headache and red, flushed skin, high fever and staring wide eyes. The skin around the mouth and lips may be pale, but the tongue is a fiery red and the hands and feet are cold. It is used as a remedy for infectious diseases such as influenza, scarlet fever, measles, whooping cough, chicken pox, mumps and the early stages of pneumonia. Also for boils, earache (particularly on the right side and worse when the head is cold or wet), cystitis, boils, conjunctivitis, tonsillitis, inflammation of the kidneys, neuralgia (sharp pain along the course of a nerve) and sore throat. Other conditions that benefit from this remedy include labour pains, soreness of the breasts in breast-feeding, fever and teething in children, with broken sleep and whitlow (an infection of a fingernail). The symptoms are worse at night and with lying down, and occur more intensely on the right side. Also, they are exacerbated by loud noises, bright lights, jarring of the body, touch or pressure and with cool surroundings.

They improve with sitting upright or standing and keeping warm or warm applications to the painful area. People suitable for belladonna usually enjoy good health, being fit, energetic and ready to tackle any task. They are amusing, sociable and popular when in good health. However, if they become ill the reverse is often true and they may be restless, irritable and possibly even violent.

Aurum metallicum

Aurum met.; gold

Gold was highly prized by Arabian physicians in the early Middle Ages who used it to treat heart disorders. In the early part of this century, it was used in the treatment of tuberculosis. Gold is now used in conventional medicine for some cancer treatments and for rheumatic and arthritic complaints. In homoeopathy, pure gold is ground down to produce a fine powder, and it is used to treat both physical and mental symptoms. It is used as a remedy for congestive circulatory disorders and heart diseases including angina pectoris. The symptoms include a throbbing, pulsing headache, chest pain, breathlessness and palpitations. It is also used to treat liver disorders with symptoms of jaundice, painful conditions of bones and joints (especially the hip and knee), inflammation of the testes and an undescended testicle in small boys (especially if the right side is affected). It is a remedy for sinusitis and severe mental symptoms of despair, depression and thoughts of suicide. The person who is suitable for this remedy tends to drive himself very hard to the point of being a workaholic. He (or she) is excessively conscientious but usually feels that he has not done enough and is oversensitive to the criticism of other people. The person may come to regard himself as a failure and become severely clinically depressed or even suicidal. Symptoms are made worse by mental effort and concentration, or physical exercise, especially in the evening or night and by emotional upheaval. They improve with cold bathing, walking in the fresh air and with rest and quiet.

Bryonia alba

Bryonia, European white bryony, black-berried white bryony, wild hops

Bryony is a native plant of many parts of Europe and grows in England, although it is rarely found in Scotland. It has large, white, branched roots with swollen, expanded portions that are highly poisonous. The smell given off is unpleasant and, if eaten, the taste is very bitter and death soon follows. The tall stems of the plant climb up supports by means of corkscrew tendrils and round black berries are produced in the autumn. Bryony was used by the physicians of ancient Greece and Rome and was described by Hippocrates. The homoeopathic remedy is made from the fresh pulped root of the plant, and is mainly used for conditions producing acute stitch-like pains, which are made worse by even slight movement and relieved by rest. These ailments usually develop slowly and accompanying symptoms include dry skin, mouth and eyes with great thirst. It is used as a remedy for inflammation of the lining of joints in arthritic and rheumatic disorders with swelling, heat and pains. Also, for chest inflammation, pleurisy, chesty bronchitis and pneumonia with severe pain and dry, hacking cough. Digestive problems that are eased by Bryonia include indigestion, colic, constipation, nausea, vomiting and diarrhoea. Breast inflammation because of breast-feeding, colic in babies, gout and lumbago may be helped by Bryonia. The symptoms are made worse by movement and bending and improve with rest and pressure applied to the painful area. People suitable for Bryonia are hardworking, conscientious and reliable but have a dread of poverty. They tend to measure success in life in financial or materialistic terms. They cope badly with any threat to their security or lifestyle, becoming extremely worried, fretful and depressed.

Calcarea carbonica

Calc. carb.; calcium carbonate

This important homoeopathic remedy is made from powdered

mother-of-pearl, the beautiful, translucent inner layer of oyster shells. Calcium is an essential mineral in the body, being especially important for the healthy development of bones and teeth. The Calc. carb. remedy is used to treat a number of different disorders, especially those relating to bones and teeth, and also certain skin conditions and symptoms relating to the female reproductive system. It is a remedy for weak or slow growth of bones and teeth and fractures that take a long time to heal. Also, for teething problems in children, pains in bones, teeth and joints, headaches and eye inflammations affecting the right side, and ear infections with an unpleasant-smelling discharge. Premenstrual syndrome, heavy periods and menopausal disorders are helped by Calc. carb., and also chapped skin and eczema.

Calc. carb. may be used as a remedy for verruca (a type of wart) and thrush infections. People who benefit from Calc. carb. are very sensitive to the cold, particularly in the hands and feet and tend to sweat profusely. They suffer from fatigue and anxiety, and body secretions (sweat and urine) smell unpleasant. Children who benefit from Calc. carb. have recurrent ear, nose and throat infections, especially tonsillitis and glue ear. Symptoms are made worse by draughts and cold, damp weather and also at night. They are worse when the person first wakens up in the morning and for physical exercise and sweating. In women, symptoms are worse premenstrually. They improve in warm, dry weather and are better later on in the morning and after the person has eaten breakfast. People suitable for Calc. carb. are often overweight or even obese with a pale complexion. They are shy and very sensitive, quiet in company and always worried about what other people think of them. Calc. carb. people are hard-working, conscientious and reliable and easily upset by the suffering of others. They need constant reassurance from friends and family and tend to feel that they are a failure. Usually, Calc. carb. people enjoy good health but have a tendency for skeletal weakness. They enjoy a wide variety of different foods and tend to overeat, but are upset by coffee and milk. They are afraid of dying and serious illness, the supernatural, madness, being a failure and becoming poor, and they tend to be claustrophobic.

Calcarea fluorica

Calc. fluor.; fluorite, calcium fluoride, fluoride of lime

This homoeopathic remedy is one of the Schussler tissue salts (*see* GLOSSARY). Calcium fluoride occurs naturally in the body in the enamel of the teeth, bones, skin and connective tissue. It is used to treat disorders of these body tissues or to maintain their elasticity. It is used to treat chronic lumbago, scars, and to prevent the formation of adhesions after operations, gout and arthritic nodules. Also, for rickets, slow growth of bones in children, enlarged adenoids that become stony because of persistent, recurrent respiratory tract infections and cataracts. It is used to strengthen weak tooth enamel and strained and stretched ligaments and muscles, e.g. around a joint. People suitable for Calc. fluor. are intelligent and punctual but tend to make mistakes through lack of planning. They benefit from the guidance of others to work efficiently and fear poverty and illness. They are often prone to piles, varicose veins, swollen glands and muscle and ligament strain. The manner of walking may be rapid with jerking of the limbs. Symptoms are made worse on beginning movement and in cold, damp, draughty conditions. They improve with warmth and heat and for continual gentle movement.

Calcarea phosphorica

Calc. phos., phosphate of lime, calcium phosphate

This homoeopathic remedy is a SCHUSSLER TISSUE SALT (*see* Glossary) and calcium phosphate is the mineral that gives hardness to bones and teeth. It is obtained by a chemical reaction between dilute phosphoric acid and calcium hydroxide, when a white precipitate of calcium phosphate is formed. Since calcium phosphate is an essential mineral in the normal, healthy development of bones and teeth, it is used to treat disorders in these tissues. It is particularly helpful as a remedy for painful bones, difficult fractures that are slow to heal, teeth prone to decay, problems of bone growth and teething in children and 'growing pains'. Also, it is beneficial during convalescence when a person is weakened and tired after an illness, and for digestive problems including diarrhoea, stomach pains and indigestion. It may be used as a remedy for tonsillitis, sore throats and swollen glands. Children who benefit from this remedy tend to be thin, pale, miserable and fail to thrive, and are prone to sickness and headaches. They are often fretful and demanding. Adults are also unhappy and discontented with their circumstances, although endeavour to be friendly towards others. They are restless and need plenty of different activities and stimulation, hating routine and needing a good reason to get out of bed in the morning. Symptoms are made worse by any change in the weather, and in cold, wet conditions, e.g. thawing snow. Also for worry or grief and too much physical activity. Symptoms improve when the weather is warm and dry, in summer, and from taking a hot bath.

Calendula officinalis
Calendula, marigold, garden marigold, marygold

This is a familiar garden plant that grows well in all parts of the United Kingdom, having light green leaves and bright orange flowers. The plant has been known for centuries for its healing properties and was used in the treatment of various ailments. The parts used in homoeopathy are the leaves and flowers, and the remedy is of value in first aid for its antiseptic and anti-inflammatory activity. It is used in the treatment of boils, stings, cuts and wounds, and to stem bleeding, often in the form of an ointment that can be applied to broken skin. It is helpful when applied to skin tears following childbirth. It is used in the form of an antiseptic tincture as a mouth wash and gargle after tooth extraction, for mouth ulcers or a septic sore throat. When taken internally it prevents suppuration (pus formation) and may be used for persistent chronic ulcers and varicose ulcers, fever and jaundice. It is a useful remedy in the treatment of children's ailments. The symptoms are made worse in damp, draughty conditions and cloudy weather and after eating. They improve with walking about and lying absolutely still.

Cantharis vesicatoria
Cantharis, Spanish fly

This remedy is derived from the body and wings of a bright green iridescent beetle that is found mainly in the southern parts of Spain and France. The beetle, *Cantharis vesicatoria*, secretes a substance called canthardin, which has irritant properties, is also poisonous and is an ancient remedy to cure warts. It was also used as an aphrodisiac, reputedly by the notorious Maquis de Sade. The beetles are dried and ground to produce a powder that is then used in homoeopathy. It is an irritant, blistering agent acting externally on the part of the body to which it is applied and internally on the bladder, urinary tract and genital organs. Hence it is used to treat conditions in which there are stinging and burning pains. An accompanying symptom is often a great thirst but a reluctance to drink. It is used to treat cystitis with cutting hot pains on passing urine, urinary frequency with pain and other urinary infections. Also, certain inflammations of the digestive system in which there is abdominal distension and burning pains and diarrhoea. In general it is used as a remedy for conditions that worsen rapidly. It is a remedy for burns and scalds of the skin, including sunburn, insect stings, and rashes with spots that contain pus. Some mental symptoms are eased by Cantharis, including angry and irritable or violent behaviour, extreme anxiety and excessive sexual appetite. Symptoms are made worse with movement, touch and after drinking coffee or chilled water. They improve when gastro-intestinal wind is eliminated and with warmth, at night time and with very light massage.

Carbo vegetabilis
Carbo veg., vegetable charcoal
The homoeopathic remedy Carbo veg. is made from charcoal, which itself is obtained from heating or partially burning wood without oxygen. The charcoal is hard and black or dark grey, and is a form of carbon that is present in all living things. Charcoal has been made for centuries, and usually silver birch, beech or poplar trees are the source of wood that is used. The homoeopathic remedy is used to treat a person who is run down, weak or exhausted, especially after a debilitating illness or operation. It is also used for postoperative shock, when there is a clammy, cold, pale skin but the person feels a sensation of heat or burning inside. It is helpful as a remedy for ailments of poor circulation such as varicose veins. Again, the skin tends to be pale, clammy and chilly with a bluish colour and the extremities feel cold. The legs may be puffy, and additional symptoms include hoarseness and laryngitis and lack of energy. Carbo veg. is a useful remedy for digestive problems, and carbon is also used for this purpose in orthodox medicine. Symptoms are

those of indigestion, heartburn and flatulence with a sour taste in the mouth. Morning headaches with accompanying symptoms of nausea and giddiness or fainting may be relieved by Carbo veg., particularly if the cause is a large, heavy meal the night before. People suitable for this remedy often complain of a lack of energy and may indeed be physically and mentally exhausted, with poor powers of concentration and lapses of memory. They usually have fixed attitudes, with a lack of interest in news of the wider world. They do not like the night and are fearful of the supernatural. Symptoms are made worse by warm, moist weather, in the evening and night, and with lying down. They are also exacerbated after eating meals of fatty foods, coffee and milk and drinks of wine. They improve with burping and with circulating cool, fresh air.

Chamomilla
Chamomile, common chamomile, double chamomile

A creeping and trailing plant that produces daisy-like flowers in summer and prefers dry, sandy soils. Chamomiles are native to Britain and others part of northern Europe and have been used in medicine since ancient times, being described by Hippocrates. When walked on, it gives off an aromatic perfume and was gathered and strewn on the floor in medieval dwellings to counter unpleasant odours. It is prized for its many medicinal uses, the flowers and leaves both being used for a number of different ailments. Herbalists use chamomile to treat skin conditions such as eczema, and for asthma and disturbed sleep. In homoeopathy, it is used for its soothing and sedative effect on all conditions producing restlessness, irritability and pains. It is a useful remedy for children's complaints such as teething where the child is fretful and cries if put down, colicky pains and disturbed sleep. Also, for toothache, when one cheek is red and the other white, that is exacerbated by heat and relieved by cold. It is used to treat a blocked ear and earache, painful, heavy periods and soreness and inflammation associated with breast-feeding. People suitable for this remedy are very sensitive to pain, which causes sweating or fainting, especially in children and women. They are irritable and fretful when ill. Symptoms are made worse if the person becomes angry or in cold winds and the open air. They improve if the person fasts for a time and if the weather is wet and warm. People who are suitable for chamomile are noisy sleepers, in that they frequently cry out or talk while dreaming. If woken suddenly from sleep they are extremely irritable and they like to poke their feet out from the bed covers to keep them cool.

Chincona officinalis

Cinchona succirubra; china, Peruvian bark, Jesuit's bark
This homoeopathic remedy, known as china, is obtained from the dried bark of the cinchona tree and contains quinine. The attractive evergreen cinchona, with its red bark, is a native of the hot tropical forests of South America, but it is also cultivated in India, Sri Lanka and southeast Asia. A preparation of powdered bark was used to treat a feverish illness suffered by the Countess of Cinchon, wife of the viceroy of Peru in 1638. After her recovery she publicized the remedy, and the tree was called cinchona from this time. The value of the bark as a cure for malaria had long been known and used by Jesuit priests. This was the first homoeopathic substance tested and proved by Hahnemann on himself.

In modern homoeopathy it is used mainly as a remedy for nervous and physical exhaustion resulting from chronic debilitating illnesses. It is used for weakness because of dehydration, sweating, chills and fever, and headaches that are relieved if firm pressure is applied. The person wants drinks during periods of chills and shivering rather than when feverish and hot. He or she usually has a washed-out unhealthy complexion with very sensitive skin. China is also used as a remedy for neuralgia, muscles that twitch because of extreme fatigue, bleeding, including nosebleeds, and tinnitus (noises in the ears). It has a helpful effect on the digestion and is used to treat gastro-intestinal wind, gall bladder disorders and digestive upset. Some mental symptoms are helped by this remedy, including irritability and tetchy behaviour that is out of character, apathy and loss of concentration and sleeplessness.

People who are suitable for this remedy tend to be artistic, imaginative and highly strung. They find it easier to empathize with the natural world rather than with the people around them. They are intense and dislike trivial conversation and fatty foods such as butter, but have a liking for alcoholic drinks. Their nature makes them prone to irritability and depression, and they tend to draw up grand schemes at night that are later abandoned. Symptoms are made better by warmth and plenty of sleep and by the application of steady continuous pressure to a painful area. They are made worse by cold, draughty weather, particularly in the autumn, and in the evening and night.

Citrullus colocynthis
Colocynth; bitter cucumber, bitter apple

The plant *Citrullus colocynthis* is a native of Turkey and is also found in parts of Asia and Africa, flourishing in dry, arid conditions. It produces yellow flowers and then yellow-orange smooth fruits, about the size of a large apple, which contain many seeds embedded in a whitish pulp. The homoeopathic remedy colocynth is obtained from the dried fruits from which the seeds have been removed. This is then ground down to produce a powder. The fruit itself is poisonous, having a violent irritant effect on the digestive tract, causing severe, cramp-like pains, inflammation and bleeding. This is caused by the presence of a substance called colocynthin. According to tradition, Elisha, the Old Testament prophet, is said to have performed a miraculous transformation of the fruit during the famine in Gilgal, making it fit for the people to eat. In homoeopathy, colocynth is used to treat colicky abdominal pains that may be accompanied by sickness and diarrhoea (including colic in young babies). Also, for neuralgia, especially of the face, sciatica, ovarian or kidney pain because of nerves, rheumatic disorders and headache.

People who are helped by colocynth are often reserved, with a tendency to bottle up anger. They have strong opinions about what is right and wrong, and may become quite agitated if someone else has a contrary viewpoint. Physical symptoms of colicky pains or neuralgia and upset stomach may follow on from becoming upset or angry. The symptoms are made worse when the person becomes irritated or angry and in cold, damp weather conditions. Also, eating meals and drinking exacerbate the symptoms. They are relieved by warmth and pressure on the painful part and drinking coffee. Abdominal flatulence also relieves the symptoms.

Cuprum metallicum
Cuprum met.; copper

Copper ore, which is found in rocks in many parts of the world, has been mined and used for many centuries in the manufacture of weapons, utensils and jewellery, etc. In earlier times, physicians made an ointment from the ground metal and this was applied to raw wounds to aid healing. Copper is poisonous in large doses affecting the nervous system and causing convulsions, paralysis and possibly death because of its effects upon respiratory muscles. Toxic effects were recognized in those who worked with the metal and who developed wasting because of poor absorption of food, coughs and respiratory symptoms, and colicky pains. The ruddy, gold-coloured metal is ground to produce a fine red powder that is used in homoeopathy to treat cramping, colicky pains in the abdomen, and muscular spasms in the calves of the legs, feet and ankles. It is also used as a remedy for epilepsy and problems of breathing and respiration such as asthma, croup and whooping cough in which there are spasms. The person may turn blue because of the effort of breathing.

The symptoms are made worse by touch, hot, sunny weather and for keeping emotions bottled up. They improve with sweating and drinking cold fluids. People who benefit from Cuprum met. have mood swings that alternate from stubbornness to passivity, weepiness and depression. They tend to be serious people who judge themselves severely and keep their emotions very much suppressed. As babies or toddlers, they may be breath-holders who turn blue with anger or as a result of a tantrum. As children, some are destructive and others are loners who dislike the company of others.

Daphne mezereum
Daphne, spurge laurel, wild pepper, spurge olive, flowering spurge, dwarf bay

This poisonous plant is native to upland areas of Europe and is cultivated in the United Kingdom. It produces cheerful bright-red flowers and dark green leaves, and the bark is the part used in homoeopathy. It is used to treat skin conditions characterized by blistering, especially erysipelas, shingles and varicose ulcers. Also, for any condition in which there is a persistent, dry cough and tightness around the chest and a mucus discharge from the nose. There may be burning pains that are worse at night.

Drosera rotundifolia
Drosera, sundew, youthwort, red rot, moor grass

This small, carnivorous (insect-eating) plant is found widely throughout Europe and in Britain, where it grows in the poor, acidic soils of bogs, damp uplands, moorlands and woodlands. It is a small plant growing close to the ground, and needs to trap insects for extra nutrients as the soil in which it grows is so poor. It is remarkable for its leaves, which are covered with long red hairs, each with a small, fluid-containing gland at the top. When the sun shines on the leaves it resembles dew, hence the name sundew. An insect landing on the leaf is trapped because this curls over and inwards, and the sticky fluid secreted by the hairs holds it fast. The secretion contains enzymes that digest the body and the nutrients are absorbed by the plant. The small, white flowers of sundew are fully open in the early morning but close up when the sun is shining strongly. In medieval times, the plant was used to treat tuberculosis and the plague, and it was employed as a remedy for skin disorders in early Asian medicine. It was noticed that sheep who inadvertently cropped sundew developed a paroxysmal type of cough like whooping cough. It was investigated and proved as a remedy for this illness in homoeopathy, and the whole plant is used to prepare the medicine. Any condition in which there is a violent, dry, persistent barking cough of a spasmodic nature, as in whooping cough, benefits from the use of sundew, which has a particular action on the upper respiratory tract. Accompanying symptoms are gagging, sickness, sweating and nosebleeds. It is also used to treat bronchitis, asthma, corns and warts, growing pains and pains in the bones.

People who benefit from this remedy are restless and fearful of being alone when they are ill, and they tend to be stubborn and lack concentration. They are suspicious and may feel that others are talking about them or concealing bad news. They are sensitive to the supernatural and are afraid of ghosts. The symptoms are worse for being too warm in bed, after midnight, with crying, lying down, laughing, singing and talking. Also, for meals of cold food and drinks. Symptoms improve out in the fresh air, with walking or gentle exercise, sitting propped up in bed, with pressure applied to the painful part and in quiet surroundings.

Euphrasia officinalis
Euphrasia, eyebright

Eyebright is an attractive wild flower that is variable in size and grows widely throughout Europe, including Britain, and in North America. It has been known since medieval times as a remedy for inflammation of the eyes, and this remains its main use in homoeopathy. The plant flourishes on well-drained, chalky soils and may be between two and eight inches in height, depending upon conditions. It is partly parasitic, deriving some nourishment from the roots of grass, and produces pretty white, purple-veined flowers with yellow centres. The whole plant and flowers are used in homoeopathy, and the remedy is used to treat eye disorders characterized by redness, inflammation, watering, burning, stinging or itching. These include conjunctivitis, blepharitis (inflammation of eyelids), injuries to the eye and dry eyes. It is also used as a remedy for allergic conditions such as hay fever, in which the eyes are very much affected, and colds producing eye symptoms. It is a remedy for the early stages of measles, headaches, some menstrual problems and inflammation of the prostate gland in men. Symptoms are worse in the evening, in windy and warm weather and for being inside. They improve in subdued light, with drinking a cup of coffee and with cold applications.

Ferrum phosphoricum

Ferrum phos.; ferric phosphate of iron, iron phosphate

Ferrum phos. is one of the SCHUSSLER TISSUE SALTS (*see* GLOSSARY), and the iron phosphate powder is obtained by chemical reaction between sodium phosphate, sodium acetate and iron sulphate. Iron is a very important substance in the body, being found in the haemoglobin pigment of red blood cells that transports oxygen to all the tissues and organs. The homoeopathic remedy is used to treat the early stages of infections, inflammations and feverish conditions, before any other particular symptoms occur. It is used to treat colds and coughs in which there may be a slowly developing fever, headache, nosebleeds, bronchitis, hoarseness and loss of the voice, earache and rheumatic pains. Digestive symptoms such as sour indigestion, inflammation of the stomach (gastritis), and vomiting and some disorders of menstruation are helped by this remedy. It is also used to treat the early symptoms of dysentery. The person tends to be pale but is prone to flushing, and feels cold in the early afternoon. There may be a rapid weak pulse. Symptoms are worse at night and in the early morning between 4 a.m. and 6 a.m. Also, they are worse for heat and hot sun, movement and jarring of the body, pressure and touch and resting on the right side and suppressing sweating by the use of deodorants, etc. Symptoms improve for cold applications and with gentle movements. People who are suitable for Ferrum phos. tend to be thin and pale but may be liable to flush easily. They are intelligent and quick to absorb new concepts, having plenty of original ideas of their own. They may be prone to digestive and respiratory complaints, stomach upsets and coughs and colds.

Gelsemium sempervirens

Gelsemium, yellow jasmine, false jasmine, Carolina
jasmine, wild woodbine

This attractive climbing plant is a native of the southern United
States and parts of Mexico. It has a woody stem that twists
around any available tree trunk, and grows on stream banks
and on the sea coast. It produces attractive, large, bell-shaped,
perfumed yellow flowers in the early spring, which belie the
poisonous nature of the plant. It has an underground stem, or
rhizome, from which arise a tangle of yellow roots that have an
aromatic smell. The root is the part used in homoeopathy and,
if eaten in significant amounts, it affects the central nervous
system, causing paralysis and possible death through failure of
the nerves and muscles of the respiratory system. In homoeopathy it is used to treat both physical and mental symptoms.
The physical ailments treated mainly involve the nervous and
respiratory systems. These include headaches that are worsened with bright light and movement, multiple sclerosis, eye
pain, especially on the right side, sore throat and influenza-like
symptoms, earache and feverish muscular pains. Accompanying symptoms include chills and shivering, flushed face and
malaise. It is used to treat some menstrual problems including
pain. Mental symptoms that are helped by Gelsemium include
fears and phobias with symptoms of fatigue, weakness, trem-
bling and apprehension. These fears may arise before an examination, interview or public performance (stage fright). Excitement or fear that causes the heart to skip a beat and extreme
anxiety causing sleeplessness are helped by Gelsemium. Symptoms are made worse in the sun and in warm, moist, humid
weather or damp and fog. They are also worse with smoking
and for excitement, anticipation, stress or bad news. Symptoms
improve with movement in the fresh air and after sweating and

drinking alcohol or a stimulant drink. They improve after uri-
nating—a large quantity of pale urine is usually passed. People
suitable for Gelsemium tend to be well-built with a blue-tinged
skin and often complain of feeling weak and tired. They are
beset by fears, and may be cowardly and too fearful to lead or
enjoy a normal active life.

Graphites
Graphite; black pencil lead

Graphite is a form of carbon that is the basis of all life. It is
found in older igneous or metamorphic rocks, such as granite
and marble, and is mined for its industrial uses, e.g. in batteries, motors, pencil leads, cleaning and lubricating fluids. It was
investigated and proved by Hahnemann after he learned that it
was being used by some factory workers to heal cold sores.
The powder used in homoeopathy is ground graphite, and it is
mainly used for skin disorders that may be caused by metabolic imbalances and stomach ulcers. It is a remedy for eczema, psoriasis, acne, rough, dry skin conditions with pustules
or blisters, scarring and thickened cracked nails and cold sores.
Also, for stomach ulcers caused by a thinning or weakness in
the lining of the stomach wall, problems caused by excessive
catarrh, loss of hair, and cramping pains or numbing of the feet
and hands. In women it is used to treat some menstrual problems. The symptoms are worse in draughty, cold and damp conditions and for eating sweet meals or sea foods. Also, the use of
steroids for skin complaints and, in women, during menstruation. Symptoms are often worse on the left side. They improve
with warmth as long as the air is fresh and it is not stuffy, when
it is dark and for eating and sleep. People suitable for Graphites
are usually well-built and may be overweight, often having dark
hair. They like to eat well but lack physical fitness, and sweat

or flush with slight exertion. They are prone to dry, flaky skin conditions that may affect the scalp. Graphites people are usually lethargic and may be irritable, lacking in concentration for intellectual activities. They are prone to mood swings and subject to bouts of weeping, especially when listening to music. A Graphites person feels that he or she is unlucky and is inclined to self-pity, often feeling fearful and timid.

Guaiacum officinale
Guaiac, resin of lignum vitae

This attractive evergreen tree is a native of the West Indies and the northern coastal regions of South America. The tree grows to a height of 40-60 feet and produces striking, deep blue flowers. The part used in homoeopathy is a resin obtained from the wood. The wood is unusual in being very dense, which means that it sinks in water, and this property caused much interest when it was first discovered in the Middle Ages. The resin is obtained by firing the cut log, and the melted resin then flows out of a hole made in the wood and is collected. This is allowed to cool and harden, and it is usually exported in large blocks that split readily into glassy fragments. The remedy is used to treat inflammation of the pharynx (pharyngitis) and tonsillitis, being very helpful in relieving painful soreness of the throat. It is particularly indicated where there is foul-smelling sputum and sweating. It is also a remedy for gout and rheumatic conditions with severe and stabbing joint pains. The symptoms are made worse by extremes of heat and cold and damp weather, and also with movement. They may be relieved by rest and keeping warm.

Hamamelis virginiana
Hamamelis, witch hazel, spotted alder, snapping hazelnut, winterbloom

This plant is a native of the eastern United States and Canada but it is also grown in Europe. It is a shrub with grey-green leaves and yellow flowers that appear in the autumn. The part used in homoeopathy is the bark of stems and twigs and the outer part of the fresh root. This has the effect of causing body tissues, especially blood vessels, to contract, and it is used to arrest bleeding. Its curative properties were known to the native North American Indians, and it was first investigated and proved in homoeopathy by Dr Hering. Its main effect is on the blood circulation of the veins, particularly when the walls of the vessels are inflamed and weakened, and bleeding does not stop easily. It is used as a remedy for haemorrhoids, or piles with bleeding, varicose veins and ulcers, phlebitis (inflamed veins), nosebleeds, heavy periods, internal bleeding and pain associated with bruising or bleeding. Some headaches are helped by Hamamelis and, also, mental symptoms of depression, irritability and impatience. The symptoms are made worse by warmth and moisture and with physical activity. They improve out in the fresh air and for concentrating on a particular task or event and for conversation, thinking and reading.

Hepar sulphuris calcareum
Hepar sulph.; sulphide of calcium
This remedy is impure calcium sulphide, which is obtained by heating crushed and powdered oyster shells with flowers of sulphur. This is an old remedy that was, at one time, applied externally to treat swellings caused by tuberculosis, gout, rheumatism and thyroid disorders (goitre) and also itching skin. It was investigated and proved by Hahnemann as a remedy for the toxic effects of mercury, which was widely used by contemporary physicians. It is now used to treat infections and any condition where there is a discharge of foul-smelling pus. It is

used to treat skin conditions where the skin is highly sensitive to touch, such as boils and acne, and also, tonsillitis, sinusitis, earache, sore throat, hoarseness and laryngitis, mouth ulcers and cold sores. A wheezing, croup-like type of cough or chesty cough that may develop into a cold or influenza is helped by Hepar sulph. This remedy helps those who, when ill, tend to produce bodily secretions that have an unpleasant sour smell. During illness, those who benefit from this remedy are irritable, difficult to please and easily offended. They are difficult patients who make unreasonable demands and hate noise or disturbance, being touched or cold air. Symptoms are worse for cold and for getting chilled when undressing during winter and for touch. They improve with warmth and warm applications and for covering the head and for eating a meal. People suitable for Hepar sulph. tend to be overweight, lethargic, with pale skin and often depressed. They feel that life has dealt with them harshly and feel the symptoms of illness and pain acutely. They may appear to be calm but tend to be anxious and restless.

Hypericum perforatum
Hypericum, St John's wort

A perennial herbaceous plant that is a native of Britain, Europe and Asia, but is cultivated throughout the world. It grows between one and three feet in height, producing elongated, oval dark green leaves that appear to be covered in minute spots or holes (hence *perforatum*, or perforate). In fact, these are minute oil-secreting glands that secrete a bright red solution. The large, bright yellow flowers appear in June, July and August and have small black dots around the edges of the petals. The crushed flowers produce a blood-coloured juice that was used, in early times, to treat raw wounds. It was also believed that the plant could be hung up to ward off evil spirits (the name *Hypericum* being derived from the Greek, meaning 'over an apparition'). There are two traditions associated with the common name, St John's wort. One links the plant with 29 August, believed to be the anniversary of the execution of St John the Baptist. The other is that the plant is named after an ancient order of knights going back to the time of the Crusades, the knights of St John of Jerusalem.

The whole fresh green plant and flowers are used in homoeopathy to produce the mother tincture. It is mainly used to treat damage to nerves and nerve pain following accidental injury. Typically, there are shooting, stabbing pains that radiate upwards, and it is indicated especially where there are many nerve endings concentrated in a particular part of the body, e.g. the fingers and toes. It is very effective in pains associated with the spinal nerves and spinal cord, concussion, head or eye injuries. It is also a remedy for wounds and lacerations producing stabbing pains indicating nerve damage, and accidental crushing injuries. It is useful for bites, stings, splinters and puncture wounds, toothache and pain following dental extractions. In addition, it is a treatment for asthma and some digestive complaints of indigestion, sickness and diarrhoea. It is sometimes helpful in the treatment of piles, or haemorrhoids, and some menstrual problems with accompanying headache. The symptoms are made worse by cold, damp or foggy weather, before a storm and getting chilled when undressing. Also for touch and for a close, stuffy atmosphere. Symptoms improve when the person remains still and tilts the head backwards.

Ignatia amara
Agnate; *Strychnos ignatii*, St Ignatius' bean
Ignatia amara is a large tree that is native to the Philippine

Islands, China and the East Indies. The tree has many branches and twining stems and produces stalked white flowers. Later, seed pods are produced, each containing ten to twenty large, oval seeds, that are about one inch long and are embedded in pulp. The seeds are highly poisonous and contain strychnine, which affects the central nervous system. Similar active constituents and properties are found in nux vomica. The tree is named after the founder of the Jesuits, Ignatius Loyola (1491-1556), and Spanish priests belonging to this order brought the seeds to Europe during the 1600s. The homoeopathic remedy is made from the powdered seeds and is used especially for emotional symptoms. It is used for grief, bereavement, shock and loss, particularly when a person is having difficulty coming to terms with his or her feelings and is inclined to suppress the natural responses. Accompanying symptoms include sleeplessness, anger and hysteria. Similar emotional and psychological problems are helped by this remedy, including anxiety and fear, especially of appearing too forward to others, a tendency to burst into fits of crying, self-doubt, pity and blame, and depression. Nervous tension headaches and digestive upsets, feverish symptoms, chills and pains in the abdomen may be helped by Ignatia. Some problems associated with menstruation, especially sharp pains or absence of periods are relieved by this remedy, as are conditions with changeable symptoms. These are worse in cold weather or conditions, with emotional trauma, being touched, for smoking and drinking coffee. They improve with warmth, moving about, eating, lying on the side or area that is painful and after passing urine.

The person for whom Ignatia is suitable is usually female and with a tendency towards harsh, self criticism and blame; she is usually a creative artistic person, highly sensitive but with a tendency to suppress the emotions. She is perceptive and intelligent but inclined to be hysterical and subject to erratic swings of mood. Typically, the person expects a high standard in those she loves. The person enjoys dairy products, bread and sour foods but sweets, alcoholic drinks and fruit upset her system. She is afraid of crowds, tends to be claustrophobic, and fears being burgled. Also, she is afraid of being hurt emotionally, and is very sensitive to pain. The person is usually dark-haired and of slim build with a worried expression and prone to sighing, yawning and excessive blinking.

Ipecacuanha

Ipecac.; *Cephaelis ipecacuanha, Psychotria ipecacuanha,* the ipecac plant

This plant is a native of South America, particularly Brazil, Bolivia and New Grenada. The plant contains the alkaloids emetine and cephaeline, and different varieties contain differing proportions of these alkaloids. The root is the part used in homoeopathy, and the preparations may be in a number of different forms. It is used to treat conditions where the main symptoms are nausea and vomiting, which are intractable and persistent, e.g. motion sickness and morning sickness. It is also used as a remedy for bronchitis, breathlessness because of the presence of fluid in the lung, whooping cough and heart failure. The symptoms are made worse by cold weather and lying down, and after a meal of pork or veal. They improve in the fresh open air and while resting with the eyes shut.

Kalium bichromicum

Kali bich.; potassium dichromate, potassium bichromate

This substance has several uses in industry (e.g. in the preparations of dyes and in batteries) as well as its medicinal purposes. The crystals of potassium dichromate are bright orange and are prepared from a chemical reaction involving the addition of a solution of potassium chromate to an acid. It is used for discharges of mucus and disorders of the mucous membranes, particularly involving the vagina and genital and urinary tracts, throat, nose and stomach. The remedy is useful for catarrhal colds and sinusitis, feelings of fullness and pressure, headache, migraine and glue ear. Also, for joint and rheumatic disorders with pains that may move about or even disappear. People who benefit from this remedy are highly sensitive to cold and chills when ill, but also experience a worsening of symptoms in hot, sunny conditions. They tend to be people who adhere very closely to a regular routine and may be somewhat rigid and inflexible. They like everything to be done properly down to the smallest detail and are law-abiding, moral and conformist. Symptoms are worse during the summer and also in wet and chilly conditions. They are at their height in the early hours of the morning between 3 and 5 a.m., and also on first waking up. Drinking alcohol and becoming chilled while taking off clothes exacerbates the symptoms. They improve with moving around and after eating a meal. Also, symptoms improve with warmth and heat (but not hot sun) and after vomiting.

Kalium iodatum
Kali iod.; *Kali hydriodicum*, potassium iodide
This is prepared by chemical reaction from potassium hydroxide and iodine and is an old remedy for syphilis. It is recommended that potassium iodide should be added to animal feed concentrates and table salt to prevent deficiency in iodine. The homoeopathic remedy is used to relieve catarrh in those who are prone to chesty conditions. It is also used to treat swollen glands, sore throats, sinusitis, hay fever and influenza-type infections. It is used to treat male prostate gland disorders. The

symptoms tend to improve with movement and from being out
in the fresh air. They are made worse by heat and touch and are
at their most severe between two and five in the early morning.
People who suit this remedy tend to be dogmatic, knowing exactly what they think about a particular subject. They may be
irritable or bad-tempered and not easy to get along with. They
have a preference for cool rather than warm or hot weather.

Kalium phosphoricum

Kali phos.; potassium phosphate, phosphate of potash
This remedy is one of the SCHUSSLER TISSUE SALTS (*see* GLOS-
SARY), and it is obtained from a chemical reaction between dilute phosphoric acid and solution of potassium carbonate. Potassium carbonate is derived from potash, the white powder
that is left when wood is burnt completely. Potassium is an essential element in the body, vital for the healthy functioning of
nerve tissue. Kali phos. is used to treat mental and physical
exhaustion and depression, particularly in young persons in
whom it may have been caused by too much work or studying.
Accompanying symptoms include jumping at noise or interruption and a desire to be alone. Also, there may be a pus-con-
taining discharge from the bladder, vagina, bowels or lungs and
extreme muscular fatigue. They may suffer from gnawing hun-
ger pains, anxiety, insomnia, tremor and have a tendency to
perspire on the face when excited or after a meal. People who
are suitable for Kali phos. are usually extrovert, hold clearly
formed ideas and are easily exhausted. They become distressed
by bad news, including that which does not affect them directly,
such as a disaster in another country. They tend to crave sweet
foods and dislike bread. Symptoms are made worse by any anxiety, in cold, dry weather and in winter and on drinking cold
drinks. Also, they are exacerbated by noise, conversation, touch

and physical activity. Symptoms improve with heat, gentle exercise, in cloudy conditions and after eating.

Lachesis
Trigonocephalus lachesis, *Lachesis muta*, venom of the bushmaster or surukuku snake

This South African snake produces a deadly venom that may prove instantly fatal because of its effects upon the heart. The venom causes the blood to thin and flow more freely, hence increasing the likelihood of haemorrhage. Even a slight bite bleeds copiously with a risk of blood poisoning or septicaemia. The snake is a ferocious hunter, and its African name, surukuku, describes the sound it makes while in pursuit of prey. The properties of the venom were investigated by the eminent American homoeopathic doctor Constantine Hering during the 1800s. He tested and proved the remedy on himself. It is effective in treating a variety of disorders, particularly those relating to the blood circulation and where there is a risk of blood poisoning, or septicaemia. It is used to treat varicose veins and problems of the circulation indicated by a bluish tinge to the skin. The remedy is useful for those suffering from a weak heart or angina, palpitations and an irregular, fast or weak pulse. There may be symptoms of chest pain and breathing difficulty. It is of great benefit in treating uterine problems, particularly premenstrual congestion and pain that is relieved once the period starts. It is also an excellent remedy for menopausal symptoms, especially hot flushes, and for infections of the bladder and rectum. It is used to treat conditions and infections where symptoms are mainly on the left side, such as headache or stroke. Also, as a treatment for sore throats and throat infections, tonsillitis, lung abscess, boils, ulcers, wounds that heal slowly, vomiting because of appendicitis and digestive disorders, fevers with chills and shivering, nosebleeds and bleeding piles.

It is used to treat severe symptoms of measles and serious infections including scarlet fever and smallpox. Symptoms are made worse by touch and after sleep and by tight clothing. They are worse for hot drinks and baths, exposure to hot sun or direct heat in any form. For women, symptoms are worse during the menopause. They improve for being out in the fresh air and drinking cold drinks and for release of normal bodily discharges. People suitable for Lachesis tend to be intelligent, creative, intense and ambitious. They have strong views about politics and world affairs and may be impatient of the views of others. They may be somewhat self-centred, possessive and jealous, which can cause problems in close relationships with others. They dislike being tied down and so may be reluctant to commit themselves to a relationship. Lachesis people have a liking for sour pickled foods, bread, rice and oysters and alcoholic drinks. They like coffee, but hot drinks and wheat-based food tends to upset them. They have a fear of water, people they do not know, being burgled and of dying or being suffocated. Lachesis people may be somewhat overweight and are sometimes red-haired and freckled. Alternatively, they may be thin and dark-haired, pale and with a lot of energy. Children tend to be somewhat jealous of others and possessive of their friends, which can lead to naughty or trying behaviour.

Ledum palustre
Ledum; marsh tea, wild rosemary

Wild rosemary is an evergreen shrub that grows in the bogs and cold upland conditions of the northern United States, Canada and northern Europe, especially Scandinavia, Ireland and parts of Asia. The bush produces elongated, dark green leaves, about one or two inches long, that are smooth and shiny on the upper surface but underneath are covered with brown woolly hairs. ('Ledum' is derived from the Greek word *ledos*, meaning 'woolly robe'). The leaves contain a volatile, aromatic oil like camphor, and the plant has been used for centuries by Scandinavian people to repel insects, moths and mice. The plant produces attractive white flowers and is valued for its antiseptic properties. The fresh parts of the plant are gathered, dried and ground to make a powder used in homoeopathy, and it is a valuable first aid remedy. It is taken internally for animal bites, insect stings, lacerations and wounds in which there is bruising and sharp stabbing pains. There is usually inflammation, redness, swelling and throbbing accompanied by feverish symptoms of chills and shivering. It is additionally used as a remedy for gout in the big toe, rheumatic pains in the feet that radiate upwards, hot, painful, stiff joints and tendons but with cold skin. People who benefit from this remedy tend to get hot and sweaty at night when ill, and usually throw off the bed coverings. They often have itchy skin on the feet and ankles and have a tendency to sprain their ankles. When ill, they are irritable and hard to please or may be withdrawn, and do not want the company of others. The symptoms are made worse by warmth or heat, touch and at night. They improve with cold applications to the painful part and for cool conditions.

Lycopodium clavatum

Lycopodium; club moss, wolf's claw, vegetable sulphur, stag's-horn moss, running pine

This plant is found throughout the northern hemisphere, in high moorlands, forests and mountains. The plant produces spore cases on the end of upright forked stalks, which contain the spores. These produce yellow dust or powder that is resistant to

water and was once used as a coating on pills and tablets to
keep them separate from one another. The powder was also
used as a constituent of fireworks. It has been used medicinally
for many centuries, as a remedy for digestive disorders and
kidney stones in Arabian countries and in the treatment of gout.
The powder and spores are collected by shaking the fresh, flowering stalks of the plant, and its main use in homoeopathy is for
digestive and kidney disorders. It is used to treat indigestion,
heartburn, the effects of eating a large meal late at night, sickness, nausea, wind, bloatedness and constipation. Also, in men,
for kidney stones, with the production of a red-coloured urine
containing a sand-like sediment and enlarged prostate gland. It
is used in the treatment of some problems of male impotence
and bleeding haemorrhoids, or piles. Symptoms that occur on
the right side are helped by Lycopodium, and the patient additionally tends to crave sweet, comfort foods. Nettle rash, psoriasis affecting the hands, fatigue because of illness and ME
(myalgic encephalomyelitis), some types of headache, cough
and sore throat are relieved by this remedy. It is used to relieve
emotional states of anxiety, fear and apprehension caused by
chronic insecurity or relating to forthcoming events, such as
taking an examination or appearing in public (stage fright). Also,
night terrors, sleeplessness, shouting or talking in the sleep and
being frightened on first waking up can all benefit from this
treatment.

The symptoms are worse between 4 p.m. and 8 p.m. and in
warm, stuffy rooms and with wearing clothes that are too tight.
They are also worse in the early morning between 4 a.m. and 8
a.m., for eating too much and during the spring. They improve
outside in cool fresh air, after a hot meal or drink and with
loosening tight clothing, with light exercise and at night. People suitable for Lycopodium tend to be serious, hard-working

and intelligent, often in professional positions. They seem to be self-possessed and confident but are in reality rather insecure with a low self-opinion. They are impatient of what they perceive as being weakness and are not tolerant or sympathetic of illness. Lycopodium people are sociable but may keep their distance and not get involved; they may be sexually promiscuous. They have a great liking for sweet foods of all kinds and enjoy hot meals and drinks. They are easily filled but may carry on eating regardless of this and usually complain of symptoms on the right side. Lycopodium people are afraid of being left on their own, of failure in life, of crowds, darkness and the supernatural, and tend to be claustrophobic. They are often tall, thin and pale with receding hair or hair that turns grey early in life. They may be bald, with a forehead lined with worry lines and a serious appearance. They tend to have weak muscles and are easily tired after physical exercise. They may have a tendency to unconsciously twitch the muscles of the face and to flare the nostrils.

Mercurius solubilis
Merc. sol.; quicksilver

The mineral cinnabar, which is found in volcanic crystalline rocks, is an important ore of mercury and is extracted for a variety of uses, including dental fillings and in thermometers. Mercury is toxic in large doses, and an affected person produces great quantities of saliva and suffers repeated bouts of vomiting. Mercury has been used since ancient times and was once given as a remedy for syphilis. A powder of precipitate of mercury is obtained from dissolving liquid mercury in a dilute solution of nitric acid, and this is the source of the remedy used in homoeopathy. It is used as a remedy for conditions that produce copious bodily secretions that often smell unpleasant, with accompanying symptoms of heat or burning and a great sensitivity to temperature. It is used as a remedy for fevers with profuse, unpleasant sweating, bad breath, inflammation of the gums, mouth ulcers, candidiasis (fungal infection) of the mouth, infected painful teeth and gums, and excessive production of saliva. Also, for a sore infected throat, tonsillitis, mumps, discharging infected ear, and a congested severe headache and pains in the joints. It is good for eye complaints, including severe conjunctivitis, allergic conditions with a running nose, skin complaints that produce pus-filled pustules, spots, and ulcers, including varicose ulcers. The symptoms are made worse by extremes of heat and cold and also by wet and rapidly changing weather. They are worse at night and for sweating and being too hot in bed.

Symptoms improve with rest and in comfortable temperatures where the person is neither too hot nor too cold. People suitable for Merc. sol. tend to be very insecure although they have an outwardly calm appearance. They are cautious and reserved with other people and consider what they are about to say before speaking so that conversation may seem laboured. Merc. sol. types do not like criticism of any kind and may suddenly become angry if someone disagrees with their point of view. They tend to be introverted, but their innermost thoughts may be in turmoil. They tend to be hungry and enjoy bread and butter, milk and other cold drinks but dislike alcohol with the exception of beer. They usually do not eat meat and do not have a sweet tooth. They dislike coffee and salt. Merc. sol. people often have fair hair with fine, unlined skin and an air of detachment. They are afraid of dying and of mental illness leading to insanity, and worry about the wellbeing of their family. They fear being burgled and are afraid or fearful during a thunderstorm.

Natrum muriaticum

Natrum mur.; common salt, sodium chloride

Salt has long been prized for its seasoning and preservative qualities, and Roman soldiers were once paid in salt, such was its value (the word 'salary' comes from the Latin word *salarium*, which refers to this practice). Sodium and chlorine are essential chemicals in the body, being needed for many metabolic processes, particularly the functioning of nerve tissue. In fact, there is seldom a need to add salt to food as usually enough is present naturally in a healthy, well-balanced diet. (An exception is when people are working very hard physically in a hot climate and losing a lot of salt in sweat). However, people and many other mammals frequently have a great liking for salt. If the salt/water balance in the body is disturbed, a person soon becomes very ill and may even die.

In ancient times, salt was usually obtained by boiling sea water, but natural evaporation around the shallow edges of salt lakes results in deposits of rock salt being formed. Rock salt is the usual source of table salt and also of the remedy used in homoeopathy. This remedy has an effect on the functioning of the kidneys and the salt/water balance of body fluids, and is used to treat both mental and physical symptoms. Emotional symptoms that benefit from Natrum mur. include sensitivity and irritability, tearfulness and depression, suppressed grief and premenstrual tension. Physical ailments that respond to this remedy are often those in which there is a thin, watery discharge of mucus and in which symptoms are made worse by heat. Hence Natrum mur. is used in the treatment of colds with a runny nose or other catarrhal problems. Also, for some menstrual and vaginal problems, headaches and migraines, cold sores, candidiasis (fungal infection) of the mouth, mouth ulcers, inflamed and infected gums and bad breath. Some skin disorders are helped by Natrum mur., including verruca (a wart on the foot), warts, spots and boils, and cracked, dry lips. It may be used in the treatment of fluid retention with puffiness around the face, eyelids and abdomen, etc, urine retention, constipation, anal fissure, indigestion, anaemia and thyroid disorders (goitre). When ill, people who benefit from this remedy feel cold and shivery, but their symptoms are made worse, or even brought on, by heat. Heat, whether from hot sun and fire or a warm, stuffy room, exacerbate the symptoms, which also are made worse by cold and thundery weather. They are worse on the coast from the sea breeze, and in the morning between 9 and 11 o'clock. Too much physical activity and the sympathy of others exacerbate the symptoms. They improve in the fresh, open air and for cold applications or a cold bath or swim. Also, sleeping on a hard bed and sweating and fasting make the symptoms better. People suitable for Natrum mur. are often women who are highly sensitive, serious-minded, intelligent and reliable. They have high ideals and feel things very deeply, being easily hurt and stung by slights and criticism. They need the company of other people but, being so sensitive, can actually shun them for fear of being hurt. They are afraid of mental illness leading to loss of self-control and insanity, and of dying. Also, they fear the dark, failure in work, crowds, being burgled and have a tendency to be claustrophobic. They worry about being late and are fearful during a thunderstorm. Merc. sol. people tend to become introverted and react badly to the criticism of others. They are highly sensitive to the influence of music, which easily moves them to tears. Natrum mur. people are usually of squat or solid build with dark or fairish hair. They are prone to reddened, watery eyes as though they have been crying, and a cracked lower lip. The face may appear puffy and shiny with an air of stoicism.

Nux vomica
Strychnos nux vomica; poison nut, Quaker buttons

The *Strychnos nux vomica* tree is a native of India but also grows in Burma, Thailand, China and Australia. It produces small, greenish-white flowers and, later, apple-sized fruits, containing small, flat, circular pale seeds covered in fine hair. The seeds, bark and leaves are highly poisonous, containing strychnine, and have been used in medicine for many centuries. In medieval times, the seeds were used as a treatment for the plague. Strychnine has severe effects upon the nervous system but in minute amounts can help increase urination and aid digestion. The seeds are cleaned and dried and used to produce the homoeopathic remedy. Nux vomica is used in the treatment of a variety of digestive complaints, including cramping, colicky abdominal pains, indigestion, nausea and vomiting, diarrhoea and constipation. Also, indigestion or stomach upset caused by overindulgence in alcohol or rich food and piles, which cause painful contractions of the rectum. Sometimes these complaints are brought on by a tendency to keep emotions, particularly anger, suppressed and not allowing it to show or be expressed outwardly. Nux vomica is a remedy for irritability, headache and migraine, colds, coughs and influenza-like symptoms of fever, aching bones and muscles and chills and shivering. It is a useful remedy for women who experience heavy, painful periods that may cause fainting, morning sickness during pregnancy and pain in labour. It is also used to treat urinary frequency and cystitis.

The type of person who benefits from this remedy is frequently under stress and experiences a periodic flare-up of symptoms. The person may be prone to indigestion and heartburn, gastritis and stomach ulcer, and piles, or haemorrhoids. The person usually has a tendency to keep everything bottled up but has a passionate nature and is liable to outbursts of anger. Nux vomica people are very ambitious and competitive, demanding a high standard of themselves and others and intolerant of anything less than perfection. They enjoy challenges and using their wits to keep one step ahead. Often they are to be found as managers, company directors, scientists, etc, at the cutting edge of their particular occupation. They are ungracious and irritable when ill and cannot abide the criticism of others. This type of person is afraid of being a failure at work and fears or dislikes crowded public places. He or she is afraid of dying. The person enjoys rich, fattening foods containing cholesterol and spicy meals, alcohol and coffee, although these upset the digestive system. Symptoms are worse in cold, windy, dry weather and in winter and in the early morning between 3 and 4 a.m. They are aggravated by certain noises, music, bright lights and touch, eating (especially spicy meals) and overwork of mental faculties. Nux vomica people usually look serious, tense and are thin with a worried expression. They have sallow skin and tend to have dark shadows beneath the eyes.

Phosphorus
Phos; white phosphorus
Phosphorus is an essential mineral in the body found in the genetic material (DNA), bones and teeth. White phosphorus is extremely flammable and poisonous and was once used in the manufacture of matches and fireworks. As it tends to catch fire spontaneously when exposed to air, it is stored under water. In the past it has been used to treat a number of disorders and infectious diseases such as measles. In homoeopathy, the remedy is used to treat nervous tension caused by stress and worry, with symptoms of sleeplessness, exhaustion and digestive upset. Often there are pains of a burning nature in the chest or

abdomen. It is a remedy for vomiting and nausea, heartburn, acid indigestion, stomach ulcer and gastroenteritis. It is also used to treat bleeding, e.g. from minor wounds, the gums, nosebleeds, gastric and profuse menstrual bleeding.

Severe coughs, which may be accompanied by retching, vomiting and production of a blood-tinged phlegm, are treated with Phos. as well as some other severe respiratory complaints. These include pneumonia, bronchitis, asthma and laryngitis. Styes that tend to recur and poor circulation may be helped by Phos. Symptoms are worse in the evening and morning and before or during a thunderstorm. They are also made worse for too much physical activity, hot food and drink and lying on the left side. Symptoms improve in the fresh open air and with lying on the back or right side. They are better after sleep or when the person is touched or stroked. People who need Phos. do not like to be alone when ill and improve with the sympathy and attention of others. They are warm, kind, affectionate people who are highly creative, imaginative and artistic. They enjoy the company of other people and need stimulation to give impetus to their ideas. Phos. people have an optimistic outlook, are full of enthusiasm but sometimes promise much and deliver little. They are very tactile and like to be touched or stroked and offered sympathy when unhappy or unwell. They enjoy a variety of different foods but tend to suffer from digestive upsets. Phos. people are usually tall, slim and may be dark or fair-haired, with an attractive, open appearance. They like to wear brightly coloured clothes and are usually popular. They have a fear of illness, especially cancer, and of dying and also of the dark and supernatural forces. They are apprehensive of water and fear being a failure in their work. Thunderstorms make them nervous.

Pulsatilla nigricans

Pulsatilla, *Anemone pratensis*, meadow anemone

This attractive plant closely resembles *Anemone pulsatilla*, the pasqueflower, which is used in herbal medicine but has smaller flowers. *Anemone pratensis* is a native of Germany, Denmark and Scandinavia and has been used medicinally for hundreds of years. The plant produces beautiful deep purple flowers with orange centres and both leaves and flowers are covered with fine, silky hairs. The whole fresh plant is gathered and made into a pulp, and liquid is extracted to make the homoeopathic remedy. It is used to treat a wide variety of disorders with both physical and mental symptoms. It is useful for ailments in which there is a greenish, yellowish discharge. Hence it is used for colds and coughs and sinusitis with the production of profuse catarrh or phlegm. Also, eye infections with discharge such as styes and conjunctivitis. Digestive disorders are helped by it, particularly indigestion, heartburn, nausea and sickness caused by eating too much fatty or rich food. The remedy is helpful for female disorders in which there are a variety of physical and emotional symptoms. These include premenstrual tension, menstrual problems, menopausal symptoms and cystitis, with accompanying symptoms of mood swings, depression and tearfulness. It is a remedy for headaches and migraine, swollen glands, inflammation and pain in the bones and joints as in rheumatic and arthritic disorders, nosebleeds, varicose veins, mumps, measles, toothache, acne, frequent urination and incontinence.

Symptoms are worse at night or when it is hot, and after eating heavy, rich food. Symptoms improve out in the cool fresh air and for gentle exercise such as walking. The person feels better after crying and being treated sympathetically by others. Pulsatilla people are usually women who have a mild, passive nature and are kind, gentle and loving. They are easily moved to tears by the plight of others and love animals and people alike. The person yields easily to the requests and demands of others and is a peacemaker who likes to avoid a scene. An outburst of anger is very much out of character, and a Pulsatilla person usually has many friends. The person likes rich and sweet foods, although these may upset the digestion, and dislikes spicy meals. Pulsatilla people may fear darkness, being left alone, dying and any illness leading to insanity. They are fearful of crowds, the supernatural and tend to be claustrophobic. Usually, they are fair and blue-eyed with clear, delicate skin that blushes readily. They are attractive and slightly overweight or plump.

Rhus toxicodendron

Rhus tox.; *Rhus radicaris*, American poison ivy, poison oak, poison vine.

This large bush or small tree is a native species of the United States and Canada. Its leaves are extremely irritant to the touch, causing an inflamed and painful rash, swelling and ulceration. Often the person experiences malaise, swollen glands, headache, feverishness and a lack of appetite. The plant produces white flowers with a green or yellow tinge in June, followed later by clusters of berries. The fresh leaves are gathered and pulped to make the remedy used in homoeopathy. It is used especially as a treatment for skin rashes and lesions with hot, burning sensations and also for inflammation of muscles and joints. Hence it is used to treat eczema, chilblains, cold sores, shingles, nappy rash and other conditions in which there is a dry, scaling or blistered skin. Also, for rheumatism, sciatica, lumbago, gout, synovitis (inflammation of the synovial membranes surrounding joints), osteoarthritis, ligament and tendon strains. Feverish symptoms caused by viral infections, such as high temperature, chills and shivering, swollen, watering eyes, aching joints, nausea and vomiting, may be helped by Rhus tox. Some menstrual problems, including heavy bleeding and abdominal pains that are relieved by lying down, benefit from this remedy. People who are helped by Rhus tox tend to be depressed and miserable when ill, with a tendency to burst into tears, and are highly susceptible to cold, damp weather. Usually they have a dry, irritating cough and thirst and are irritable, anxious and restless. The symptoms are made worse in stormy, wet, windy weather and at night, and when the person moves after a period of rest. Also, for becoming chilled when undressing. Warm, dry conditions and gentle exercise improve and lessen the symptoms. Rhus tox people may be initially shy in company, but when they lose this are charming, entertaining and lively and make friends easily. They are usually conscientious and highly motivated and serious about their work to the extent of being somewhat workaholic. Rhus tox people often have an inner restlessness and become depressed and moody when affected by illness. They may be prone to carry out small compulsive rituals in order to function.

Ruta graveolens

Ruta grav.; rue, garden rue, herbygrass, ave-grace, herb-of-grace, bitter herb

This hardy, evergreen plant is a native of southern Europe but has been cultivated in Britain for centuries, having been first brought here by the Romans. It thrives in poor soil in a dry and partially shaded situation, producing yellow-green flowers. The whole plant has a distinctive, pungent, unpleasant smell and was once used to repel insects, pestilence and infections. It has been used medicinally throughout history to treat ailments in both animals and people, and was used to guard against the plague. It was believed to be effective in guarding against witchcraft, and Hippocrates recommended it as an antidote to poisoning. Rue was believed to have beneficial effects on sight and was used by the great artists, such as Michelangelo, to keep vision sharp. In the Catholic High Mass, brushes made from rue were once used to sprinkle the holy water, hence the name herb-of-grace. Taken internally in large doses, rue has toxic effects causing vomiting, a swollen tongue, fits and delirium.

The homoeopathic remedy is prepared from the sap of the green parts of the plant before the flowers open. It is indicated especially for bone and joint injuries and disorders, and those affecting tendons, ligaments and muscles where there is severe, deep, tearing pain. Hence it is used for synovitis (inflammation of the synovial membranes lining joints), rheumatism, sprains, strains, bruising, fractures and dislocations and also sciatica. Also, it is a useful remedy for eyestrain with tired, aching eyes, redness and inflammation and headache. Chest problems may be relieved by Ruta grav., particularly painful deep coughs, and some problems affecting the rectum, such as prolapse. Pain and infection in the socket of a tooth after dental extraction may be helped by this remedy. A person who is ill and who benefits from Ruta grav. tends to feel low, anxious, depressed and dissatisfied both with himself (or herself) and others. The symptoms are usually worse in cold, damp weather, for resting and lying down and for exercise out of doors. They improve with heat and gentle movement indoors.

Sepia officinalis
Sepia; ink of the cuttlefish

Cuttlefish ink has been used since ancient times, both for medicinal purposes and as a colour in artists' paint. The cuttlefish has the ability to change colour to blend in with its surroundings and squirts out the dark brown-black ink when threatened by predators. Sepia was known to Roman physicians who used it as a cure for baldness. In homoeopathy it is mainly used as an excellent remedy for women experiencing menstrual and menopausal problems. It was investigated and proved by Hahnemann in 1834. It is used to treat premenstrual tension, menstrual pain and heavy bleeding, infrequent or suppressed periods, menopausal symptoms such as hot flushes, and postnatal depression. Physical and emotional symptoms caused by an imbalance of hormones are helped by Sepia. Also, conditions in which there is extreme fatigue or exhaustion with muscular aches and pains. Digestive complaints, including nausea and sickness, abdominal pain and wind, caused by eating dairy products, and headaches with giddiness and nausea are relieved by Sepia. Also, it is a remedy for incontinence, hot, sweaty feet and verruca (a wart on the foot). A woman often experiences pelvic, dragging pains frequently associated with prolapse of the womb. Disorders of the circulation, especially varicose veins and cold extremities, benefit from sepia.

Symptoms are worse in cold weather and before a thunderstorm, and in the late afternoon, evening and early in the morning. Also, before a period in women and if the person receives sympathy from others. The symptoms are better with heat and warmth, quick vigorous movements, having plenty to do and out in the fresh open air. People suitable for Sepia are usually, but not exclusively, women. They tend to be tall, thin and with a yellowish complexion, and are rather self-contained and indifferent to others. Sepia people may become easily cross, especially with family and close friends, and harbour resentment. In company, they make a great effort to appear outgoing and love to dance. A woman may be either an externally hard, successful career person or someone who constantly feels unable to cope, especially with looking after the home and family. Sepia people have strongly held beliefs and cannot stand others taking a contrary opinion. When ill, they hate to be fussed over or have the sympathy of others. They like both sour and sweet foods and alcoholic drinks but are upset by milk products and fatty meals. They harbour deep insecurity and fear being left alone, illness resulting in madness, and loss of their material possessions and wealth. One physical attribute is that they often have a brown mark in the shape of a saddle across the bridge of the nose.

Silicea terra
Silicea; silica

Silica is one of the main rock-forming minerals and is also found in living things, where its main function is to confer strength and resilience. In homoeopathy, it is used to treat disorders of the skin, nails and bones and recurring inflammations and infections, especially those that occur because the person is somewhat rundown or has an inadequate diet. Also, some disorders of the nervous system are relieved by Silicea. The homoeopathic remedy used to be derived from ground flint or quartz but is now prepared by chemical reaction. The remedy is used for catarrhal infections such as colds, influenza, sinusitis, ear infections including glue ear. Also, for inflammations producing pus, such as a boil, carbuncle, abscess, stye, whitlow (infection of the fingernail) and peritonsillar abscess. It is beneficial in helping the natural expulsion of a foreign body, such as a splinter in the skin. It is a remedy for a headache beginning at the back of the head and radiating forwards over the right eye, and for stress-related conditions of overwork and sleeplessness.

Symptoms are worse for cold, wet weather, especially when

clothing is inadequate, draughts, swimming and bathing, becoming chilled after removing clothes and in the morning. They are better for warmth and heat, summer weather, warm clothing, particularly a hat or head covering, and not lying on the left side. People who are suitable for Silicea tend to be thin with a fine build and pale skin. They often have thin straight hair. They are prone to dry, cracked skin and nails and may suffer from skin infections. Silicea people are usually unassuming, and lacking in confidence and physical stamina. They are conscientious and hard-working to the point of working too hard once a task has been undertaken. However, they may hesitate to commit themselves through lack of confidence and fear of responsibility. Silicea people are tidy and obsessive about small details. They may feel 'put upon' but lack the courage to speak out, and may take this out on others who are not responsible for the situation. They fear failure and dislike exercise because of physical weakness, often feeling mentally and physically exhausted. They enjoy cold foods and drinks.

Sulphur
Sulphur, flowers of sulphur, brimstone
Sulphur has a long history of use in medicine going back to very ancient times. Sulphur gives off sulphur dioxide when burnt, which smells unpleasant ('rotten eggs' odour) but acts as a disinfectant. This was used in mediaeval times to limit the spread of infectious diseases. Sulphur is deposited around the edges of hot springs and geysers and where there is volcanic activity. Flowers of sulphur, which is a bright yellow powder, is obtained from the natural mineral deposit and is used to make the homoeopathic remedy. Sulphur is found naturally in all body tissues, and in both orthodox medicine and homoeopathy is used to treat skin disorders. It is a useful remedy for dermatitis, ec-

zema, psoriasis and a dry, flaky, itchy skin or scalp. Some digestive disorders benefit from it, especially a tendency for food to rise back up to the mouth and indigestion caused by drinking milk. Sulphur is helpful in the treatment of haemorrhoids, or piles, premenstrual and menopausal symptoms, eye inflammations such as conjunctivitis, pain in the lower part of the back, catarrhal colds and coughs, migraine headaches and feverish symptoms. Some mental symptoms are helped by this remedy, particularly those brought about by stress or worry, including depression, irritability, insomnia and lethargy. When ill, people who benefit from sulphur feel thirsty rather than hungry and are upset by unpleasant smells. The person soon becomes exhausted and usually sleeps poorly at night and is tired through the day. The symptoms are worse in cold, damp conditions, in the middle of the morning around 11 a.m., and in stuffy, hot, airless rooms. Also, for becoming too hot at night in bed and for wearing too many layers of clothes. Long periods of standing and sitting aggravate the symptoms, and they are worse if the person drinks alcohol or has a wash. Symptoms improve in dry, clear, warm weather and for taking exercise. They are better if the person lies on the right side.

Sulphur people tend to look rather untidy and have dry, flaky skin and coarse, rough hair. They may be thin, round-shouldered and inclined to slouch or be overweight, round and red-faced. Sulphur people have lively, intelligent minds full of schemes and inventions, but are often useless on a practical level. They may be somewhat self-centred with a need to be praised, and fussy over small unimportant details. They enjoy intellectual discussion on subjects that they find interesting and may become quite heated although the anger soon subsides. Sulphur people are often warm and generous with their time and money. They enjoy a wide range of foods but are upset by milk and eggs. They have a fear of being a failure in their work, of heights and the supernatural.

Tarentula cubensis
Tarentula cub.; Cuban tarantula
The bite of the Cuban tarantula spider produces a delayed response in the victim. About 24 hours after a bite, the site becomes inflamed and red, and swelling, fever and abscess follow. The homoeopathic remedy, made from the poison of the spider, is used to treat similar septic conditions, such as an abscess, boil, carbuncle or whitlow (an infection of the fingernail) and genital itching. Also, it is a remedy for anthrax and shock, and is of value as a last-resort treatment in severe conditions. The infected areas are often tinged blue, and there may be burning sensations of pain that are especially severe at night. It is of particular value in the treatment of recurring boils or carbuncles. The symptoms tend to improve with smoking and are made worse by physical activity and consuming cold drinks.

Thuja occidentalis
Thuja; tree of life, yellow cedar, arbor vitae, false white
  cedar
This coniferous, evergreen tree is a native species of the northern United States and Canada and grows to a height of about 30 feet. It has feathery green leaves with a strong, aromatic smell resembling that of camphor. The leaves and twigs were used by the Indian peoples to treat a variety of infections and disorders, and the plant has long been used in herbal medicine. It is an important remedy in aromatherapy. The fresh green leaves and twigs are used to prepare the homoeopathic remedy, which is especially valuable in the treatment of warts and wartlike tumours on any part of the body. It is a useful remedy for shin-

gles and also has an effect on the genital and urinary tracts. Hence it is used to treat inflammations and infections such as cystitis and urethritis and also pain on ovulation. It may be given as a remedy for infections of the mouth, teeth and gums, catarrh and for tension headaches.

People who benefit from Thuja tend to sweat profusely, and it helps to alleviate this symptom. They tend to suffer from insomnia and when they do manage to sleep, may talk or cry out. They are prone to severe left-sided frontal headaches that may be present on waking in the morning. Symptoms are worse at night, from being too hot in bed and after breakfast. Also, at 3 a.m. and 3 p.m. and in weather that is cold and wet. Symptoms are felt more severely on the left side. Symptoms improve for movement and stretching of the limbs, massage and after sweating. People suitable for Thuja tend to be insecure and unsure about themselves. They try hard to please others but are very sensitive to criticism and soon become depressed. This may lead them to neglect their appearance. Thuja people are often thin and pale and tend to have greasy skin and perspire easily.

Urtica urens
Urtica; stinging nettle

One of the few plants that is familiar to all and that, for hundreds of years, has been valued for its medicinal and culinary uses. Nettles have always been used as a source of food both for people and animals, the young leaves being a nutritious vegetable with a high content of vitamin C. Nettles were thought to purify the blood, and an ancient cure for rheumatism and muscular weakness was the practice of 'urtication', or lashing the body with stinging nettles. The hairs covering the leaves of the nettle release a volatile liquid when touched, which causes the familiar skin reaction of painful, white bumps to appear. The fresh, green parts of the plant are used to prepare the homoeopathic remedy, which is used as a treatment for burning and stinging of the skin. Hence it is used to treat allergic reactions of the skin, urticaria, or nettle rash, insect bites and stings and skin lesions caused by burns and scalds. Also, for eczema, chicken pox, nerve inflammation and pain (neuritis and neuralgia), shingles, rheumatism, gout and cystitis in which there are burning, stinging pains. The person who benefits from this remedy is prone to inflamed, itching and irritated skin complaints and may be fretful, impatient and restless. Symptoms are made worse by touch and in cold, wet weather, snow and for contact with water. Allergic skin reactions may occur if the person eats shellfish such as prawns. The symptoms improve if the affected skin is rubbed and also if the person rests and lies down.

Glossary of Terms used in Homoeopathy

aggravations a term first used by Dr Samuel Hahnemann to describe an initial worsening of symptoms experienced by some patients, on first taking a homoeopathic remedy, before the condition improved. In modern homoeopathy this is known as a *healing crisis*. To prevent the occurrence of aggravations, Hahnemann experimented with further dilutions of remedies and, in particular, vigorous shaking (SUCCUSSING) of preparations at each stage of the process.

allopathy a term first used by Dr Samuel Hahnemann meaning 'against disease'. It describes the approach of conventional medicine, which is to treat symptoms with a substance or drug with an opposite effect in order to suppress or eliminate them. This is called the 'law of contraries' and is in direct contrast to the 'like can cure like', the 'law of similars' or *similia similibus curentur* principle, which is central to the practice of homoeopathy.

centesimal scale of dilution the scale of dilution used in homoeopathy based on one part (or drop) of the remedy in 99 parts of the diluent liquid (a mixture of alcohol and water).

classical the practice of homoeopathy based on the work of Dr Samuel Hahnemann and further developed and expanded by other practitioners, particularly Dr Constantine Hering and Dr James Tyler Kent.

constitutional prescribing and constitutional types the homoeopathic concept, based on the work of Dr James Tyler

Kent, that prescribing should be based on the complete make-up of a person, including physical and emotional characteristics, as well as on the symptoms of a disorder.

decimal scale of dilution the scale of dilution used in homoeopathy based on one part (or drop) of the remedy in nine parts of the diluent liquid (a mixture of alcohol and water).

healing crisis the situation in which a group of symptoms first become worse after a person has taken a homoeopathic remedy, before they improve and disappear. The healing crisis is taken to indicate a change and that improvement is likely to follow. It is usually short-lived (*see also* AGGRAVATIONS).

homoeopathy the system of healing based on the principle of 'like can cure like' and given its name by Samuel Hahnemann. The word is derived from the Greek *homeo* for 'similar' and *pathos* for 'suffering' or 'like disease'.

laws of cure, law of direction of cure three concepts or 'laws' formulated by Dr Constantine Hering to explain the means by which symptoms of disease are eliminated from the body.

(1) Symptoms move in a downwards direction.

(2) Symptoms move from the inside of the body outwards.

(3) Symptoms move from more important vital organs and tissues to those of less importance.

Hering was also responsible for the view in homoeopathy that more recent symptoms disappear first before ones that have been present for a longer time. Hence symptoms are eliminated in the reverse order of their appearance.

materia medica detailed information about homoeopathic remedies, listed alphabetically. The information includes details of the symptoms that may respond to each remedy, based on previous research and experience. Details about the source of each remedy are also included. This information is used by a homoeopathic doctor when deciding upon the best remedy for each particular patient and group of symptoms.

miasm a chronic constitutional weakness that is the aftereffect of an underlying suppressed disease that has been present in a previous generation or earlier in the life of an individual. The concept of miasm was formulated by Samuel Hahnemann who noted that some people were never truly healthy but always acquired new symptoms of illness. He believed that this was because of a constitutional weakness that he called a miasm, which may have been inherited and was caused by an illness in a previous generation. These theories were put forward in his research writings entitled *Chronic Diseases*. Three main miasms were identified, PSORA, SYCOSIS and SYPHILIS.

modalities a term applied to the responses of the patient, when he or she feels better or worse, depending upon factors in the internal and external environment. These are unique from one person to another, depending upon the individual characteristics that apply at the time, although there are common features within each constitutional type. Modalities include responses, fears and preferences to temperature, weather, foods, emotional responses and relationships, etc, which all contribute to a person's total sense of wellbeing. Modalities are particularly important when a person has symptoms of an illness in prescribing the most beneficial remedy.

mother tincture (symbol O) the first solution obtained from dissolving a substance in a mixture of alcohol and water (usually in the ratio of 9/10 pure alcohol to 1/10 distilled water). It is subjected to further dilutions and SUCCUSSIONS (shakings) to produce the homoeopathic remedies.

nosode a term used to describe a remedy prepared from samples of infected diseased tissue, often to treat or prevent a particular illness. They were first investigated by Wilhelm Lux, not without considerable controversy. Examples are *Medorrhinum* and *Tuberculinum*.

organon *The Organon of Rationale Medicine.* is one of the most important works of Samuel Hahnemann, published in Leipzig in 1810, in which he set out the principles and philosophy of modern homoeopathy. The *Organon* is considered to be a classic work and basic to the study of homoeopathy.

polycrest a remedy suitable for a number of illnesses, disorders or symptoms.

potency the dilution or strength of a homoeopathic remedy. Dr Samuel Hahnemann discovered that by further diluting and SUCCUSSING (shaking) a remedy, it became more effective or potent in bringing about a cure. It is held that the process of diluting and shaking a remedy releases its innate energy or dynamism, even though none of the original molecules of the substance may remain. Hence the greater the dilution of a remedy, the stronger or more potent it becomes. Hahnemann called his new dilute solutions 'potentizations'.

potentiate the release or transfer of energy into a homoeopathic solution by succussing or vigorous shaking of the mixture.

principle of vital force 'vital force' was the term given by Samuel Hahnemann to the inbuilt power or ability of the human body to maintain health and fitness and fight off illness. Illness is believed to be the result of stresses, causing an imbalance in the vital force, which assail all people throughout life and include inherited, environmental and emotional factors. The symptoms of this 'disorder' are illness and are held to be the physical indications of the struggle of the body's vital force to regain its balance. A person with a strong vital force will tend to remain in good health and fight off illness. A person with a weak vital force is more likely to suffer from long-term, recurrent symptoms and illnesses. Homoeopathic remedies are believed to act upon the vital force, stimulating it to heal the body and restore the natural balance.

provings the term given by Samuel Hahnemann to experimental trials he carried out to test the reactions of healthy people to homoeopathic substances. These trials were carried out under strictly controlled conditions (in advance of the modern scientific approach), and the symptoms produced, the results, were meticulously recorded. Quinine was the first substance that Hahnemann investigated in this way, testing it initially on himself and then on close friends and family members. Over the next few years he investigated and proved many other substances, building up a wealth of information on each one about the reactions and symptoms produced. After conducting this research, Hahnemann went on to prescribe carefully the remedies to those who were sick. Provings are still carried out in modern homoeopathy to test new substances that may be of value as remedies. Usually, neither the prescribing physician nor those taking the substance—the 'provers'—know the identity of the material or whether they are taking a placebo.

psora one of three MIASMS identified by Samuel Hahnemann, believed to be because of suppression of scabies (an itchy skin infection caused by a minute burrowing mite). Psora was believed to have an inherited element or to be because of suppression of an earlier infection in a particular individual.

Schussler tissue salts Wilhelm Heinrich Schussler was a German homoeopathic doctor who introduced the biochemic tissue salt system in the late 1800s. Schussler believed that many symptoms and ailments resulted from the lack of a minute, but essential, quantity of a mineral or tissue salt. He identified twelve such tissue salts that he regarded as essential and believed that a cure could be obtained from replacing the deficient substance. Schussler's work was largely concentrated at the cell and tissue level rather than embracing the holistic view of homoeopathy.

similia similibus curentur the founding principle of homoeopathy that 'like can cure like' or 'let like be treated by like', which was first put forward by Hippocrates, a physician of ancient Greece. This principle excited the interest of Paracelsus in the Middle Ages, and was later restated and put into practice by Hahnemann with the development of homoeopathy.

simillimum a homoeopathic remedy that in its natural, raw state is able to produce the same symptoms as those being exhibited by the patient.

succussion vigorous shaking of a homoeopathic remedy at each stage of dilution, along with banging the container holding it against a hard surface causing further release of energy.

sycosis one of the three major MIASMS identified by Samuel Hahnemann and believed to result from a suppressed gonorrhoeal infection. Sycosis was believed to have an inherited element or to be because of suppression of an earlier infection in a particular individual.

syphilis the third of the three major MIASMS identified by Samuel Hahnemann believed to result from a suppressed syphilis infection. Syphilis was believed to have an inherited element or to be because of suppression of an earlier infection in a particular individual.

trituration the process, devised by Samuel Hahnemann, of rendering naturally insoluble substances soluble so that they can be made available as homoeopathic remedies. The process involves repeated grinding down of the substance with lactose powder until it becomes soluble. The substance usually becomes soluble at the third process of trituration. Each trituration is taken to be the equivalent of one dilution in the centesimal scale. Once the substance has been rendered soluble, dilution can proceed in the normal way.